CHINESE WOMEN
AND CHRISTIANITY

1860-1927

American Academy of Religion Academy Series

edited by
Susan Thistlethwaite

Number 75
CHINESE WOMEN
AND CHRISTIANITY

1860-1927

by
KWOK Pui-lan

KWOK Pui-lan

CHINESE WOMEN
AND CHRISTIANITY

1860-1927

Scholars Press
Atlanta, Georgia

CHINESE WOMEN AND CHRISTIANITY
1860-1927

by
KWOK Pui-lan

© 1992
KWOK Pui-lan

' **Library of Congress Cataloging in Publication Data**

Kwok, Pui-lan.
    Chinese women and Christianity, 1860-1927 / Kwok-Pui-lan.
    p. cm. — (American Academy of Religion academy series ; no.
    75)
    Includes bibliographical references.
    ISBN 1-55540-669-6 (alk. paper) ; ISBN 1-55540-670-X (alk. paper pbk.)
    1. Women—China—Religious life. 2. Women in church work—China.
I. Title. II. Series.
BV4527.K86 1991
275.1'081'082—dc20   91-42763
                                          CIP

Printed in the United States of America
on acid-free paper

Table of Contents

Acknowledgements

I would like to thank former and present faculty and students of the Theology Division, Chung Chi College, the Chinese University of Hong Kong, for their continual support of my spiritual quest. Grateful acknowledgement is due my colleagues in the Women's Theological Center, Boston, sisters in the Asian Women Theologians, Northeast U.S. group, numerous feminist scholars in the Boston region, and the faculty and students of Harvard Divinity School for providing intellectual stimulation and a theological home for me during the years I stayed in Boston.

While I was studying the lives of women in modern China, I benefited from many conversations with Benjamin I. Schwartz, with whom I had the opportunity to study prior to his retirement. I am also grateful to the many people who helped me at different stages of the research and writing. Tu Wei-ming, Franklin Woo, Sharon Welch, and Jane Hunter offered helpful insights and comments. Gordon D. Kaufman, who saw the importance of the study from the beginning, has been a source of unfailing support. Paul A. Cohen patiently guided me in the craft of historical scholarship, and because of his meticulous reading, the book is much improved. Beverly Moon and Janice Wickeri helped to make the manuscript more readable by their skillful editing.

Library staff of the following institutions have answered my queries and made available important resources, some of which have seldom been used before: Congregational Library, Houghton Library, Harvard-Yenching Library, Yale Divinity School Library, the Burke Library of Union Theological Seminary, New York, General Commission on Archives and History, the United Methodist Church, Archives of National Board, Y.W.C.A. of the U.S.A., and the Library of the National Committee of Chinese Christian Three-Self Patriotic Movement, Shanghai. Thanks also to Houghton Library of Harvard University and the United Church Board for World Ministries for permission to quote from the American Board of Commissioners for Foreign Missions papers.

I would like to thank the Anglican Diocese of Hong Kong and Macao, the United Board for Christian Higher Education in Asia, and Harvard Divinity School for financial support of my graduate studies, as well as the United Methodist Church, the World Council of Churches, and the Foundation for Theological Education in South East Asia for grants in support of my dissertation writing, and the Presbyterian Church, U.S.A., for funding a research trip to China.

Finally, I am grateful to my husband Wai Pang for being an understanding listener and helpful critic and to my daughter An Pu for finding ways to enjoy herself while I worked at the computer.

Abbreviations

ABC	American Board of Commissioners for Foreign Missions, Archives. Houghton Library, Harvard University, Cambridge, Massachusetts.
CR	*The Chinese Recorder and Missionary Journal*
Fuzhou Report [year]	Annual report [year] of the Fuzhou station of the American Board of Commissioners for Foreign Missions in China.
JHXB	*Jiaohui xinbao* (The church news)
NCC 1922	*The Christian Church as Revealed in the National Christian Conference, 1922*
NDB	*Nüduobao* (The woman's messenger)
Nianjian	*Zhonghua Jidu jiaohui nianjian* (Chinese Christian church year book)
Pangzhuang Women [year]	Annual report [year] of woman's work for Pangzhuang station of the American Board of Commissioners for Foreign Missions in China
Records 1877	*Records of the General Conference of the Protestant Missionaries of China Held at Shanghai, May 10-24, 1877*
Records 1890	*Records of the General Conference of the Protestant Missionaries of China Held at Shanghai, May 7-20, 1890*
Records 1907	*China Centenary Missionary Conference Records: Report of the Great Conference Held at Shanghai, April 5th to May 8th, 1907*
WWFE	*Woman's Work in the Far East*
WGGB	*Wanguo gongbao* (The globe magazine)
Year Book	*The China Mission Year Book*, 1910-1925 *The China Christian Year Book*, 1926-1938

Introduction

In 1821, a Chinese woman named Mrs. Liang, née Li, was baptized into the church by her husband Liang Fa, who three years later became China's first pastor. No one else was present to witness the ceremony. The couple read some passages from the Bible, said a prayer, and perhaps sang a hymn before Mrs. Liang confessed her faith and Liang Fa sprinkled water on her head. The ceremony took place in a shabby cottage in a village about fifty miles southwest of Guangzhou. Having no baptism font, the couple used a Chinese rice bowl instead. Mrs. Liang was the first woman converted to Protestant Christianity in China.[1] In a hundred years' time, the number of female Christians would increase to 128,704, about thirty-seven percent of the Christian population.[2]

The story of Chinese women in Protestant Christianity has seldom been told. The relation of women to the unfolding drama of the missionary movement in China has never been recognized as the *problematik* of serious scholarly study. In the past, the relationship between Chinese women and Christianity has been interpreted chiefly by missionaries. In the early twentieth century, the Briton John Macgowan and the American Arthur H. Smith in their memoirs of Christian mission in China highlighted Christianity's contribution to the elevation of the status of women. The titles of their books, *How England Saves China* and *The Uplift of China,* reflected both their feelings of cultural superiority and their aggressive attempts to change other nations.[3] In a much more reserved tone, Kenneth S. Latourette, in his monumental study, *A History of Christian Missions in China,* also affirmed that Christianity brought revolutionary changes to Chinese women.[4]

More recently, historians interested in the cultural exchange between the East and the West have offered their evaluations and interpretations. Paul A. Cohen, writing about the impact of Christian missions on nineteenth-century China, states that the missionary enterprise was "ideally suited to stimulate change" in the area of the emancipation of women. As examples, he cites the provision of female education, the anti-footbinding movement, and the criticism by missionaries of concubinage, infanticide, and arranged marriage.[5] From another angle, Jane Hunter was more interested in the transmission of values in the personal encounter between women missionaries and Chinese women. She suggests that the most significant contribution of missionary women lay in the role models provided by their own lives rather than in the work they accomplished.[6]

Although missionaries and historians studied the interaction between Chinese women and Christianity out of different motives, both have looked at this encounter more from the side of missionaries and have arrived at a positive evaluation of Christianity. In this book, however, I examine the interaction from the perspective of Chinese women and integrate their experience within the wider social and cultural changes as well as the women's movement taking place in China. This approach reveals clearly that the relationship between Chinese women and Christianity changed over time and was much more complex than hitherto assumed.

The study begins with the treaties of 1858-1860, which allowed missionaries to preach anywhere in China and finishes in 1927 with the anti-Christian movement (1922-1927) marking the end of a missionary era. The woman's work of Christian missions reached a small number of women, who crossed the cultural boundary to join the Protestant church, a brand new social institution in nineteenth-century China. Although a tiny minority in society, Christian women were the first group of Chinese women to organize themselves in order to publicly address women's oppression. By means of a careful historical reconstruction, the present study attempts to answer questions such as why did Chinese women join the church? What were the symbolic resources they found significant in Christianity for their spiritual life? How did they adapt to church life with its unfamiliar rituals and new prescriptions for women? Did their Christian identity affect the development of their feminist consciousness?

By means of this book, I hope to contribute further to our knowledge of the relationship of Chinese Christian women to their faith, to the social reform activities associated with nineteenth and twentieth-century Chinese Christianity, and to the feminist movement of the day. Christian women, more than their Chinese sisters, have had more sustained exposure to Western civilization through the Christian church, mission schools, hospitals, and Christian benevolence. Their responses to the Christian missionary enterprise give us rare information on how Chinese women reacted to foreign influences and religion in particular.

From another perspective, the results of the study will also broaden our understanding of Christianity in terms of how it adapts to and functions in a totally new cultural context. For example, some of the Christian symbolism needed to be interpreted and adjusted to the religious needs of both male and female Chinese audiences. In many churches, male and female worshippers had to be segregated because of Chinese proprieties. Western Christian institutions, such as the Young Women's Christian Association and the Woman's Christian Temperance Movement underwent changes when introduced to China.

The data for this historical study are drawn from a wide variety of sources, from well-known missionary accounts to overlooked religious journals, from Christian church yearbooks to Chinese women's obituaries. Since resource materials of all the Christian missions in China are too numerous for one study, I have limited myself to the study of Protestant Christianity, focusing primarily on the mission boards of the United States. Two collections feature prominently in the study: (1) the tracts and pamphlets sent back from China by missionaries of the American Board of Commissioners for Foreign Missions (hereafter, the American Board) and deposited at the Harvard-Yenching Library, and (2) the mission papers of the same organization, housed at the Houghton Library of Harvard University.

The substantial use of missionary materials and the writings of Chinese male Christians is unavoidable because most of the early Chinese Christian women were illiterate. Chinese Christian women only began to write in Christian journals and magazines in the late nineteenth century. When using the writings of missionaries, I have taken special care to compare and contrast different accounts to verify the data and to avoid the one-sided interpretation of some missionaries. I have also tried to analyze and evaluate the missionary reports within the wider Chinese social and cultural context. Special attention is given to how Chinese Christian women at the turn of the century interpreted the work of Christian missions and history of Christianity in China.

The writings of Chinese Christian women, gathered together here for the first time, appeared as autobiographies and short articles scattered throughout church yearbooks, college bulletins, pamphlets, and religious journals, especially in the *Chinese Recorder, Nüduobao* (The woman's messenger), and *Nüqingnian* (The Y.W.C.A. magazine). The authors, mostly students and graduates of mission schools, have written profusely on topics that include women's fashion and hairstyle, female education, love and marriage, employment of women, nationalism, and religious faith. This first hand information allows us to have a glimpse of the inner world of women and their subjective response to changing circumstances in China.

The book is divided into five chapters. The chapters are organized in a thematic manner, but also follow a somewhat chronological order as Christian women expanded their roles in the church and society during that period. Chapter one sets the stage for the study, providing historical background on pertinent issues relating to the encounter of Chinese women with Christianity. In chapter two, by careful analysis of tracts, catechisms, and popular Christian literature, we will examine how the missionaries adapted the Christian message to a different religious system. Our purpose here is to demonstrate that the feminization of Christian symbolism increased the appeal of Christianity for both women and men in China. Chapter three analyzes the participation of women within specific Christian congregations and patterns of female religious leadership. The involvement of Christian women in social reforms during the turbulent years of the late nineteenth and early twentieth centuries will be discussed in chapter four. In the final chapter, we will attempt to listen to the voices of these women as conveyed by their own writings as we focus on the dynamic relationship between women's consciousness and their religious faith. The conclusion both summarizes the results and draws out the implications of the present study for further exploration.

I have used the pinyin system for romanization throughout the study. Proper names of individual Chinese, where Chinese characters are available, are romanized in the standard form (for example, Ding Shujing). Where characters are not available, the name given in the source is cited. To help readers who are more familiar with the Wade-Giles system, I have included the Wade-Giles romanization in parentheses after some more well-known names. It should be noted that women were known by different names, for example, Jiang Hezhen was also rendered as Mei Jiang Hezhen, Anna Kong Mei, and Mrs. H. C. Mei. I have used their maiden names wherever possible both in the text and in the notes, to avoid confusion. Only when the maiden name is not known is a woman referred to by her married name, that is, as Mrs. so and so. The glossary at the end provides a reference to the Chinese names, terms, and titles I have been able to determine.

Notes

1. Mai Zhanen (George H. McNeur), *Liang Fa zhuan* (Life of Liang Fa) (Hong Kong: The Council on Christian Literature, 1959), 24-25.
2. M. T. Stauffer ed., *The Christian Occupation of China: General Survey of the Numerical Strength and Geographical Distribution of the Christian Forces in China, 1918-1921* (Shanghai: China Continuation Committee, 1922), 293.
3. John Macgowan, *How England Saved China* (London: T. Fisher Unwin, 1913); and Arthur H. Smith, *The Uplift of China* (New York: Young People's Missionary Movement, 1907).
4. Kenneth S. Latourette, *A History of Christian Missions in China* (New York: Macmillan Co., 1929), 485.
5. Paul A. Cohen, "Christian Missions and Their Impact to 1900," in *The Cambridge History of China,* vol. 10, *Late Ch'ing 1800-1911,* ed., John King Fairbank (Cambridge: Cambridge University Press, 1978), 582-583.
6. Jane Hunter, *The Gospel of Gentility: American Women Missionaries in Turn-of-the-Century China* (New Haven: Yale University Press, 1984), 1-51.

CHAPTER I

Women, Christian Mission, and the Chinese Context

When the Protestant missionaries arrived in China in the early nineteenth century, Christianity was treated as a heterodoxy, similar in status to other popular Buddhist and Daoist (Taoist) sects. Under the Guangzhou system, foreigners were allowed to live in Guangzhou for only a few months each year, without the company of their wives and family members.[1] Missionaries, who were both foreigners and male, could hardly reach Chinese women because of the segregation of the sexes in Chinese society. The Treaty of Nanjing (1842), which brought the Sino-British Opium War to an end, allowed missionaries and their families to settle down and preach the Gospel in the five treaty ports of Guangzhou, Xiamen, Fuzhou, Ningbo, and Shanghai. Through the opening of girls' schools and home visitation, the wives of missionaries were able to establish some contacts with neighboring women.

The treaties of Tianjin (1858) and Beijing (1860), following the second Opium War, accorded missionaries greater freedom to buy property and to preach anywhere in China. At first, the wives of missionaries continued to assume the chief responsibility for working among Chinese women, but during the late 1860's, women's mission boards were formed on both sides of the Atlantic, commissioning single women to go into the mission field. The steady increase of female missionaries in China changed the contours of Protestant missions. Not only did they establish "woman's work" as a distinct component of missionary activities, they also called attention to the importance of women's issues.

Chinese women joined the Protestant Christian church at a very slow pace. Among the six Protestant Christians converted in 1842, we do not know if any were women.[2] The first missionary conference in 1877 estimated the number of female communicants to be 4,967,[3] the majority of whom came from the poor and lower classes. At the turn of the century, Christian missions began to attract women from families of officials and literati, primarily through their mission schools in the large cities. The national report of 1922 indicated that women comprised thirty-seven percent of the Protestant Christian population, with a heavy concentration in the two coastal provinces of Guangdong and Fujian.[4]

In the following, I will try to provide a historical background to the interaction between Chinese women and Christian mission. Many Chinese women were devout followers of popular religions which gave them a sense of identity and offered them means of mutual support. Some religious sects also allowed women to perform certain leadership and ritualistic roles. The popular appeal of these folk religions among women will be analyzed because Christianity had to compete with them for followers. Even when some women decided to give up their indigenous beliefs and convert to Christianity, they had to overcome many difficulties because of their sex. The general anti-Christian atmosphere and the barriers of mission work among women will be discussed. With evangelistic zeal, women missionaries gradually started mission work among the female populace. An overview of ''woman's work'' of the missions will be presented, focusing on evangelism, female education, and medical service. Lastly, I will discuss the relationship between Chinese women and women missionaries in order to understand the complexities of the cross-cultural encounter.

Women's Popular Religious Practices

Chinese women, especially those living in the rural areas, worshipped many gods and goddesses and participated in a wide range of religious activities. They visited temples, burned incense, and prayed before religious images; in addition, they celebrated religious festivals with elaborate rituals, paid tribute to the dead, and consulted diviners and oracles on particular occasions. These diverse religious phenomena formed a cultural substratum in society, creating a symbolic and moral universe quite different from the predominant Confucian culture upheld by intellectuals and the elite.

Popular religion in China was very complex because it had intricate ramifications in other segments of Chinese culture.

C. K. Yang, in his book *Religion in Chinese Society*, distinguishes between institutional and diffused religion; the latter refers to religious practices that permeate and infuse other social institutions. Yang indicates that it is the pervasive diffused religion that undergirds secular institutions and the general social order in Chinese society.[5] For instance, ancestor worship cannot be labeled as "religion" alone, because of its much wider implications for the family and clan. Another example is the celebration of religious festivals in local villages, which includes not only religious rituals but also a communal meal and theatrical performances. Thus, when some missionaries argued that the Chinese converts should not be required to contribute money to the worship of local deities, the villagers pointed out that these same Christians participated in and enjoyed other aspects of the festivals associated with these gods.[6]

In the symbolic universe of Chinese popular religion, certain important female religious figures attract both male and female adherents. The worship of Guanyin (the goddess of mercy) is so pervasive that one scholar in the history of religions calls it "the cult of half Asia."[7] The term Guanyin is made up of the two Chinese characters for "see" and "sound," signifying the special capacity of the goddess to understand and appreciate the supplications of her followers. In some religious sects of Buddhism, a powerful female divinity, the Eternal Mother *(Wusheng laomu)* features prominently. The Eternal Mother, who gave birth to the yin and the yang, is believed to send down intermediaries to save human beings so that they can be reunited with her in paradise.[8]

In the coastal provinces of Guangdong and Fujian, where missionaries first began their activities, many women and men worshipped Mazu (goddess of heaven), the patron deity of fishing peoples and seafarers. Folk legends describe Mazu as living near the seashore in a village in Fujian. From there she exhibits the miraculous power to calm the stormy sea and mighty gales, bringing the ships of her brothers safe to shore. Popular devotion to these powerful goddesses attracted the attention of missionaries and foreigners. *The Chinese Repository*, a journal founded by the American missionary Elijah C. Bridgman, published articles on Guanyin and Mazu in the early 1840's.[9] The worship of Mazu was seen by missionaries as a serious rival to the Christian religion. W. H. Medhurst of the London mission denounced it as superstitious in a small tract where he argued that the power to control nature lies with God and not with a mythological female figure. The tract was later revised and re-issued in the Fuzhou dialect for the convenience of Fujian readers by Justus Doolittle, an American missionary who was heavily involved in tract production.[10]

Liang Fa, the first Chinese pastor, was also aware of the popular devotions to these female goddesses. A sincere follower of Guanyin before his conversion,[11] he later criticized the Chinese popular religions as superstitious and heterodox. In his influential tract *Quanshi liangyan* (Good words to admonish the age), he displayed a highly skeptical attitude toward those people, especially women, who worshipped Guanyin, Madam Golden Flower *(Jinhua furen)*, and other goddesses.[12] Liang attempted to show that only the Christian God was the true God and that Christianity was higher than all other religions. Nevertheless, these popular devotions had enormous appeal for women, since they included female representations of the divine and had direct bearings on women's experiences, such as childbirth and menstruation.

Followers of popular religions sometimes organized themselves into religious sects with their own initiation rites and patterns of organization. Daniel L. Overmeyer argues that the religious sects provided an alternative social structure for marginalized people, whose lives could be mercilessly threatened by the whims of emperors, failure at examinations, famines, or floods. These popular religious sects were characterized by "predominantly lay membership, hierarchical organization, active proselytism, regular performance of religious rituals, possession of their own scripture texts, and a tendency toward collective security and action."[13] According to Overmeyer, these sects fulfilled important functions in the Ming and Qing dynasties (1360-1644; 1644-1911), such as offering mutual assurance in group ritual and support, providing channels for personal religious cultivation, fostering personal and group identity, and creating opportunities for leadership beyond the immediate family and clan.[14]

One interesting feature in popular religious sects was women's role and participation in these groups. Overmeyer's meticulous study of Chinese folk Buddhism indicates that women had a relatively higher status in the popular sects: "Women were not only members; during the Ming and Qing there are several accounts of women who were leaders of sects and congregations, or even sect founders."[15] Likewise, Susan Naquin, in her study of the rebellion of a White Lotus sect in 1813, points out that women could be sect masters, custodians of secret scriptures from one generation to the next, and teachers of both male and female sect members. Such characteristics of the sectarian tradition, Naquin concludes, attracted women "who wished to escape from the restrictions imposed on them by the hierarchical nature of the society."[16]

Thus, the popular religious sects posed challenges to Christianity at two different levels: (1) they represented a radically different symbolic universe with their own sacred symbols, and (2) they had a social organization that provided an alternative for people at the lower end of the social ladder, including women. Treated as a heterodoxy and opposed by the literati and upper classes, Christianity had to compete with these popular religions for female followers. In some instances, women who were former leaders of religious sects exerted some influence in Christian circles after their conversion. During the latter half of the nineteenth century, the Christian church served as a haven for the adherents of some religious sects, especially when the Qing government tightened its control over and suppressed heterodoxy. The popular religious sects, therefore, provide a very important religious context within which to understand how Christianity adapted itself to the Chinese situation.

Barriers to Mission Work among Women

Statistics indicate that women joined the church at a rather slow pace in the several decades following 1860, when the missionaries were first allowed to preach in the interior of China. The social and cultural barriers facing the early female converts can hardly be overstated. Rich and upper class families would not allow their female family members to join a foreign religion; most probably they would have exerted unpleasant pressure on them if they decided to do so. Women had to give up many social customs and folk religious practices in order to adopt the worship and customs of the church. Although Chinese women were not as secluded as upper-class Indian women in their zenanas, decent women were not supposed to appear in public, let alone worship together with men in a church.

In the 1860's, the journey to and from church could be a "continued torture." John Macgowan of Xiamen recalled that middle-aged and elderly women of his church were teased and ridiculed by people using the most abusive language when they passed by shops and temples on their way to worship.[17] In certain places, the physical limitation created by women's bound feet would have caused an additional obstacle, especially when the church building was far away from the home. In Beijing, some missionaries solved this problem by giving women "cart money" to hire a cart so that they could come to church.[18]

Apart from these social and physical barriers, the anti-Christian atmosphere, especially in the Lower Yangtze region of China, would have dissuaded some women from even coming close to the mission compound. Anti-missionary writings accused missionaries of horrible crimes such as gouging out the eyes of dead people to make medicine or kidnapping children and causing physical harm to them.[19] Among the many accusations, some were specifically targeted at women's participation in the church. Anti-missionary propaganda charged that it was against social propriety for women to mix with men in a church, and accused churchgoers of participating in adulterous relations during Christian gatherings. For instance, one influential anti-missionary booklet, *Pixie jishi* (A record of facts to ward off heterodoxy), wrote:

> Every seventh day, they have worship, called Mass or worship. Stopping all their work, the old and the young, the male and the female, assemble at the Roman Catholic church. After taking his seat, the priest praises the merit of Jesus. . . . The congregation chants the scriptures; then, they commit adultery with one another in lusty pleasure.[20]

The male missionaries were portrayed as having a huge sexual appetite, luring Chinese women into promiscuous relations. Some anti-missionary writings even charged that in Christian marriage, the priest required the newly wed bride to have sexual intercourse with him before with the groom.[21] Missionaries were also alleged to have used charms and medicine pills to gain access to women. For example, during the poison scare of 1871, rumors were spread from Guangzhou on up the coast that the missionaries had put poison into the wells and would only give medicine to people, especially women, if they promised to become followers.[22]

Heterodoxy in China was often associated with the breakdown of social morality, and some secret Daoist sects were accused of practising certain forms of sexual orgies in their religious meetings. The writers of anti-Christian tracts might have had this religious background in mind when they accused the Christian community of indecent sexual behavior. In a society where sexual propriety was to be observed, the unconventional participation of Chinese women in church gatherings aroused great curiosity and suspicion. Women's religious activities, such as receiving baptism, making confession, joining religious orders, and offering service to the church were also questioned and attacked.[23]

Furthermore, the Chinese gentry saw the introduction of a new religious system as iconoclastic, threatening the social fabric of the traditional order. The Christian teaching that all human beings are brothers and sisters before God, for example, would undermine hierarchical social relationships in the family and society. Some of the anti-Christian writings accused Christianity of upsetting the established social order stipulated by Confucian teachings. They falsely charged that Christianity allowed fathers and daughters, brothers and sisters, mothers and sons to marry each other. Several texts even stated explicitly that Christianity elevated the status of women to be highter than that of men, allowing for women to rule the nation and make all important decisions.[24]

After the Tianjin incident (1870), which took the lives of twenty-one foreigners and some thirty to forty Chinese Christians, the Chinese government proposed a Missionary Circular to regulate missionary activities. Among other stipulations, article two stated that "Chinese women should henceforth be prohibited from entering foreign churches and female missionaries should no longer be permitted to labor in China."[25] Reactions to this particular article indicated that some missionaries were already aware of the importance of women in the church; for instance, Griffith John of the London Mission wrote: "In demanding the abolition of female schools, and disallowing the attendance of women at religious services, the Chinese government is aiming at the very life of our churches."[26] The Missionary Circular, however, was never carried out due to the opposition of foreign governments.

Anti-missionary propaganda and outbursts continued into the 1890's, sometimes causing damage to mission properties and physical harm to the missionaries and their families. Aware of the growing anti-Christian sentiment, the Christian mission boards called for the sending of more female missionaries, especially single women, to work among the female populace. In the latter half of the nineteenth century, Chinese women were approached through house-to-house visitations and the mission schools. Most of the converts were illiterate women drawn from the lower class and the rural areas. While younger girls and older women could find time to attend religious activities, married women were often hindered from doing so because of household chores.

Christian missions slowly reached the rich and educated class at the turn of the century, when the Chinese were more open to the West. After the aborted attempt at social reform in 1898 and the subsequent Boxer Uprising of 1900, more and more people recognized the need to strengthen their country through Western knowledge. Upper class and rich families began to send their sons and daughters to learn English and the sciences in prestigious schools run by the missions. Christian missions enjoyed unprecedented growth during the first two decades of the twentieth century. Further, the Christian population increased more than fourfold (from 85,000 in 1900 to 366,524 in 1920), and the number of missionaries and their wives reached 6,000 in 1919.[27]

Just as Chinese women began to enrol in the Christian schools and join the church in greater numbers, they witnessed a far-reaching women's movement unfolding in China. During the May Fourth movement of 1919, progressive female students demonstrated on the street, demanding sexual equality, economic independence, and political participation in the government. In the midst of the rising consciousness of women, some observers were careful to note that according to the biblical account in Genesis, women were created second to men, and further, that the Christian church did not treat men and women on an equal basis.[28] The anti-Christian writings of the 1920's criticized Christianity as patriarchal and oppressive to women, in addition to being unscientific and culturally imperialistic. It was ironic that Christianity, condemned in the nineteenth century for putting women on a pedestal, was now accused of being both conservative and out-dated and of failing to keep abreast of the times. On the other hand, the anti-Christian movement prompted Chinese Christians to reflect seriously on their faith and to adapt Christianity to the Chinese context. Chinese Christian women, in particular, had to defend their identities both as Christians and as women.

Woman's Work of the Missions

Missionary activities among women began slowly after the Treaty of Nanjing allowed the wives of missionaries to settle with their husbands in the treaty ports. While the male missionaries were preaching in the chapels or distributing religious tracts in the crowded streets, their wives would hold small Bible classes and visit Chinese women in their homes. In 1844, the first mission school for girls in China was opened in Ningbo by an English woman, Miss Aldersey of the Society for the Promotion of Female Education in the Far East. The school started with a handful of students, among whom was Mrs. Tseng Laisun, a well-known figure in the missionary community.[29] In the early 1850's, Sophia Doolittle and Lucy E. Hartwell also organized day and boarding schools for boys and girls in Fuzhou.[30] Because these early schools had great difficulty in recruiting students, the missionaries sometimes had to pay a small sum to the family as an inducement.

With the coming of single female missionaries in the mission field, "woman's work" became a distinct component in the missionary enterprise. At the first missionary conference of 1877, A. P. Happer of Guangzhou and Martha F. Crawford, the wife of T. P. Crawford of Dengzhou, Shandong, were appointed to write papers for the session on "Woman's Work for Woman." Together they listed many areas of woman's work, including home visitation, day and boarding schools for girls, religious meetings for women, the training of Bible women, handicraft classes, and the preparation of reading materials for female readers.[31] The papers engendered much discussion, as missionaries debated the effectiveness of different strategies to reach women, and many probably would agree with Martha F. Crawford that "the men can never be Christianized unless the women also are Christianized."[32]

Missionary work among women fell into three categories: evangelism, female education, and medical service. In the cities, the Christian church was the center for evangelistic work, with different religious activities organized for women, such as Bible classes, prayer meetings, and Sunday schools. In the rural churches, where church members and prospective audiences were scattered throughout numerous villages, evangelism had to be carried out through frequent visitation and itinerancy. At the initial stage of a Christian mission, the women missionaries usually devoted much of their time to evangelism, but with the addition of a number of schools and sometimes a hospital as the missions grew, they had to supervise an extensive enterprise. Person-to-person evangelism was often left to the Bible women, who were employed for home visitation and teaching women to read the Bible.

Evangelism was probably the most difficult and least rewarding branch of woman's work. The number of female converts increased very slowly in the nineteenth century despite efforts of women missionaries to overcome cultural and language barriers in reaching Chinese women. Missionaries of the American Board who worked in big cities such as Beijing, Tianjin, and Fuzhou, often reported that women found it difficult to attend church services because of their social seclusion.[33] In addition, anti-missionary riots, such as the poison scare of 1871, deterred women from participating in religious activities.[34] The situation seems to have changed only at the turn of the century, when the Chinese attitude toward the West became more favorable. The Christian churches were then able to attract women from the upper and intellectual classes as converts.

One of the most significant contributions of Christian missions was the opening of schools for girls. In traditional China, daughters of rich families might be able to receive some private tutoring together with the sons, but girls from poorer families were largely illiterate. By providing free education, food, and accommodation, the early mission schools offered an opportunity for girls of the lower class to receive an education. The mission schools were originally set up to provide wives for Chinese helpers and to train Bible women and teachers for evangelistic work.[35] It was only around the 1890's that the educational goals of mission schools for girls were broadened to provide a liberal education, modeled after girls' schools in the West.

Since the early girls' schools were instruments of proselytism, it was not surprising to find them "Sunday schools every day." Religious instruction featured prominently in the curriculum. For example, the Bridgman Academy, one of the oldest girls' schools in northern China, reported in the 1870's that more than three-quarters of each day was devoted to the study of Christian literature.[36] Later, other subjects were added to the curriculum of mission schools, such as Chinese characters, history, geography, arithmetic, and the simple sciences, preparing students to be better wives and mothers who could set up Christian homes to influence their neighborhoods.[37]

The number of girls in the mission schools increased steadily. In 1860, there were only 12 schools with approximately 196 pupils, and in 1877, the number of schools rose to 38 with 524 pupils. When the Chinese opened their first school for girls in Shanghai in 1897, there were more than three-hundred mission schools with an enrollment of more than seven thousand girls.[38] Under mounting pressure, the Empress Dowager issued an edict permitting the establishment of schools for girls in 1901, although a national system of government-supported girls' schools was not instituted until 1907. Chinese private schools for girls mushroomed in the early twentieth century; for instance, 12 schools were founded in Shanghai between 1901 and 1907, and by 1908, Beijing reported 20 schools for girls.[39] In 1908, the number of girls in government-supported schools already exceeded that of mission schools.[40] A national report in 1922 indicated that there were more than 60,000 female students in mission schools; the ratio of girls to boys was less than one to two in Christian primary schools, and less than one to five in middle schools. Even so, Christian schools continued to educate a much higher percentage of girls than government schools.[41]

The most significant development of female education in twentieth-century China was the establishment of women's colleges. Built on the earlier work of Bridgman Academy, the North China Union College for Women began to offer a limited number of college-level courses in 1905. In Nanjing, the Ginling Women's College was founded in 1915 under the sponsorship of a number of mission boards, together with the support of Smith College in Massachusetts. Members of the class of 1919 at Ginling were the first women in China to receive the bachelor of arts degree. Further south in Fuzhou, the Hwa Nan College for Women offered a full college course in 1917, with the support of the Methodist Women's Foreign Missionary Society in America.[42]

Western medical techniques were made available in China when Peter Parker of the American Board opened the Canton Medical Missionary Hospital, treating a blind woman as his first patient in 1835.[43] But the segregation of the sexes in society made it inconvenient for male doctors to treat women patients. Lucinda Coombs, the first female missionary doctor, reached Beijing in 1873; after that, a small number of women physicians were commissioned by the mission boards.[44] In 1890, there were twenty-three of them working in fifteen Chinese cities; most of these women came from the United

States,[45] where women had already been admitted to medical schools in 1850, whereas European universities began to offer medical education to women only in the 1870's.

The missionary hospitals had very primitive equipment. A survey made in the 1920's showed that the majority of the hospitals did not have a pure water supply, and about one-third did not possess bedding for patients, protection against flies, means of sterilizing bedding or mattresses, or a laboratory of any kind.[46] Female missionary doctors treated a large number of out-patients every day, besides taking care of in-patients and visiting patients in their homes. With limited time and resources, the missionary doctors also had to train their own assistants and nurses for the hospitals. Medical missionary work was better received than other missionary activities, partly because medical doctors commanded respect in Chinese society and partly because of its immediate effect in relieving suffering. Mission hospitals were also meant to be instruments for spreading the Gospel. Bible women were sent to distribute religious literature to women who were waiting their turn to see a doctor or to receive medicine. Chapel services were held for in-patients, and occasionally a school was organized to teach patients how to read and write.

Woman's work was primarily supported by money raised by the women's boards of the different missions. The women missionaries of the major American mission boards, such as the Congregationalist and the Methodist, submitted annual reports to their respective women's boards. To foster interest and galvanize support for work in China, women missionaries published the quarterly *Woman's Work in China* beginning in 1877 in Shanghai; it was superceded by *Woman' Work in the Far East* in 1890. Support for woman's work reached a climax during the years between 1880 and 1920, when the women's boards sent out missionaries not only to Christianize the world but also to effect cultural transformation according to Western values and ideals. After World War I, support for women's boards declined because of financial difficulties brought about by the war and the decline of interest in Christian mission due to an increase in the secularization of Western societies.

Chinese Women and Women Missionaries

Although the Missionary Circular had proposed the limitation of women missionaries, there was an influx of single female missionaries in the field beginning in the 1870's. In 1866, missionary accounts reported that there were only 17 single women missionaries working in China; the majority had been sent by the China Inland Mission founded by Hudson Taylor.[47] A decade later, the number climbed up slowly to 63, when woman's work began to gain some attention in missionary circles. By 1890, the number reached 316, and together with the wives of missionaries, the total number of women in the mission field outnumbered that of men (707 women to 589 men).[48] The predominance of women missionaries made at least one missionary remark: "We are feminizing Christianity and we are responsible for the Chinese belief that 'Christianity is splendid for women and children, but it is not for men.'"[49]

The particular circumstances of China called for the sending of female missionaries. Although the male missionaries could work among women in certain places, anti-missionary attacks in other situations made it awkward for the male missionaries to approach women directly. Besides, women missionaries seemed to be less threatening to the populace. Even after the anti-missionary outbreaks, they were still cordially treated; for instance, Lucy E. Hartwell reported that after the poison scare of 1871, her neighbors, especially women, still greeted and talked with her.[50] In places where antipathy towards Christian missions was exceptionally strong, female missionaries were sent as pioneers to open the mission field. The China Inland Mission sent women missionaries to initiate mission work in the heartland of China, in the provinces of Shanxi, Shaanxi, and Gansu.[51] As if sowing seeds among the rocks, Christian missionaries encountered great difficulties at the beginning; nevertheless, women missionaries wrote that Chinese women were more receptive to foreigners than Chinese men, who were far more unfriendly to outsiders.

The demand for female missionaries in China received a favorable response by the women's boards, newly formed on both sides of the Atlantic. The upsurge of interest in missionary activities during the latter half of the nineteenth century had very complex causes. The evangelical revival movement certainly played no small part in fueling women's religious fervor, but the mission field also provided new challenges and opportunities not readily available at home. In the case of America, the newly opened female colleges enlarged the pool of prospective candidates, and the mushrooming of women's benevolent and voluntary associations provided the social context for church women to organize themselves after the Civil War.[52] In 1869, Congregationalist women organized a women's board, saying, "the time seems fully to have come, to extend the blessing of the gospel to the women of the heathen lands."[53] Within a couple of years, the Women's Foreign Missionary Society of the Methodist Episcopal Church and the Women's Board of the Presbyterian Church were also founded.[54]

At first, missionaries in China doubted whether single women should be sent to the mission field, because some were afraid that married missionaries would have the extra burden of having to take care of them. Harriet F. Baldwin, the wife of Caleb C. Baldwin of Fuzhou, for example, expressed such reservations in the early 1870's: "It seems to me there *must be* work enough for *ten* ladies, and if one could be found who felt that she could have an establishment of her own, keep house by herself—counseled and advised by kind friends she would find there, I think she could make herself useful among the Church."[55] Gradually, the atmosphere became more receptive as single women demonstrated that without family burdens, they could devote more time to mission work and travel around as itinerants. At the first missionary conference of 1877, A. P. Happer concluded his presentation with a supplication that more female missionaries be sent: "May the Great Captain of our Salvation, as He leads forth the ransomed hosts of the Lord to the conversion of the world, greatly multiply from every land the number of women workers for women. . ."[56]

Jane Hunter's study of American women missionaries in China at the turn of the century indicates that a high percentage of women missionaries came from middle-class families in the small towns of the Midwest.[57] With a strong evangelical commitment and a belief in the Victorian values of feminine domesticity, these women went across the ocean, intent on developing a missionary career in a strange land. Once in China, they experienced a sense of freedom and liberation denied to them in their own societies. Despite their repeated claims to live a life of unselfishness and self-sacrifice, they found the mission field offered them unexpected authority and opportunities for achievement, adventure, and status.[58] Hunter describes how women missionaries adjusted themselves to this new environment:

> At first they were troubled by the discrepancy between their expected demeanor of modesty and self-effacement, and their experience of authority. Gradually, however, the

experience of authority transformed self-expectations, and missionary women came to discover inner certainties to match their circumstances. Gradually, they developed colonial temperaments to accord with their colonial status.[59]

It is rather difficult to generalize the response of Chinese women to these Western women with "pale skin, long noses, deep-set eyes, and furry hair,"[60] who had come a long way for the sake of their salvation. At first, many village women were curious to have a look at a foreign woman, and they would try to touch her clothes, or visit her to see how she lived. Later, some might develop closer personal and emotional ties with these foreign missionaries during home visits and Bible study classes. A few women missionaries, such as Mrs. Griffith John, Mrs. Joseph Edkins, and Mrs. William Muirhead, were loved by their Chinese followers, both men and women, who mourned their deaths and wrote poems in their memory.[61] In addition, some of the graduates of mission schools also expressed gratitude to their missionary teachers for their guidance and loving kindness.[62] On the other hand, however, village women found that some foreign missionaries were too harsh with them, losing patience sometimes when teaching them how to read and write. Thus, they preferred to consult with and learn from the Chinese Bible women, who were more understanding. Other educated Chinese women also found some missionaries to be too ethnocentric, treating Chinese women as if they were much inferior and ignorant.[63]

Judging from the small number of Chinese women who joined the Christian church, the women missionaries did not quite succeed in bringing their Chinese sisters into the Christian fold. From another vantage point, some scholars stress the role of women missionaries in the development of feminist consciousness of women in China. Jane Hunter has argued that the most significant contribution of female missionaries was frequently their own example, rather than their missionary agenda.[64] Their personal lives demonstrated that a woman could lead an independent life, pursuing a career as teacher, doctor, or missionary. Alison R. Drucker, on the other hand, stresses the contribution of foreign women in the feminist movement in China, citing their involvement in the anti-footbinding movement as an example.[65]

While some women missionaries did act as women's advocates in China, their ethnocentrism resulting from their privileged position in semi-colonial China should not be overlooked. Female missionaries originally came to China to save the souls of their "heathen sisters." Judging from their own standards, however, they found that their sisters could not possibly be "saved" without first adopting some of their cultural values, such as monogamy, the nuclear family, and personal hygiene. It is often difficult to draw a fine distinction between genuine cultural transmission and ethnocentrism, the more so if the parties involved hold unequal power. In order to justify their existence in China, missionary reports and literature focused on the pitiful condition of Chinese women, reinforcing the belief of uncritical readers in their own cultural superiority.

Some women missionaries found egoistical satisfaction in treating Chinese women like children under their control. To their great surprise, these Chinese "daughters" sometimes acted in ways beyond their control and expectations. When in 1872 Mary Porter demanded that girls in her school unbind their feet, she could not have dreamed of what this would lead to. As her biographer says:

> The best result of the unbinding of feet in the Peking school was not foreseen by the missionaries. The girls, by submitting to this break with established custom, were brought into heavy trials costing them pain and mortification. But these long continued trials firmly borne developed strength and independence of character. They learned to think and act for themselves.[66]

As products of their own time, many women missionaries were bound by the Victorian ideology of female domesticity and subordination. Some of them could not quite appreciate the wider feminist movement in twentieth-century China, criticizing that the girls had gone too far and acted too much like men. For example, Matilda C. Thurston and Luella Miner, principals of Ginling College and North China Union College for Women respectively, were surprised to see their college students demonstrating on the streets during the May Fourth period, despite discouragement from the teachers.

The cross-cultural encounter between women missionaries and Third World women has been interpreted in conflicting ways. Missionary women were portrayed as saints in their "hagiographic" biographies, but as villains boasting a selfish egoism in other writings. My observation is that missionary women were neither saints nor villains but human beings caught up in an historical drama that was beyond their control and that produced results they had not intended. The missionary movement provided both Western and Chinese women an opportunity to understand their own cultural conceptions and to learn something from another culture. It was up to individual participants, however, to make good use of the opportunity. Meaningful human encounter often involves a give-and-take process requiring "hard work and genuine openness," as indicated by Irwin T. Hyatt, Jr., in his book on three missionaries in Shandong.[67]

In this chapter, we have seen that Chinese women participated in a wide range of folk religious practices. Several powerful goddesses, who addressed the particular needs of women, featured prominently in the popular belief system. This cultural and religious substratum posed important challenges to Christianity as we shall see in the following chapters. Mission work among women encountered many obstacles because of social seclusion of women, opposition of family members, and sexual propriety required by the society. Anti-Christian propaganda, portraying male missionaries as harboring lustful desires and accusing church members of committing adultery with one another, further hindered women from joining church activities.

The situation resulted in a separation of mission work along the gender line, with women missionaries working primarily among Chinese women and children. Women missionaries first came as evangelists, but as time went by, they often took up additional roles as teachers, school principals, or hospital administrators. As role models for their students, patients, and female church members, they demonstrated what women could accomplish in their careers. But their ethnocentrism and sense of cultural superiority hindered them from establishing equal relationships with Chinese women. While criticizing Chinese culture as oppressive to women, some women missionaries failed to appreciate that they were also bound by the Victorian concepts of womanhood. The relationship between Chinese women and Christianity took place in the midst of these tensions, ambiguities, and complexities of the cross-cultural encounter.

Notes

1. Mary Morton Morrison, the wife of Robert Morrison, the first Protestant missionary to China, had to stay together with their children in Macao, see Marshall Broomhall, *Robert Morrison: A Master Builder* (New York: George H. Doran Co., 1924?), 61.
2. Luella Miner, "The Place of Woman in the Protestant Missionary Movement in China," *Year Book* 9 (1918): 341.
3. *Records 1877,* 486.
4. The number of female communicants was highest in Guangdong (24,373) and second in Fujian (15,451), see M. T. Stauffer, ed., *The Christian Occupation,* 293.
5. C. K. Yang, *Religion in Chinese Society: A Study of Contemporary Social Functions of Religion and Some of Their Historical Factors* (Berkeley and Los Angeles: University of California Press, 1970), 290-340.
6. The contribution of money for religious festivals had been an issue in anti-missionary incidents; see, for example, "French communication to Zongli yamen" 18 January 1862 and "Zongli yamen to the governors of Guangdong and Guangxi" 19 January 1862 in vol. 1 of *Jiaowu jiaoan dang* (Archives on missionary affairs and cases), ed., Institute of Modern History, Academia Sinica, (Taibei: Institute of Modern History, Academia Sinica, n.d.), 4-6.
7. C. N. Tay, "Kuan-yin: The Cult of Half Asia," *History of Religions* 16 (1976): 147-174.
8. Daniel L. Overmeyer, *Folk Buddhist Religion: Dissenting Sects in Late Traditional China* (Cambridge, Mass.: Harvard University Press, 1976), 135-145.
9. "Sketch of Teën Fe, or Matsoo Po, the Goddess of Chinese Seamen," *Chinese Repository* 10 (1841): 84-87; and "Sketch of Kwanyin, the Chinese Goddess of Mercy," *Chinese Repository* 10 (1841): 185-191.
10. W. H. Medhurst, *Mazupo shengri zhi lun* (On the birthday of Mazu) (Singapore: Jianxia shuyuan, 183?), and Justus Doolittle, comp., *Quanshan liangyan* (Good words exhorting one to virtue) (n.p., 1856). Item one.
11. P. Richard Bohr, "Liang Fa's Quest for Moral Power," in *Christianity in China: Early Protestant Missionary Writings,* ed., Suzanne Wilson Barnett and John King Fairbank (Cambridge, Mass.: Committee on American-East Asian Relations of the Department of History, Harvard University, 1985), 37-38.
12. Liang Fa, *Quanshi liangyan* (Good words to admonish the age), in Mai Zhanen, *Liang Fa zhuan*, Appendix, 6.

13. Daniel L. Overmeyer, "Alternatives: Popular Religious Sects in Chinese Society," *Modern China* 7/2 (April 1981): 154.
14. Ibid., 156-169.
15. Ibid., 165.
16. Susan Naquin, *Millenarian Rebellion in China: The Eight Trigrams Uprising of 1813* (New Haven: Yale University Press, 1976), 41.
17. "Chivalry to Women as Christian Sentiment," *CR* 22 (1891): 266.
18. W. S. Ament, "Report of Peking Station for the Year Ending April 30, 1884," ABC 16.3.12 (8), no. 10. But Timothy Richard in Shandong reported that crippled women would walk ten miles to attend church services; see *Forty-five Years in China: Reminiscences by Timothy Richard, D. D. Litt. D.* (New York: Frederick A. Stokes Co., 1916), 122-123.
19. Paul A. Cohen, *China and Christianity: The Missionary Movement and the Growth of Chinese Anti-Foreignism, 1860-1870* (Cambridge, Mass.: Harvard University Press, 1963), 50.
20. See "Tianzhujiao xieji shuo" (Catholic heterodoxy), in *Pixie jishi* (A record of facts to ward off heterodoxy) (n.p., 1871), 1.
21. Lu Shiqiang, "Wanqing Zhongguo zhishi fenzi dui Jidujiao yili de pichi (1860-1898)" (Chinese intellectuals' criticism of Christian doctrines in late Qing, 1860-1898), *Lishi xuebao* (Journal of history) 2 (1974): 153.
22. Ellsworth C. Carlson, *The Foochow Missionaries, 1847-1880* (Cambridge, Mass.: East Asian Research Center, Harvard University, 1974), 128-129. See also Carl T. Smith, "The Protestant Church and the Improvement of Women's Status in 19th Century China," *Ching Feng* 20 (1977): 109-110.
23. Lu Shiqiang, *Zhongguo quanshen fanjiao de yuanyin* (The origin and causes of the anti-Christian movement by the Chinese officials and gentry) (Taibei: Institute of Modern History, Academia Sinica, 1966), 32.
24. Lu Shiqiang, "Wanqing Zhongguo zhishi fenzi dui Jidujiao," 153.
25. Paul A. Cohen, *China and Christianity*, 252-253.
26. Griffith John, "The Chinese Circular on Mission," *CR* 4 (1871): 150. John had reported a steady increase of female constituents in his church; see R. Wardlaw Thompson, *Griffith John: The Story of Fifty Years in China* (New York: A. C. Armstrong and Son, 1906), 218-219.
27. M. T. Stauffer, ed., *The Christian Occupation*, 38; see also "Appendix H," xc.
28. See Zhang Qinshi (C. S. Chang), *Guonei jin shinian lai zhi zongjiao sichao* (Religious thought in China during the last decade) (Beijing: Yenching School of Chinese Studies, 1927), 239; and Peng Jinzhang, "Jidujiao shi mieshi nüxing mo?" (Does Christianity despise women?), *Zhenli zhoukan* (Truth weekly) 42 (13 January 1924): 1.

29. Mrs. Tseng Laisun was also rendered as Mrs. Tsang Laisun or simply Laisun. See Luella Miner, "The Place of Woman," 323. For a discussion on the family of Mrs. Tseng Laisun, see Carl T. Smith, *Chinese Christians: Elites, Middlemen, and the Church in China* (Hong Kong: Oxford University Press, 1985), 70-74.

30. Ellsworth C. Carlson, *The Foochow Missionaries*, 52-53.

31. See the papers on "Woman's Work for Woman" by A. P. Happer and Martha F. Crawford (Mrs. T. P. Crawford) in *Records 1877*, 139-147, 147-152.

32. Martha F. Crawford, "Woman's Work for Woman," 152.

33. For example, W. S. Ament, "Report of Peking Station for the Year Ending April 30, 1884," ABC 16.3.12 (8), no. 10; and Emily S. Hartwell's letter of 9 February 1887, ABC 16.2.5. (3), no. 224.

34. Lucy E. Hartwell's letter of 30 December 1871, ABC 16.3.5 (1), no. 167.

35. Ellsworth C. Carlson, *The Foochow Missionaries*, 86; Kenneth S. Latourette, *A History of Christian Missions*, 450; and "Annual Report of Bridgman Academy, 1874-1875," ABC 16.3.12. (3), no. 112.

36. "Report of the Committee on Education, April 26, 1873," ABC 16.3.12 (3), no. 102.

37. China Educational Commission, *Christian Education in China: A Study Made by an Educational Commission Representing the Mission Boards and Societies Conducting Work in China* (New York: The Foreign Missions Conference of North America, 1922), 257.

38. Ida Belle Lewis, *The Educatioin of Girls in China* (New York: Teachers College, Columbia University, 1919), 24.

39. Margaret Burton, *The Education of Women in China* (New York: Fleming H. Revell Co., 1911), 112, 125.

40. Ida Belle Lewis, *The Education of Girls in China*, 24, 34.

41. M. T. Stauffer, ed., *The Christian Occupation*, 302, 304.

42. Jessie Gregory Lutz, *China and the Christian Colleges, 1850-1950* (Ithaca, N.Y.: Cornell University Press, 1971), 132-138.

43. Sara Waithill Tucker, "The Canton Hospital and Medicine in Nineteenth Century China, 1835-1900," (Ph.D. diss., Indiana University, 1983), 1.

44. K. Chimin Wong and Wu Lien-teh, *History of Chinese Medicine: Being a Chronicle of Medical Happenings in China from Ancient Times to the Present Period* (Tientsin: Tientsin Press, 1932), 277.

45. *Records 1890*, 710.

46. Harold Balme, *China and Modern Medicine: A Study in Medical Missionary Development* (London: United Council for Missionary Education, 1921), 105.

47. See Howard Taylor, *Hudson Taylor and the China Inland Mission: The Growth of a Work of God* (London: Morgan and Scott, 1920), 89.

48. *Records 1877*, 487; and *Records 1890*, 735.
49. John F. Goucher remarked in the "Report of the Foreign Missions Conference of North America," in 1917, as quoted in the editorial, *CR* 49 (1918): 214.
50. Lucy E. Hartwell's letter of 30 December 1871, ABC 16.3.5 (1), no. 167.
51. Marshall Broomhall, *The Jubilee Story of the China Inland Mission* (London: Morgan and Scott, 1915), 123-128.
52. See Jane Hunter, *The Gospel of Gentility*, 1-51.
53. Mrs. Albert Bowker and Mrs. J. A. Copp, "To Christian Women, in Behalf of Their Sex in Heathen Lands," *The Missionary Herald* 64 (1866): 139.
54. For the history of American women in mission, see Helen B. Montgomery, *Western Women in Eastern Lands: An Outline Study of Fifty Years of Women's Work in Foreign Missions* (New York: Macmillan Co., 1911); and R. Pierce Beaver, *All Love Excelling: American Protestant Women in World Mission* (Grand Rapids, Mich.: Wm. B. Eerdmans, 1968).
55. Harriet F. Baldwin's letter of 21 June 1871, ABC 16.3.5 (1), no. 91. Emphasis hers.
56. *Records 1877*, 147.
57. Jane Hunter, *The Gospel of Gentility*, 28-29.
58. Ibid., 51.
59. Ibid., 265.
60. Ibid., 2.
61. See *JHXB* 5 (7 June 1873): 276b-278; *WGGB* 10 (5 January 1878): 285-286b; 10 (12 January 1878): 301-301b; and 12 (28 February 1880): 246-247. Some Chinese journals and books indicate their pagination at the middle of two pages. I use the page number to denote the front page and add a "b" when referring to the back page.
62. For example, Huang Ying (Lu Yin) was impressed by Charlotte Jewell, the principal of Mary Gamewell School in Beijing; see "Lu Yin zizhuan" (Autobiography of Lu Yin), in vol. 1 of *Lu Yin xuanji* (Selected works of Lu Yin), ed., Qian Hong (Fushou: Fujian People's Press, 1985), 560-561. Further, Zeng Baosun was grateful to Principal Barnes for her care and guidance; see *Zeng Baosun huiyilu* (The memoir of Zeng Baosun) (Hong Kong: Chinese Christian Literature Council, 1970).
63. Sophia H. Chen (Chen Hengzhe), "A Non-Christian Estimate of Missionary Activities," *CR* 65 (1934): 111.
64. Jane Hunter, *The Gospel of Gentility*, 26.
65. Alison R. Drucker, "The Influence of Western Women on the Anti-footbinding Movement, 1840-1911," in *Women in China: Current Directions in Historical Scholarship*, ed., Richard W. Guisso and Stanley

Johannesen (New York: Philo Press, 1981), 179-199.

66.   A. H. Tuttle, *Mary Porter Gamewell and Her Story of the Seige of Peking* (New York: Eaton and Mains, 1907), 69.

67.   Irwin T. Hyatt, Jr., *Our Ordered Lives Confess: Three Nineteenth-Century American Missionaries in East Shantung* (Cambridge, Mass.: Harvard University Press, 1976), 237.

CHAPTER II

The Feminization of Christian Symbolism

Chinese women have been attracted to the Christian church for many different reasons. Some joined because of the influence of relatives or friendship with missionaries, while others valued opportunities to learn to read, to sing Christian hymns, and to play certain roles in the Christian community. At times, women have been driven to seek refuge with the missionaries and the church because of sociopolitical pressures, such as economic difficulties, political chaos, famine, and undesirable arranged marriages.[1] Although the religious content of Christianity might not be the most important cause for women's conversion, it is still important to explore the symbolic resources available to them and to find out how the Christian message was made applicable to their situation.

Since the majority of female converts were illiterate, the basic tenets of Christian faith had to be presented orally, through preaching and teaching, especially by women missionaries and Bible women. However, only some of the sermons that circulated at Fujian can be located, and we have little knowledge of the oral teachings of missionaries.[2] In general, women missionaries rarely published in Chinese, and their English writings and correspondence seldom discussed religious dogmas or how the Gospel was adapted to suit a Chinese audience. One viable way to clarify the gospel message that was communicated is to analyze the reading materials from which the Chinese women were taught, including the Bible, the Lord's Prayer, the catechism, and simple tracts. In the lower forms of mission primary schools, students were taught the Christian *Sanzi jing* (Trimetrical classic), which was written in rhymed couplets of three characters, modeled after the Chinese style.[3] These basic reading materials, together with other religious writings by both the missionaries and the Chinese, help us to reconstruct the religious milieu of the time.

The Chinese language is radically different from Indo-European languages. As Jacques Gernet, a French sinologist says, "a model of a language more different from that of Greek, Latin or Sanskrit cannot be imagined."[4] Frustrated by the difficulty of learning the Chinese language, some early missionaries believed the "evil one" had invented Chinese for the purpose of keeping Christianity out of China.[5] Not only is there no exact equivalent for the term *God*, the missionaries seemed to be in a quandary to find the right words for rendering such expressions as Holy Spirit, conversion, priesthood, and Protestantism. The choice of a particular Chinese term is not a simple matter of translation but involves a representation of the symbolism and concept concerned, because the Chinese term invariably brings with it the connotations and ramifications of its Chinese context. This is evident in the translation of the term *God* into Chinese, because whatever term is chosen, it will bring with it a previous life of its own.

The communication of the Gospel took place against the rich and diverse Chinese religious background. Protestant missionaries had to borrow from Chinese religious ideas to convey their message, as did their Nestorian and Roman Catholic predecessors, who came during the seventh and the sixteenth centuries, respectively. In the symbolic universe of the Chinese, there were both masculine and feminine dimensions; for example, the Dao is manifested through the interplay of the yin and the yang, giving rise to all things. Some prominent female religious figures such as Mazu and Guanyin drew a large number of followers, both male and female, in popular religion. This diffused and pluralistic religious system differed significantly from the Christian belief in a monotheistic God, portrayed predominantly in male metaphors as the Father and the Son.

In the transposition of Christian symbolism and concepts to the Chinese context, I will argue there was a process of "feminization of Christian symbolism" especially in the nineteenth century. By this I mean an emphasis on the compassion of God, the use of more inclusive metaphors for the divine, the stress on Jesus' relation with women, and the downplaying of the sinfulness of Eve. The concept of a "feminization" of the Christian religion was introduced by historian Barbara Welter in her study of American religion in the first half of the nineteenth century. She observed that as women became more prominent in worship and church life, the sermons preached at the pulpit began to introduce the ideas of a Father-Mother God and a feminized Christ who exemplified meekness and humility. Popular hymns, too, focused on Christ's love and God's mercy.[6] From the Chinese perspective, feminization of Christian symbolism took place in a different setting, because Christianity needed to "incarnate" within a religious system that did not repress the feminine dimension.

A feminized Christianity increased its appeal not only to Chinese women, but to men, too, since traditionally both men and women worshipped goddesses in Chinese religion. The juxtaposition of Christianity and Chinese culture created a symbolic world quite different from Christianity in the West. Western feminist theologians, such as Mary Daly and Rosemary Radford Ruether, criticize the core symbolism of Christianity as androcentric, which can be used to provide religious legitimation for male domination.[7] Chinese Christian women, however, did not experience Christianity in the same way because Christian symbolism and concepts underwent modifications when they assumed a Chinese dress. Furthermore, as we shall see in the following discussion, religious symbolism may not function in the same manner in a cross-cultural context.

Attempting to recontruct the symbolic world communicated by Christianity, I shall examine the Chinese term for God, the image of God as father, Jesus and the salvation story, the relationship between Jesus and women, and the female symbolism of Eve and Mary. My purpose is both to analyze the process of feminization of Christian symbolism and to understand what were the symbolic resources available to women who joined the Christian church.

The Chinese Term for God

The "term question," an expression used by missionaries, refers to the unsettling debate concerning how to render the Hebrew and Greek terms *Elohim* and *Theos*, or God, into the Chinese language. As William Milne, one of the early Protestant missionaries noted, "the Chinese language possesses no single appellation expressive of the idea which Christians connect with the words God, deity, etc."[8] The term question not only epitomizes the differences that exist between Chinese and Indo-European languages, but it also informs us how the missionaries and Chinese Christians adapted the doctrine of God into the Chinese context.

The controversy first began in the seventeenth century, when the Jesuits proposed to use *tian* ("heaven") or *shangdi* ("supreme ruler") for God, but the Dominicans and Franciscans insisted on using *tianzhu*, or Master of Heaven. The battle waged for nearly a century, and although Pope Clement XI decreed in 1715 that the term *tianzhu* should be used, the issue was far from being settled. When Protestant missionaries arrived in the early nineteenth century, they wished to use another term for God to distinguish their religion from Roman Catholicism. Robert Morrison and William Milne used *shen* in their first translation of the New Testament, but they also employed many other terms in their Chinese religious writings.[9] In his popular tract, Milne wrote that the true God has many aliases, such as *shen, zhu, shenzhu, shentian, tiandi zhi dazhu*, or just *tian*.[10] Other writers, such as W. H. Medhurst and Charles Gützlaff, preferred to use *shangdi*, and Liang Fa, the only Chinese writing at this early period, used *shentian shangdi* for Yahweh and *shen* as the generic term for deity.

The protestant term question originated in the 1840's, when the representatives of the mission bodies met to prepare·a new translation of the Bible, later known as the Delegates Version. As it turned out, the choice of the Chinese term for God became "a contest between British and American sinologues," with the British favoring *shangdi* and the Americans preferring *shen*. In 1877, when the first general missionary conference was held at Shanghai, the missionaries agreed not to discuss the issue in order to avoid a further schism.[11] To elicit opinion from the Chinese Christians, Young J. Allen and John Roberts invited the readers to discuss "the *shenghao* question" (as it was called in Chinese) in the *Wanguo gongbao* (The globe magazine).[12] With enthusiasm and vigor, some fifteen Chinese writers joined the debate before the journal finally decided to put an end to the discussion. The term question trailed on, with both sides publishing numerous articles and pamphlets on the subject, until the disastrous Boxer incident unexpectedly ushered in a new era of cooperation among missionaries and the debate gradually died down.[13] Even today, however, Chinese Roman Catholics continue to use *tianzhu*, while mainline Protestants use *shangdi* and evangelical Christians prefer the term *shen*.

The debate on the translation of the term *God*, which happened nowhere else with such intensity, brings into focus the peculiarity of the Chinese language. Unlike the Indo-European languages, Chinese language lacks inflection. As S. Wells Williams, a missionary who later became a professor of Chinese language, remarked: "No word in Chinese undergoes any change to represent its use as a verb, noun, or adjective; to indicate its position in the nominative, genitive, or accusative cases; or to show its number, gender, or tense. They are all, like our ten digits, unalterable."[14] In the Hebrew and Greek Bibles, the terms *elohim* or *theos* can be used to refer both to the supreme God as well as to deity in general, for instance, "I am the Lord your *God*. . . You shall have no other *gods* before me," (Exod. 20:2-3). Chinese nouns, without any designation for the singular or the plural, and without capitalization or any such devices, cannot function in the same way without causing confusion.

But the difference in language only reflects the deeper divergence in mental categories and thought processes. The missionaries believed there is a supreme being, who creates and rules the universe, and God is the name for this "self-existent, eternal, almighty Being, the Creator of heaven and earth."[15] In contrast, the Chinese conceive of cosmogony as a dynamic, continuous, and organismic process in which there is no creator who stands outside the universe.[16] "The analogy behind their thinking is not a man making a pot," as A. C. Graham vividly describes it, "but rather a tree growing from its hidden root and branching out."[17] In order to bridge the gap between these two mental worlds, William J. Boone, the American Missionary Bishop of the Protestant Episcopal Church, suggested translating God as *shen*, the generic name the Chinese use for the highest class of beings to whom they offer religious worship.[18] But his opponents argued that the Chinese worship many religious objects, not all of them can be classified as *shen*, and besides, the term *shen* hardly evokes the sense of power and majesty of the supreme being. Instead, W. H. Medhurst and James Legge proposed to use *shangdi*, the Chinese term for the highest being with supreme authority and ruling power.[19] Boone and others, defending their choice, challenged that Shangdi is the proper name for the highest Chinese "idol," which should not be identified with the Christian God.

The term question basically concerns finding a Chinese term to convey the concept of a monotheistic and transcendent God in the pluralistic religious system in China. In the protracted discussion on the "oneness" and "plurality" of the highest deity, the issue of gender frequently emerged, and I would like to focus on this aspect of the debate. In Chinese cosmology, *taiji* ("the ultimate") gives rise to the yin and yang, the interplay of which gives rise to the myriad of things. Many missionaries, interpreting the Chinese religious system with their Western mind-set, considered the Chinese cosmogony to be both dualistic and mechanistic. Boone, for example, cited this as evidence against the use of the term *shangdi* for God:

> [I]f Shangti [Shangdi] stood quietly by and permitted the *Yin* and *Yang* to grind until heaven and earth and all things were made, we cannot regard him as God (*propriè*); and if he did not exist at that time as an idle spectator, he is not self-existent from eternity; and this is equally fatal to his claim to be regarded as truly and properly God.[20]

Noting that the yin and the yang are sometimes represented as earth and heaven, and that the Chinese make sacrifices to these two principles during the winter and summer solstices, Boone stated that heaven and earth are their two highest gods, which he found incompatible with Christian monotheism.[21] Some twenty years later, S. Wells Williams extended Boone's argument to draw the conclusion that *shangdi*, which is synonymous with heaven, bears the "male principle of nature," for in Chinese cosmogony, heaven is male and earth is female, denoting a matrimonial relation.[22] To supplement his argument, Williams compared heaven and earth in Chinese cosmology to the Greek and Syrian gods and goddesses:

> In Peking, where the *Tien tan* [tiantan] and *Ti tan* [ditan], the altars to Heaven and Earth, are laid out in all their magnitude on the south and on the north of the imperial palace, they are fully understood to be of equal divine powers, complementary to each other as much as Zeus and Hera among the Greeks, or Baal and Astarte among the Syrians.[23]

To defend themselves against the charge of dualism, the *shangdi* advocates employed several strategies. According to Medhurst, the Chinese do not ascribe the creation of the world to any one being, but they do attribute to Tian or Shangdi the production and superintendence of all things.[24] In the Chinese classics, there are instances where Shangdi is portrayed in anthropomorphic language, such as the command, the will, and the virtue of Shangdi. Rejecting the idea that Chinese cosmology is mechanistic, Medhurst affirmed that the world comes forth through the command of Shangdi, and if the Chinese ever ascribe "the production of all things to the five elements, or the *yin* and *yang*, it is only as these elements and principles are employed by him, who in their estimation is the Divinity."[25]

Both Milne and Medhurst tried to draw out the different nuances suggested by the Chinese terms *tian* and *di* ("ruler"). Milne, who adopted the use of *shangdi* in his later years, asserted that *shangdi* is different from all other terms, such as *tian, shangtian,* and *shen,* for they each have a "companion, or (to avert to the Chinese sexual system of the world), in fact, a consort or spouse," but it is not mentioned that Shangdi has any companion.[26] Similarly, Medhurst preferred the use of *di* ("ruler") to *tian,* because it does not carry the dualistic overtones: "Te [di] is never considered as synonymous with heaven and earth together, but with heaven only; there is no reference to the dual system when Te [di] is used."[27]

But the most intriguing defense for the term *shangdi* came from Legge, who argued that the sacrifices in winter and in summer were made not to two gods but to Shangdi alone, for, in his view, the Chinese were monotheistic in ancient times and only later did they begin to worship more than one deity. For Legge, heaven and earth are the works of God, and they point to two different aspects of the divine. "When we consider heaven, we are filled with awe: we are moved to reverence and honour Him, whose throne they are. When we consider the earth, we are penetrated with a sense of His kindness." Using the parental images, Legge portrayed God with both male and female characteristics, for heaven represents divine majesty and the earth represents divine care, "the former teaches us of God's more than parental authority; the latter of His more than maternal love."[28]

Influenced by their own dualistic thinking and anthropocentric understanding of the divine, most missionaries could not fully appreciate the universal dynamism symbolized by the yin and the yang. Boone has certainly gone too far in his hypostasis of heaven and earth as two deities. Medhurst could find no problem in the identification of Shangdi with heaven, but he rejected the heaven-earth duality. S. Wells Williams discredited Shangdi as the "male principle of nature," and contrary to both Milne and Medhurst, he

maintained that Shangdi has a female counterpart. In their denunciation of the dual system of the Chinese, these missionaries seemed
most uncomfortable with the female representation of the divine. In
the seventeenth century, some Roman Catholic missionaries were
reported also to have objected to the Chinese praying to earth.[29]

Among the missionaries, Legge, the illustrious translator of
Chinese classics, was most appreciative of Chinese culture. He went
one step further than most of the missionaries to identify the Shangdi
of the Chinese with the Christian God, and once he even ascended
with his shoes off the altar of heaven, where Shangdi was worshipped. However, in his polemic against his rivals, Legge overstressed
the personal characteristics of the term *shangdi* and failed to
present adequately the cosmological dimension of the Chinese
religious system.[30]

When we turn to the debates among the Chinese Christians, we
can see that some were more free to adopt the symbol of God into
their tradition because they did not share some of the missionaries'
assumptions. Their writings in *Wanguo gongbao* clearly indicated
that they could understand and follow the major tenets of the
controversy. For example, they debate the generic terms used for
deity in Chinese, the difference between God the creator and other
deities in Chinese folk religion, the relation between *shangdi* and
heaven, and finally, whether *shangdi* was equivalent to the Christian God.[31] The religious writings of the Chinese and the direct
observation of the missionaries both confirmed that the majority of
Chinese Christians preferred *shangdi* rather than *shen*.[32] In certain
cases, even when the missionaries used *shen*, Chinese Christians still
chose the term *shangdi*, and their strong preference, for instance in
Fujian, motivated the missionaries to change to *shangdi* as well.[33]
The choice of *shangdi* over *shen* could be attributed to many
reasons: the term *shangdi* is embedded in the Chinese classics,
denoting the highest idea of supreme ruler, while *shen* refers to the
numerous popular deities, who hardly command respect. Some
Chinese Christians were, perhaps, eager to demonstrate that Christianity was not a foreign religion. For them, the Chinese classics
pointed to the same God, who was called by another name, Yahweh,
in the Christian Bible.[34]

While proponents of *shen* emphasized the differences between
the Chinese religious system and Christianity, such as the lack of an
idea of a creator and the worship of heaven and earth as parts of

nature in Chinese tradition,[35] the advocates of *shangdi* underscored their similarities. The latter sought to demonstrate that an anthropomorphic understanding of the creator does not contradict Chinese cosmology, which conceives of the ultimate dwelling in all things. The Neo-Confucian philosophy provided the advocates for *shangdi* with the framework to understand the universal principle (*li*) undergirding all things (*wu*), and they did not seem to have any difficulty imagining *shangdi* as creator and, at the same time, immanent throughout creation. Citing Zhu Xi and Cheng Yi, they contended that the material form of heaven, which is call *tian* ("heaven"), cannot be separated from the ruling aspect, which is called di ("ruler"). Like James Legge, they argued that sacrifices to heaven and earth were made to *shangdi*, and that the fact that sacrifice was made not to heaven alone demonstrates that *shangdi* is not to be equated with the natural heaven.[36]

Many Chinese Christians who adopted the term *shangdi* for God did not separate immanence from transcendence, the material from the spiritual, the human realm from the cosmological. Contrary to the dualistic thinking of the missionaries, their mode of thought could be characterized as correlative thinking, which saw each part in connection with the whole.[37] They were interested in how ultimate reality can be immanent in its parts yet more than the parts, to hold the cosmic organism together. The missionaries, on the other hand, were concerned more with distinguishing God from all creation, and for them, the notion of "one above many" is essential.[38] Since Chinese Christians did not think so much in dualistic terms, the yin and yang polarity, or even the gender of God, did not surface as an issue in their discourse on the term question.

Our discussion shows that Chinese Christians played an important role in the term question by helping to make the alien symbol of a monotheistic God more accessible. They opted for an indigenous and respectable term for God, and they incorporated the doctrine of God into their wholistic and cosmological religiosity. Because of their non-dualistic thinking, Chinese Christians did not absolutely reject the female representation of the divine, seeing God the creator dwelling in all things, including the sun and the moon, the heaven and the earth. While many missionaries blamed the Chinese language for its inadequacy in expressing spiritual truth, the term controversy drove home to many Chinese Christians the limitation of any language to name what cannot be named. Pan Xunru of Shanghai summarized the term debate most succinctly: "Whether we use *shangdi* or *shen*, it is, I am afraid, just as Laozi has said, we have no name for it, we just arbitrarily name it."[39]

God the Father

Although the family is the basic institution of Chinese society, the Chinese have not projected a divine father of all humankind. Medhurst had noticed this peculiar characteristic of Chinese culture, as he wrote:

> It is strange, however, that while Confucius recommends such an excessive veneration for parents, he should have overlooked the reverence due to the Father of our spirits; and while he traced up the series from parents to ancestors, requiring the highest degree of honor to be paid to our first progenitors, that he should not have considered Him from whom all beings spring, and who is entitled to our first and chief regard.[40]

In the seventeenth century, some of the more orthodox Roman Catholic missionaries found the worship of ancestors to be irreconcilable with the worship of God, and the famous Rites Controversy led to direct confrontations between popes and Chinese emperors and contributed to the eventual expulsion of missionaries from China in 1724. Later, when Protestant missionaries arrived in China, they had to distinguish the worship of God from ancestor worship, but on the other hand, they also wished to capitalize on the Chinese reverence to their ancestors and hoped to extend it to God.

Chinese tracts and religious literature, written by both male and female missionaries, frequently referred to God as the Heavenly Father. Although some of them had questioned the gender of *shangdi* in the Chinese context, none of them seemed to have been troubled by their use of the male image for God. God as the Father is used in the New Testament, where Jesus himself calls God *Abba* (or "Papa"), denoting his intimate relationship with Him. When the missionaries used the phrase Heavenly Father, they highlighted the love and protection of God, especially in their rhetoric directed against those indigenous deities that the Chinese feared. In his popular tract, Milne wrote, "*shangtian shenzhu* is the father of all human beings, who bestows us with all the rich blessings, and we should have filial piety toward Him."[41]

The image of God as father was presented not only in religious writings, but more importantly, it was reenacted in Christian worship services. Many of the new inquirers, including women, were taught to recite the Lord's Prayer, which begins with "Our Father, who art in heaven." The trinitarian formula, God the Father, Son, and Holy Spirit, was invoked frequently in baptism and in Christian liturgies. In the hymns sung in the churches, the father image of God was used in the context of his loving kindness and care, for example:

> God is compassionate and merciful,
> nurtures and protects all the people.
> But the people are not grateful,
> they turn instead to worship idols and false gods.[42]

The image of the Heavenly Father can be related to the familial context in very different ways. It can be used either to reinforce the family system or to challenge it. In the writings of the missionaries, notably in a collection of essays on filial piety, most of the authors did not conceive the fatherhood of God as challenging the filial piety due to parents and ancestors. What they tried to denounce were the ritualistic sacrifices made to the ancestors.[43] Trying to extend the reverence due to one's father to the Heavenly Father, the missionaries did not call into question the patriarchal family system. Beginning in the 1890's, however, some missionaries, notably Young J. Allen, sought to introduce a more egalitarian notion of the sexes based on the belief that God is our common father and we are all his children. For Allen, God creates and loves both men and women, and Christianity promotes the equality of the sexes.[44]

In fact, the Chinese also recognized the revolutionary potential in the belief of God as the common father of human beings. For example, in the Taiping movement, the leader Hong Xiuquan incorporated the notion of the common fatherhood of God in his revolutionary rhetoric to unify his community to fight against the Manchus. It is not surprising, therefore, to find the anti-Christian tracts condemning the belief in God the Father as undermining hierarchical social relations in China. The combative *Pixie jishi* writes, "The world only has the Heavenly Father (God), the Heavenly Mother (the Virgin), and the Heavenly Elder Brother (Jesus), and there is no more distinction between those above and those below."[45] If all become brothers and sisters, it continues, the five relationships in Chinese society will be destroyed. As we have mentioned, Christianity was accused of subverting the social relationships, encouraging sexual impropriety, and even advocating the domination of women over men.[46]

As for Chinese Christians, although they also referred to God as Heavenly Father, their writings seldom dwelled on the love and kindness of the Father. When some open-minded Christians wrote in support of the anti-footbinding movement and better treatment for women, they described God as the creator of men and women, rather than God as the common father of all.[47] The father image of God seemed to be difficult for the Chinese to appropriate. For instance, the author of an article in *Wanguo gongbao* in 1875 said that the Chinese found it strange to call God *tianfu* ("Heavenly Father"), because they did not understand how heaven can have a father. It went on to explain that we call God "Father" to denote his relationship with us, and that we refer to him as "Heavenly Father" to express our respect.[48] Another inquirer was puzzled by the fact the "*tianfu* is not heaven, not earth, not *li* [principle], not *qi*, not nature, not human, not object, nor ghost." The editor of the journal explained that God is the great father who creates heaven and earth and all the myriad things, the progenitor of all the peoples, and the common father of all the nations.[49]

Apart from the difficulty of juxtaposing the anthropomorphic "Father" with the naturalistic "Heaven," the father image also had other limitations in the Chinese cultural context. The father in the Chinese family was expected to be strict and stern to his children, so that fatherhood could not be used plausibly to express the encompassing love of God and his close relationship with creation. Frank Rawlinson, the editor of the influential *Chinese Recorder*, raised this issue in discussing the problems of the naturalization of Christianity in China:

> The concept "father," however, is not the one best adapted for use in China to suggest the character of the Supreme Father as the father, together with the teacher and emperor, was expected to hold himself aloof and be reticent. It does not, therefore, easily suggest the idea of intimate relationship with the Supreme Father so prominent in Jesus' thought. The Chinese concept needs a richer content.[50]

Moreover, the image of God as the father without a female counterpart does not harmonize with family symbolism. If we are to honor our parents on earth, it seems incomplete that we only have a single parent, a father in heaven without a mother. Thus in the famous vision of the Taiping leader Hong Xiuquan, the heavenly court was portrayed as a divine family, with a Heavenly Father and Mother, and with Jesus as the Elder Brother and his wife as the Elder Sister-in-Law. Hong called himself the Younger Brother of Jesus, saying he was the sun and his wife the moon.[51] Hong's vision can be seen as an attempt to indigenize Christian symbolism in the Chinese familial context, and it should not be dismissed as nothing more than a misunderstanding or a blasphemy on his part.

The problems surrounding the father image of God necessitated the use of other images, and several prominent missionaries as well as Chinese Christians referred to God as both father and mother. The idea of God as father and mother is not unique to China, however. The American Shakers in the nineteenth century also believed in the Father-Mother God, and the Mormons posited a dual parenthood within the Godhead.[52] But the use of this dual image of God in China as early as the 1830's by people who obviously did not belong to these sectarian traditions merits our attention. The image of a Father-Mother God was used in several contexts in China, but most frequently to describe God as our source and creator. In a small tract on the doctrine of God, Charles Hartwell, an American missionary in Fuzhou, stated that trees have their roots, rivers have their source, fruits have their seeds, and God is "the origin of all living things, the ruler of all nations and the father and mother of all the peoples."[53] Gützlaff also used the father-mother image to describe God's protection and nurturance: "Human beings depend on the grace of God, just like babies who cannot eat when they are hungry, cannot dress up when they are cold, but have to depend on their father and mother. . . . God loves humankind, much more than the love of the father and mother."[54] This was echoed by Mary Elizabeth Andrews, whose selection of biblical verses included reference to God's love and compassion resembling that of a mother: "Can a woman forget her sucking child, that she should have no compassion on the son of her womb? Even these may forget, yet I will not forget you" (Isa. 49:15).[55]

Liang Fa also employed the father-mother metaphor to refer to the grace of God in the context of the forgiveness of sin:

> God, the great father and mother of all the people on
> earth, is patient with his people, just like fathers and
> mothers are patient with their children. God is waiting
> to forgive their sins, if they will only repent of their sins
> and turn their evil hearts to accept God's forgiveness and
> to live in his grace. God does not wish to condemn them
> to death or to imprison their souls in hell to suffer from
> the punishment of eternal fire.[56]

The father-mother image was not only used in the familial context
of care and nurturance but also in the political context of rule and
power. In the Chinese tradition, the king or emperor is often
referred to as the father-mother of the people, and the magistrates
as the father-mother officials.[57] Kuang Rixiu, an Anglican from
Hong Kong, explained that *shangdi* means the judge or ruler to whom
the masses of people turn to, and a child also calls his father and
mother "ruler." He continued that *shangdi* is "the master who rules
over the world and human beings, the great father and mother of
all the peoples."[58]

In summary, we can see that the father image of God cannot
be easily appropriated in the Chinese context without causing
tension. The notion that God is the common father of all humankind
has the potential to challenge the authority of fathers in the family.
Furthermore, the stern image of the Chinese father does not
adequately convey the loving kindness of God, and God as a single
parent disrupts the symmetry and harmony of the familial symbolism.
Some writers of the religious tracts, therefore, were driven to use the
more inclusive metaphor of a father-mother God.

Jesus and the Salvation Story

The Christian catechism and the trimetrical classic were widely taught
to the men and women who came to church and to girls and boys
in the mission schools. An analysis of their basic contents helps us
to understand the gospel message of Jesus as the Savior and the structure of the salvation story. The American Board collection of Chinese
tracts in the Harvard-Yenching Library has different versions of the
Christian trimetrical classic, ranging in date from 1832 to 1913,[59] and
various catechisms dated from 1829 to 1892.[60]

The Christian trimetrical classic starts with a succinct summary
of the doctrine of God: "In the beginning, there is God, who makes

people and all things, and creates heaven and earth. Omniscient, omnipresent, omnipotent, he is the true ruler."[61] The different versions of the catechism all begin by defining God as the creator, who is to be distinguished from all other false deities.[62] The "idols," or man-made images, the sun, and the moon are only part of the creation, and do not deserve our devotion. God is a spirit who has no image or shape, without beginning or end. Intelligence, majesty, mercy, and righteousness are his attributes.

God is revealed in the Bible, which is more valuable than all the Chinese classics, for those books are written by human beings and do not reveal the salvation of the soul and life after death. God creates the first human being and gives him a soul by breathing into his nostrils. He places Adam and Eve in the garden of Eden, but they disobey him by listening to the temptation of the serpent and eating the fruit of the tree of knowledge. Because of their sin, they are driven away from the garden, and their fall taints all human beings, who become sinners under curse and punishment.

From the Fall, most catechisms and trimetrical classics move directly to salvation in Jesus Christ, leaving out the entire history of the Old Testament. The catechism of Helen S. Nevius mentions briefly Noah and Abraham, and the kingdom of Judah under David and Solomon. The little attention paid to the Old Testament is a characteristic not only of the catechism but of most of the religious tracts as well, since many missionary writers came from evangelical backgrounds, and their message was basically Christocentric. This negligence prompted one missionary to write an article listing some thirty reasons why the Old Testament is important to Christian religious life.[63] Without knowledge of the Old Testament, the majority of Chinese Christians could not conceive of God acting in history, as one who enters into a covenantal relationship with his people. The gospel message presented was highly individualistic, concerned with personal salvation from sin, punishment, and death.

The catechism continues to discuss the birth of Jesus, the Son of God, but the special circumstances surrounding Jesus' birth are not emphasized. Since the focus of the story is on the atonement, the narrative highlights the cross and the resurrection, without giving much attention to the life and ministry of Jesus. The Son of God came to die for us, because we all inherit original sin from our ancestors and we commit sin ourselves. Jesus, as our mediator, bore our punishment, and his merits (*gonglao*) can be computed to our names. In order to help us believe in Jesus, the gracious God sends us the Holy Spirit, who is one with the Father and the Son. At the end of the world, Jesus will come again to judge the good and the wicked; those who believe in him will go to heaven, a place of happiness and glory, while the rest will descend to hell and eternal damnation. Therefore, we must repent of our sin, trust in Jesus, loving him and following his teachings.

The Christian belief in the depravity of human beings is contrary to Mencius' teaching that human nature is basically good, and the various theories of atonement, such as ransom or propitiation, are alien to Chinese thought. To help its readers understand these foreign doctrines, the trimetrical classic introduces a medical metaphor to bridge the cultural gap. The human predicament is compared to a person with sickness, and Jesus' salvation is likened to a good medicine that can cure all diseases; those who refuse the good medicine are not doing themselves any good.[64]

After conversion, the duties of the Christian include reading the Bible, praying to God, and attending church services. Baptism and Holy Communion are the two most important sacraments in the church. Baptism symbolizes the cleansing of the heart with the blood of Jesus, just as the body is cleansed with water. Holy Communion, symbolizing the sacrifice of Jesus' body and blood, was instituted by Jesus himself, who gave the bread and the wine to his disciples at the Last Supper. The final part of the catechism consists usually of the Lord's Prayer and the Ten Commandments; some include the Apostle's Creed as well.

In writing the Christian catechism and religious tracts, the missionaries had to borrow from the religious ideas of the Chinese to express the Christian doctrines. In the seventh century when Christianity was first introduced into China, the Nestorians adopted many terms from Buddhism for their use, and Buddhism was then experiencing its peak of influence in China. Centuries later, when Roman Catholic and Protestant missionaries arrived, they also discovered that Buddhism provided many religious ideas and concepts that were able to convey a Christian message.[65] Acknowledging that Buddhism was a helpful preparation for Christianity, W. A. P. Martin, a missionary highly respected in the Qing court, listed some twenty Buddhist terms and phrases that occurred most frequently in Christian books, such as *heaven, hell, devil, soul, the next world, sin, repentance, and conversion.* "So half the doctrines of Christianity are introduced to the Chinese in a dress borrowed from Buddhism,'' he commented.[66]

Nevertheless, the missionaries had different opinions regarding this large-scale borrowing from Buddhist terminology. Many expressed concern that the adoption of Buddhist terms, which originated in a different context, would distort the Christian message. In his elucidation of Christian terminology in Chinese, John C. Gibson pointed out that the term *tianting* (''heavenly hall'') is a poor translation for heaven, for it sounds more like a Chinese *yamen* (''court'') than the glorious throne of God, the home of the redeemed. The word *zui* (''sin'') does not convey the idea of the guilt of sin, but implies the breach of criminal law. *Xinde* (''faith''), as used in the Chinese context, is understood more as a moral attainment than confidence or trust.[67] But however inappropriate these terms might be, the missionaries really did not have any others from which to choose. One missionary lamented:

> Who has been fortunate enough to discover a name for sin which does not dash us on the Scylla of civil crime or engulph [*sic*] us in the Charybdis of retribution for the faults of a former life? Use whatever language you please to express the resurrection, and the uninitiated will understand it to mean transmigration.[68]

On the other hand, some missionaries, like Martin, could see no problem of seizing the terms of the land, ''sprinkling them with holy water and consecrating them to a new use.''[69] Noting that some Buddhist terms might cause confusion, Joseph Edkins, who had seriously studied Chinese Buddhism, also affirmed that the borrowing of Buddhist terms was helpful for proselytism.

> I do not in any way doubt that Buddhist doctrines have been, for the Christian teacher, most important preparation for Christianity, and that through the spread of these doctrines the Chinese people look upon Christianity with much less strangeness and accept its doctrines with much less difficulty them [*sic*] otherwise they would have been able to do.[70]

View from the Chinese perspective, the propagation of Christianity in Buddhist terminology might have dismayed the intellectuals who had little respect for popular Buddhism. For example, some

Chinese literati claimed that Christianity had stolen the Buddhist ideas of heaven and hell to lure people to believe in their doctrines.[71] For the average village folk, however, these borrowings certainly made the foreign religion more accessible. If we compare the structure of the salvation story with the religious beliefs of some Buddhist sectarian groups, which had a great appeal for women, we can discern certain resemblances in the religious motifs and themes, for example, the incarnation of the buddhas and bodhisattvas in order to save all sentient beings, the ascent to heaven and descent to hell, the traditions of self-cultivation and merit, and eschatological expectations.[72]

The one significant difference, however, is the gender of the saving agent, because Chinese Buddhist sects venerate the Wusheng laomu, or the Eternal Mother, instead of a male savior. In popular beliefs, Guanyin and Mazu also embody some salvific motifs, and they offer their followers protection and blessing. Interestingly, the first Protestant missionary, Robert Morrison, was asked by a follower whether Jesus was a man or woman, since God is said to have no temper or anger.[73] In anti-Christian writings, the worship of Jesus was often contrasted with the worship of Guanyin.[74] At least one missionary, Laura M. White, has compared the earthquake during Jesus' death and his miraculous resurrection to similar motifs in the Guanyin story.[75]

For Chinese women, who were raised in a more inclusive religious environment, worship of Jesus might be one more way to attain the Western Paradise, and the salvation offered by Jesus was seen in the context of a pluralistic belief, in which both male and female could be salvific figures. The maleness of Jesus did not seem to be an issue for women and Christian women emphasized there was no distinction between the sexes in Christ in their religious writings. For example, Zeng Baosun, a prominent female educator wrote: "In Christ there is no distinction between men and women, and He has set the same moral standard for both sexes."[76] Chinese men, however, seemed to identify more with Jesus' maleness. For example, the Taiping leader Hong Xiuquan referred to Jesus as his Heavenly Elder Brother. In the 1920's, when Jesus was upheld as the moral example for Christians and his humanity was emphasized by Chinese theologians,[77] male Christians would easily identify Jesus with the Chinese sages who were usually male.

Jesus and Women

Since the catechism and the trimetrical classic do not tell much about the life of Jesus, we have to look for other sources to understand the teaching of early Protestant missionaries to China on Jesus' relationship with women. In the American Board collection of Chinese religious literature, four tracts and pamphlets on the life and ministry of Jesus provide some helpful materials.[78] The earliest one of these was written in 1834 by Charles Gützlaff, while the other three were published in the 1870's. Charles Hartwell's tract contains the stories of the creation of the world and the Fall, in addition to the life of Jesus, and Chester Holcomb's work follows more closely the words of the scriptures, although he rearranges the sequence of the story. The longest one is written by Simeon Foster Woodin, which consists of the four gospels consolidated into one chronological narrative.[79] All four narratives contain many gospel stories of Jesus with women, and women occupy a central place in the works of both Hartwell and Holcomb. The emphasis on the women close to Jesus reflected the climate of the time, when an increasing number of women missionaries arrived in China and more attention was paid to woman's work.

In the preface to his book, Gützlaff explains his wish to make the Gospel easier for the readers by presenting a concise summary of Jesus' life based on materials from the four gospels. The attempt to present Jesus' life in a somewhat chronological order, based on all four gospels, is followed by both Holcomb and Woodin. The merging of the gospel narratives has the immediate effect of increasing the number of episodes wherein Jesus encounters women. For example, Gützlaff's account generally follows the basic scheme of the synoptic gospels supplemented with materials from John's gospel, including Jesus talking to the Samaritan woman at the well (John 4:1-30) and the raising up of Lazarus, the brother of Martha and Mary (John 11:1-46).[80] In addition, both versions of the woman anointing Jesus with oil are included: in the first, a sinful woman washes Jesus' feet and anoints them with ointment (Luke 7:36-38), and in the second, a woman anoints Jesus' head with costly oils (Mark 14:3-9 and Matt. 26:6-13).[81] Although in Gützlaff's arrangement the episodes involving women increase, he arranges these stories among episodes of Jesus teaching to the people or Jesus performing miracles, so that the women are not so conspicuous in the narrative.

In sharp contrast, Holcomb's account gives a more prominent place to women, though Holcomb also adopts the same method of merging the gospel narratives as Gützlaff does. While Gützlaff rewrites the entire gospel narrative, sometimes shortening the stories, Holcomb follows the words of the scriptures more faithfully, preserving the original depth and detail of the stories. Holcomb's portrayal of the life of Jesus adheres to the Lukan scheme, and except for the Samaritan woman at the well, his account includes almost all of the gospel stories about women. Women become more prominent in the narrative, because Holcomb condenses the gospel by leaving out many parables and teachings of Jesus, as well as Jesus' argument with the Pharisees and his private discussion with the disciples. Women are described as active participants in Jesus' mission, following him and providing for his needs. As faithful disciples of Jesus, they stood by him at the cross and were first to witness his resurrection. Holcomb captures also the reader's attention by mentioning women in the titles of the various sections, such as "Jesus Preaches the Gospel and Women Provide Food." "Woman Anoints Jesus' Head with Ointment," and "The Angel Announces the Resurrection of Jesus to the Believing Women."[82]

Among the several versions of the life of Jesus, Charles Hartwell's work merits special recognition because of its writing style and its adaptation to the Chinese context. It is arranged in lesson form, written in Fuzhou dialect. At the end of each lesson, a short ballad summarizes and reiterates the major facets of the story. Scholars who study Chinese popular culture point out that ballads were especially favored by rural women, "women like to gather in a reading circle and listen to one of their number 'sing' ballads. The ballads are in simple and rhythmic popular language, especially designed for women to read or sing."[83] It was often reported that women who came to church liked to sing, and Hartwell might have had in mind those women who regularly went to his home and learned to read from his wife.[84]

Hartwell includes the following stories about women in his tract: Mary gives birth to Jesus; Jesus changes water to wine in response to his mother's request; he straightens the woman who is bent over for eighteen years and calls to life the son of a widow at Nain. Jesus forgives the woman who pours ointment on his feet and raises up

Jairus' daughter. Women come near to Jesus and bring their children with them. Jesus drives the demon out of the daughter of the Canaanite woman and raises up Lazarus, the brother of Martha and Mary. Women cry under the cross as Jesus is crucified but Jesus appears to them after his resurrection.

Furthermore, in his editorial remarks, Hartwell underscores the positive role played by women. In the story of Jesus blessing the children, the synoptic texts do not specify who it is that brings the children, but Hartwell adds that women drew close to Jesus, bringing their children with them (Matt. 19:13-15, Mark 10:13-16; and Luke 18:15-17).[85] In the story of the raising of Lazarus from the dead, Hartwell emphasizes that it is the sisters (Martha and Mary) who believe in Jesus and request him to heal their brother (John 11:1-46).[86] His tract would have a special appeal to women, because it highlights Jesus' compassion for the widow of Nain, whose only son had died, as well as his mercy shown to the little daughter of Jairus and to the Canaanite woman whose daughter was possessed by an unclean spirit.

In addition to religious tracts and pamphlets, there are also pictures about the life of Jesus that provide another perspective on Jesus' relations with women. In the newspaper *Jiaohui xinbao* (The church news) published by Young J. Allen, excerpts from and commentaries on the Bible formed a regular feature, and they were usually illustrated. During the first year of the journal's publication (1868-1869), Allen recounted the story of the life of Jesus. Nearly half of the excerpts on Jesus' ministry had something to do with women, and these women were shown in the pictures, for example, Mary and Jesus, the Samaritan woman at the well, Peter's mother-in-law, the widow at Nain, a woman pouring ointment over Jesus' feet, women witnessing the cross and resurrection, and so on.[87] These pictures and illustrations were recognized as important resources in conveying the Gospel to the poorly educated and to women; indeed, one Beijing reader wrote to the journal requesting that more pictures be included.[88] In a short book entitled *Fuyin cuoyao* (Selections from the gospels), the illustrations were drawn by Ada Haven, later Mrs. C. W. Mateer. Women appear in nearly half of the pictures, and they are portrayed surrounding Jesus, talking to him, and witnessing to his resurrection.[89] In several illustrations, the women occupy the front stage, while Jesus is relegated to the background.

These tracts and illustrations on the life of Jesus suggest that the missionaries emphasized the close relationship between Jesus and the women who followed him. Although we have few Chinese writings on the subject by the women missionaries, it is highly plausible that they, too, underscored Jesus' love for and acceptance of women. Many women missionaries came from an evangelical background and had a strong conviction that their lives had been changed by Jesus, prompting them to come to China to uplift their "heathen" sisters. In a paper read before the Shanghai Missionary Association, Mary Martin, the wife of Timothy Richard, cited the teaching and life of Jesus to elucidate the Christian idea of womanhood. She argued that Jesus' treatment of women had helped elevate the status of women. She emphasized, for instance, his submissive respect for his mother, his teaching profound spiritual truths to women, his intimate friendship with Martha and Mary, his appreciation of the poor widow who gave only two mites, his healing the woman who suffered from a hemorrhage, his sympathy for the woman caught in sin, and his appearance to Mary Magdalene after his resurrection.[90]

The missionaries might not have consciously chosen to preach a Gospel that gives women a prominent place, but the social and religious factors contributed to this process. The slow rate of proselytism and the strong resistance from Chinese men made woman's work more crucial to the survival of the church. The segregation of the sexes divided mission work along gender lines, and women missionaries became more conscious of their role in advocating the welfare of women. In the late nineteenth century, some outspoken missionaries, both men and women, looked on the low status of women in Chinese society as a sign of the inferiority of Chinese culture, contrasting it with Jesus' attitude toward women. In the Chinese Christian community, the message that Jesus treats women with love and dignity served as an important basis to argue for equality between the sexes, especially in the wake of the May Fourth movement. Zhang Zimou, for example, affirmed that "Jesus treated women as equals with men," citing Jesus' preaching to women, his accepting the anointment by a woman, and his praise of the widow's donation. He, accordingly, criticized and denounced those Chinese customs that regard women as inferior to men.[91] When the anti-Christian movement attacked Christianity as discriminatory against women, Peng Jinzhang admitted that both the Old Testament and Paul's teachings contain elements of sexual inequality, but he pointed to Jesus' egalitarian treatment of women as the basis for his defense.[92] Chinese Christian women also referred to Jesus' attitude toward women to support their demand for equal status and recognition in the church and in society. We shall discuss their writings in more detail in the last chapter.

Eve and Mary

In Christian tradition, the two major female symbols are Eve and Mary. Eve symbolizes the transgression and sinfulness of women, for she listened to the serpent and tempted Adam to sin. In contrast, Mary is elevated as a model of holiness, obedience, and virginity for women to emulate. The veneration of Mary is very significant in Greek Orthodoxy and Roman Catholicism, but not so important in Protestantism. We shall trace the development of these two symbolic figures within the Chinese context to see how they were adapted to Chinese culture.

The story of the Fall is mentioned in all of the catechisms and in the Christian trimetrical classics, but Eve is not condemned for having tempted Adam or for having sinned first. Most versions of the trimetrical classic indicate that human beings sin, using the generic term *ren* ("human being") without specifying either the number or the gender:

> There is the evil one,
> who uses flowery words,
> to tempt human being(s),
> who commits sin against heaven.[93]

One version mentions that both Adam and Eve were tempted, they disobeyed the law, and both ate the fruit.[94] Referring to the original sin, the trimetrical classic says, "Because of the sin of *shizu* ["ancestor(s)"], the progeny born are all evil."[95] The Chinese term *shizu* can be used to indicate either the plural or the singular, and the singular in this case is most likely to be understood as Adam.

In the five versions of the catechism that I have studied, three attribute the Fall to both Adam and Eve without mentioning the temptation of Eve.[96] Two versions describe the story of the serpent tempting Eve, who took the fruit and gave it to Adam, but the narratives do not suggest that Eve was particularly to blame.[97] The catechisms describe the punishment after the Fall of Adam and Eve, who were driven away from Eden and had to do harsh labor to feed themselves. However, it is not mentioned that Adam and Eve received separate punishments. Eve had to suffer the pain of childbirth and her husband would rule over her. Adam had to till the soil and work hard for his living (Gen 3:16-17).

Nor did the missionaries put extra blame on Eve in their commentaries on the Fall. For example, John Roberts, in his commentary on Genesis 3, first blamed Adam for succumbing to his appetite before describing how Eve was tempted by the serpent.[98] In his short commentary, Charles Hartwell said that Eve did not obey God and ate the fruit of the forbidden tree, but Adam also ate it and their sin was just the same.[99]

Several reasons may be advanced to explain why religious writings did not stress the sinfulness of Eve. Most of the catechisms and tracts to which we have referred were written between 1860-1890, the period during which an increasing number of Chinese women were joining the church. We can draw the cross-cultural comparison that in nineteenth-century America, as more and more women were sitting in the pew, the church tended to downplay the relation between Eve and sin and to explore other, more promising models to show the character of women was suitable for religion and that women could be a benevolent force in society.[100]

Another reason may be that the missionaries perceived women as victims of society and did not consider them to be particularly sinful and vicious. Sidney A. Forsythe's study of the correspondence of missionaries of the American Board in China indicates that while the missionaries tended to have a negative and derogatory stereotype of Chinese men, they considered Chinese women to be more "innocent" and less dangerous.[101] At the turn of the century, veteran missionaries such as Young J. Allen and Arthur H. Smith helped propagate the view that Chinese women were oppressed by society and were victims of patriarchal social structures.[102] Female missionaries, on the other hand, emphasized the possibilities of women as social "leaven" in Chinese society.[103] Such views of women might not be shared by Chinese Christian men. Huang Pinsan, a Baptist from Shanghai, for instance, commented that both in China and in the West, more blame was put on women than on men. He noted that 1 Timothy states that Eve was created second, and that it was she who was deceived and fell into sin (1 Tim. 2:13).[104]

The third reason is that when the writers discussed the concept of sin, they usually had in mind the sins committed by men, partly because their readers were mostly male. Liang Fa listed the following as sinful in his tract: idol worship, prostitution, adultery, promiscuity, homosexuality, masturbation, robbery, gambling, murder, alcoholism, and so forth.[105] Other missionary writings shared a similar view of sin. For example, Gützlaff cited disobedience, adultery, greed, jealousy, murder, pride, cheating, and other vices.[106] It is interesting to compare this with a list from the same period of things that a woman was not supposed to do, such as laughing out loud, being talkative, gossiping, lying, indulgence in clothing, tempting men, pretending to be sick, and worrying.[107] Since women were not conceived to have a propensity to commit grave sins such as rape and robbery, the writers did not dwell on the sinfulness of Eve as an archetype for fallen women.

Religious symbols took on new meaning as the society changed, and in the twentieth century, when women were exploring their new roles in society, Laura M. White, the editor of *Nüduobao*, interpreted the sin of Adam and Eve anew for her readers. For centuries, she said, Chinese women have been treated as playmates and slaves, and today, Chinese Adams should rise up and treat women as their helpers and love them as their equals. As for Chinese Eves, their temptations included self-pride, superficiality, indulgence in vanity, laziness, and trying to be like men. She exhorted women to seek inner freedom, to share happiness with others, and to build families based on love, gentility, and purity, comparable to the first family in Eden.[108]

If Eve was the negative model, the mother of Jesus was often seen by the Christian church as a perfect example of a devout, pious, and obedient woman. However, the Protestant missionaries did not exalt the mother of Jesus, nor did they try to promote reverence toward Mary like other Christians. We can suggest two major reasons: first, they wished to distinguish their form of Christianity from Roman Catholicism, which promoted the veneration of saints and the Virgin Mary, a practice they thought to be too similar to the Chinese veneration of their ancestors and sages. The Protestant Memorial to the throne in 1895 mentioned that Christians respect Mary, the mother of Jesus, and the saints, but do not worship them or ask for their intercession, because Jesus Christ is the only mediator.[109] Writing on the difference between Roman Catholicism and Protestantism, a Chinese Methodist from Shanghai mentioned further that Protestants do not make images of the Virgin Mary.[110]

Secondly, the immaculate conception and the virgin birth were not easy matters for the uninitiated. Suspicious of the mystery of Jesus' birth, anti-Christian propaganda even suggested that Mary might have been involved in some promiscuous relations and Jesus might have been born out of wedlock.[111]

In the early twentieth century, when anti-Christian writings were less rampant and the Chinese society was looking for new images for motherhood, more discussions about the mother of Jesus appeared in religious journals. In 1907, the Baptist *Zhenguangbao* (True light magazine) included the Virgin Mary in its history of praiseworthy Christian women. The article on Mary begins by saying that she was a chaste woman from among the Hebrew people, and even mentions the names of Mary's father and mother. It continues by portraying the virgin birth, the escape to Egypt, Mary worrying while young Jesus talked with the wise men in the temple of Jerusalem, Mary and Jesus at the marriage feast in Cana, and finally, Mary standing and crying before the cross.[112] The story presents Mary as a patient, affectionate, and faithful mother, who was devoted to the ministry of her son.

In the first issue of *Nüduobao*, Laura M. White printed the famous picture of the Sistine Madonna, which occupied almost an entire page. The accompanying article states that goddess worship is to be found in many religions in the world, for example, among the Egyptians, Greeks, Germans, and the Chinese. White suggested that the goddess symbolizes purity, compassion, patience, gentleness, and sacrifice for the sake of the world. In Christianity, Mary is venerated as a model not only for women but for all of humankind. Although many of the characteristics listed are stereotypically feminine qualities, the article mentions further that Mary was courageous, intelligent, and self-possessed. Daring to follow Jesus to the cross, Mary accepted his death graciously and carried on with her own duties after Jesus' death.[113] A later editorial spells out more clearly that Mary set up a model of motherhood to be emulated. Mary's courage in the exile to Egypt saved Jesus' life, her care for Jesus was responsible for his growth, her deep devotion to her son made her an understanding parent, and her love for Jesus was demonstrated most evidently at the cross. Mary is hailed not only as the mother of Jesus but also as the mother of all Christians.[114]

In another article, White contrasted the mother of Jesus with the popular Chinese deity Guanyin. She recounted the story of the immaculate conception, Mary's care for the child Jesus, and her commitment to her son even to his death. Then she traced the story of Guanyin, particularly her chastity and sacrifice for the salvation of others. In the end, White said Mary and Guanyin shared similar motifs much as incarnation, prayer and salvation, self-cultivation, and the union between the human and the divine, despite the fact that the two originated from different contexts.

Our exploration of the Christian symbols and concepts in the Chinese context demonstrates that they take on new meanings when presented in the Chinese language and adapted to the religious background of the land. The situation is further complicated by the fact that the presenter of the message, in this case the missionary, comes from a linguistic and cultural background different from that of the audience. For example, the word *zui* ("sin") may be intended by the missionary to mean one thing, but the audience may understand it to refer to another. The religious image of father does not function in the same way cross-culturally, because people have different experiences of the familial system. Members of the audience, drawing on their own experiences, interpret the religious symbols and doctrines in ways that the missionary can hardly control. In his interpretation theory, Paul Ricoeur has referred to this phenomenon as "the surplus of meaning."[115]

The adaptation of Christian symbols to the Chinese context had two distinct levels. The missionaries consciously adapted Christianity to make it more congenial to the Chinese. They utilized Chinese religious terminology and concepts to express Christian ideas, explored more inclusive metaphors for God, and shifted their emphases on some aspects of Christian symbolism. On another level, the writings of Chinese Christians indicated that they also adapted Christian symbols to the cultural environment in which they had grown up. Their adaptations may have been more daring and may have gone further than those of the missionaries. For instance, the wholistic consciousness of the Chinese, which understands the universe as an organic whole (one part in coordination with another), challenged the more dualistic worldview of the missionaries. Chinese Christians, transposing their cosmological awareness onto their understanding of God, sought to expand and to add on new meaning to the anthropomorphic images. Since the Chinese symbolic universe does not exclude the feminine dimension, the Chinese

Christians did not deem it necessary to repress the female representation of the divine as much as the missionaries did.

The anthropomorphic image of God as father cannot be incorporated into the cosmological understanding of the universe without
creating tension. In the religious tracts, the writers also used other
metaphors, such as the source, root, and seed, in addition to the father
image to denote God's creativity. Since the stern Chinese father does
not quite convey the loving kindness of God, a more inclusive
metaphor, a Father-Mother God has been used. Jesus as the Son of
God was often called into question because of the mystery surrounding his birth. The heavy borrowings from Buddhist terminology
juxtaposed the Jesus story with popular Buddhist beliefs, in which
both male and female equally can be salvific figures.

The difficulty of proselytism and the resistance of Chinese men
to conversion efforts made work among women more important. To
appeal to women, Jesus' relationship with women was emphasized,
and women were depicted as sincere followers of Jesus and active
in his ministry, bringing the Gospel to children and other family
members. A shift of message can be seen also in the portrayal of
Eve, who is not condemned as the first sinner, because most of the
missionaries perceived Chinese women as less wicked than their male
counterparts. In fact, they were considered to be the victims of an
oppressive society. Most of the missionaries believed in the domesticity of women, and to build a Christian home was seen as woman's
vocation. Mary, as the model of motherhood, is described as an
intelligent and understanding mother in earthly and practical terms,
contrasting with the veneration of the Virgin Mary in Roman
Catholicism.

The discussion above clearly points to a feminization of Christian symbolism when Christianity was introduced to China. Furthermore, it also shows that religious symbols may function differently
in a cross-cultural context. Western feminist theologians are percep-
tive in their critique of the image of God as father which can be
used to legitimize patriarchy in Western culture. In the Chinese
context, however, the image of God as father could also be used to
challenge the hierarchical and patriarchal kinship relations. Chinese
gentry, in their refutation of Christianity, recognized that God as the
father of all human beings could lead to more egalitarian relationships between human beings. Chinese women in the twentieth
century also used the image of God as father to relativize the

claims of authority in the patriarchal family.

Current cross-cultural studies in gender and symbolism caution us that gender-specific religious symbolism does not simply mirror human relations and must be interpreted in context.[116] This means that the male images and metaphors for God may not simply provide religious sanction for male dominance in some cultural contexts. When transposed to China, the image of God as the utimate father can also be used iconoclastically to challenge the powerful grip of fathers over their children in the Chinese mainstream tradition. On the other hand, the rich tradition of goddess worship in China does not signify that women enjoyed higher status than men in Chinese society.[117] Furthermore, as Caroline Walker Bynum has indicated, women and men may not experience the same religious image, whether male or female, in exactly the same way.[118] Careful analysis is, therefore, absolutely necessary when we are dealing with the ways in which religious symbolism is communicated to another cultural setting, as in the case of Christianity in China.

Notes

1.   Joseph W. Esherick gives the reasons why some Chinese believed in Christianity, although he does not specifically refer to women; see *The Origins of the Boxer Uprising* (Berkeley and Los Angeles: University of California Press, 1987), 86-91.

2.   William Milne, *Xiangxun shisan ze* (Thirteen sermons) (Xiamen: Huaqi yusuo, 1855); and Charles Hartwell, *Quan xiangren shize* (Ten sermons) (Fuzhou: Taiping jie fuyin tang, 1874).

3.   For a discussion on the Christian trimentrical classic as an educational material, see Evelyn S. Rawski, "Elementary Education in the Mission Enterprise," in *Christianity in China: Early Protestant Missionary Writings*, ed., Suzanne Wilson Barnett and John King Fairbank, 146-151.

4.   Jacques Gernet, *China and the Christian Impact: A Conflict of Cultures*, trans., Janet Lloyd (Cambridge: Cambridge University Press, 1985), 241.

5.   Helen B. Montgomery, *Western Women in Eastern Lands*, 90.

6.   Barbara Welter, "The Feminization of American Religion, 1800-1860," in her *Dimity Convictions: the American Woman in the Nineteenth Century* (Athens, Ohio: Ohio University Press, 1976), 86-89

7.   See Mary Daly, *The Church and the Second Sex* (Boston: Beacon

Press, 1968), and her *Beyond God the Father: Toward a Philosophy of Women's Liberation* (Boston: Beacon Press, 1973); and Rosemary Radford Ruether, *Sexism and God-talk: Toward a Feminist Theology* (Boston: Beacon Press, 1983).

8. William Milne, "Some Remarks on the Chinese Term to Express the Deity," *Chinese Repository* 7 (1838): 315. Originally published in *Indo-Chinese Gleaner* 3/16 (1821): 97-105; an extract is found in *Chinese Repository* 7 (1838): 314-321.

9. James Legge suggested that Morrison was influenced by a partial translation of the Bible he saw in the British Museum before coming to China, and that version, completed by some Roman Catholic missionaries in Guangzhou around 1738, used *shen* for God. See Legge, *Letters on the Rendering of the Name God in the Chinese Language* (Hong Kong: Hong Kong Register Office, 1850), 28-29.

10. William Milne, *Zhang Yuan liangyou xianglun* (Dialogue between the two friends Zhang and Yuan) (Fuzhou: Huaqi yusuo, 1849), 3.

11. The conference asked James Legge to prepare a paper, but the delegates decided not to debate on the term question, and the paper was left out of the official record of the conference. The paper was published by Legge's friends as *Confucianism in Relation to Christianity: A Paper Read before the Missionary Conference in Shanghai, on May 11th, 1877* (Shanghai: Kelly and Walsh, 1877).

12. John Roberts, "Shenghao lun lieyan" (Preface to the discussion on holy titles), *WGGB* 9 (21 July 1877): 675-675b.

13. After the Boxer incident, the missionaries at Beijing suggested *shangdi* for God and *ling* for Spirit as steps toward union. The proposal seemed to have received wide support; see *CR* 34 (1903): 152 and *CR* 35 (1904): 323-325, 551-557.

14. S. Wells Williams, "The Controversy among the Protestant Missionaries on the Proper Translation of the Words *God* and *Spirit* into Chinese," *Bibliotheca Sacra* 35/140 (1878): 737.

15. William J. Boone, "An Essay on the Proper Rendering of the Words *Elohim* and *Theos* into the Chinese Language," *Chinese Repository* 17 (1848): 50.

16. The characterization of "organismic" is used by Joseph Needham; see vol. 2 of *Science and Civilization in China*, by Joseph Needham and Wang Ling (Cambridge: Cambridge University Press, 1956), 291-293. For the discussion of Chinese cosmogony, refer to Tu Wei-ming, "The Continuity of Being: Chinese Visions of Nature," in *Confucian Thought: Selfhood as Creative Transformation* (New York: State University of New York Press, 1984), 35-50.

17. A. C. Graham, *Two Chinese Philosophers: Ch'êng Ming-tao and Ch'êng Yi-ch'uan* (London: Percy Lund, Humphries, and Co., 1958), 108.

18. William J. Boone, "An Essay on the Proper Rendering," 24.

19. W. H. Medhurst, "An Inquiry into the Proper Mode of Rendering the Word God in Translating the Sacred Scriptures into the Chinese Language," *Chinese Repository* 17 (1848): 105-109; and James Legge, *An Argument for Shang Te as the Proper Rendering of the Words Elohim and Theos in the Chinese Language: With Strictures on the Essay of Bishop Boone in Favour of the Term Shin, etc. etc.* (Hong Kong: Hong Kong Register Office, 1850), 25.

20. William J. Boone, "Defense of an Essay on the Proper Rendering of the Words *Elohim* and *Theos* into the Chinese Language," *Chinese Repository* 19 (1850): 370-371.

21. Ibid., 443.

22. S. Wells Williams, "The Controversy," 766.

23. Ibid., 767.

24. W. H. Medhurst, "An Inquiry into the Proper Mode," 109.

25. W. H. Medhurst, "Reply to the Essay of Dr. Boone on the Proper Rendering of the Words *Elohim* and *Theos* into the Chinese Language," *Chinese Repository* 17 (1848): 638.

26. William Milne, "Some Remarks on the Chinese Term," 319-320.

27. W. H. Medhurst, "An Inquiry into the Proper Mode," 128.

28. James Legge, *The Notions of the Chinese Concerning God and Spirit: With an Examination of the Defense of an Essay on the Proper Rendering of the Words Elohim and Theos into the Chinese Language by William J. Boone, D. D.* (Hong Kong: Hong Kong Register Office, 1852), 51.

29. Jacques Gernet, *China and the Christian Impact,* 199.

30. James Legge, *The Notions of the Chinese,* 105-106.

31. The Chinese debate can be found in *WGGB* 9 (1877): 674b-675; and *WGGB* 10 (1877-1878): 3, 8, 57b-58, 71b-72, 86b-88b, 169-175b, 212b-213, 225b-228b, 295-295b, 325-328b 353b-354, 400, 408b-411b, 450b-455b, 507-507b, 535-536, 549-550, 562-563, 590-591, 591-592.

32. See Ququ zi, "Shenghao lun" (On holy titles), *WGGB* 10 (15 June 1878): 590b. In 1876, Carstairs Douglas observed that about three-fourths of the Chinese Christians used *shangdi*; see "*Spirit* and *God*: How Should They Be Translated?" *CR* 7 (1876): 69. Later in 1904, Chauncey Goodrich also confirmed that *shangdi* was the term that the Chinese Christians loved to use; see "Tracts and Terms," *CR* 35 (1904): 391.

33. Carstairs Douglas, "*Spirit* and *God*," 69.

34. For example, He Yuquan from Hong Kong wrote an important essay showing how Chinese classics point to the same religious way as the Bible. His article also referred to James Legge; see "Tiandao hecan" (A comparison of the Dao in Confucianism and Christianity), *WGGB* 10 (29 September 1877): 86b-88b; 10 (8 December 1877): 225b-228b.

35. Huang Pinsan, "Shenghao lun" (On holy titles), *WGGB* 9 (21 July 1877): 674b-675.

36. See the discussion in Wang Bingkun, "Huihao yi" (On honorary titles), *WGGB* 10 (26 January 1878): 325-328; and Kuang Rixiu, "Shenghao lunheng" (On holy titles), *WGGB* 10 (25 May 1878): 549-550.

37. Refer to Joseph Needham, vol. 2 of *Science and Civilization in China*, 279-291; and Benjamin I. Schwartz, *The World of Thought in Ancient China* (Cambridge, Mass.: Belknap Press, 1985), 369-378.

38. Chad Hansen points out that Greek philosophy is concerned with the "one above many" and Chinese thinking is more interested in the relation between "the part and the whole"; see *Language and Logic in Ancient China* (Ann Arbor: University of Michigan Press, 1983).

39. Pan Xunru, "Shenghao lun" (On holy titles), *WGGB* 10 (22 September 1877): 72. Wang Bingkun of Guangzhou also said that the creator cannot be named, and we respectfully use the name *shangdi*, see "Huihao yi," 326.

40. W. H. Medhurst, *China: Its State and Prospects, with Special Reference to the Spread of the Gospel Containing Allusions to the Antiquity, Extent, Population, Civilization, Literature, and Religion of the Chinese* (Boston: Crocker and Brewster, 1838), 155.

41. William Milne, *Zhang Yuan liangyou xianglun,* 22.

42. *Songzhu shengshi* (Chinese hymnal) (Beijing: Meihua shuju, 1875), hymn no. 50, page 37b; see also hymn no. 10, page 8 and hymn no. 32, page 27.

43. See Charles Hartwell, ed., *Guang xiao ji* (On filial piety) (Fuzhou: Nantai jiuzhu tang, 1882), passim.

44. Young J. Allen, "Jidujiao youyi yu Zhongguo shuo" (Christianity is beneficial to China), *WGGB* n.s. 7/83 (December 1895): 6b-7; and juan 10 of *Quandi wu dazhou nüsu tongkao* (Women of all lands) (Shanghai: Christian Literature Society for China, 1903), 36-37.

45. "Tianzhujiao xieji shuo," in *Pixie jishi*, 2b.

46. Ibid., 2-3.

47. Cao Jingrong (Cao Ziyu), "Chanzu lun" (On footbinding), *JHXB* 2 (21 May 1870): 182; and Baozhuo zi, "Quanjie chanzu" (Exhortation against footbinding), *WGGB* 15 (14 October 1882): 84b-85.

48. "Tianfu shangdi bian" (On God the father), *WGGB* 7 (3 July 1875): 599b.

49. "Lun tianfu erzi zhi jie" (On the meaning of the two characters tianfu ["heavenly father"]), *WGGB* 10 (11 August 1877): 4b.

50. Frank Rawlinson, *Naturalization of Christianity in China* (Shanghai: Presbyterian Mission Press, 1927), 128.

51. See Hong Xiuquan, "The Taiping Heavenly Chronicle," in vol. 2 of *The Taiping Rebellion: History and Documents*, ed., Franz Michael

(Seattle: University of Washington Press, 1971), 51-77. Rudolf Wagner points out Liang Fa did not mention the "Heavenly Mother" in his tract; see *Reenacting the Heavenly Vision: The Role of Religion in the Taiping Rebellion* (Berkeley: Institute of East Asian Studies, University of California, 1982), 44.

52. Barbara Welter, "The Feminization of American Religion, 1800-1860," 87.

53. Charles Hartwell, *Shangdi zonglun* (On the doctrine of God) (Fuzhou: n.p., 1878), 1

54. Charles Gützlaff, *Songyan zanyu* (Eulogy and praise) (Singapore: Jianxia shuyuan, 1838), 12b.

55. Mary Elizabeth Andrews, *Shengjing yaoyan* (Important words of scripture) (Beijing: Huabei shuhui, 1890), 27b.

56. Liang Fa, *Qiufu mianhuo yaolun* (Important discourse on seeking happiness and avoiding misfortune) (Singapore: Jianxia shuyuan, 183?), 38b.

57. Benjamin I. Schwartz, *The World of Thought in Ancient China*, 415.

58. Kuang Rixiu, "Shenghao lunheng," 549b.

59. W. H. Medhurst, *Sanzi jing* (Trimetrical classic) (editions dated from 1823 to 1855 in Harvard-Yenching Library); Sophia Martin Little, *Xunnü sanzi jing* (Trimetrical classic to instruct girls) (n.p., 1832); Chauncey Goodrich, *Sanzi jing zhujie* (Trimetrical classic with commentary) (n.p., 1865); Charles Hartwell, *Shengjiao sanzi jing* (Sacred trimetrical classic) (editions dated 1870 to 1913 in Harvard-Yenching Library); and Henry Blodget, *Sanzi jing* (Trimetrical classic) (n.p., 1875).

60. Liang Fa, *Zhendao wenda qianjie* (A catechism on the true way) (Malacca, 1829); E. Doty, *Yesu zhengjiao wenda* (A catechism on the Christian true religion) (Xiamen, 1854); Caleb C. Baldwin, *Shengxue wenda* (A catechism on sacred learning) [Fuzhou colloquial], 8 juan (Fuzhou, 1864); Henry Blodget, *Zhenli wenda* (A catechism on truth) (Beijing, 1873); Helen S. Nevius, *Yesujiao wenda* (Christian catechism) (Fuzhou, 1880); and Otis Gibson, *Chuxue wenda* (Easy questions for beginners) [English and Cantonese] (Fuzhou, 1892).

61. Charles Hartwell, *Shengjiao sanzi jing* (Fuzhou: Taiping jie fuyin tang, 1870), 1.

62. I am primarily following Helen S. Nevius's *Yesujiao wenda* in discussing the content of the catechism. Her catechism was reprinted many times and widely used in northern China. Timothy Richard commended it as the most influential tract besides William Milne's *Zhang Yuan liangyou xianglun*; see Irwin T. Hyatt, Jr., *Our Ordered Lives Confess*, 76.

63. William Ashmore, "Why We Should Study the Old Testament," *CR* 23 (1892): 249-255.

64. W. H. Medhurst, *Sanzi jing* (1843), 9; Chauncey Goodrich, *Sanzi jing zhujie*, 3b; Charles Hartwell, *Shengjiao sanzi jing* (1870), 9; and Henry Blodget, *Sanzi jing*, 10.

65. See Arthur F. Wright, "The Chinese Language and Foreign Ideas," in *Studies in Chinese Thought,* ed., Arthur F. Wright (Chicago: University of Chicago Press, 1953), 286-301.

66. W. A. P. Martin, "Is Buddhism a Preparation for Christianity?" *CR* 20 (1889): 203.

67. John C. Gibson, "Christian Terminology in Chinese," *CR* 23 (1892): 255-259; 24 (1893): 51-54.

68. Signed by C., "In What Form Shall We Give the Bible to the Chinese," *CR* 21 (1890): 454.

69. W. A. P. Martin, "Is Buddhism a Preparation for Christianity?" 202.

70. Joseph Edkins, "Buddhist Phraseology in Relation to Christian Teaching," *CR* 9 (1878): 295.

71. Lu Shiqiang, *Zhongguo guanshen*, 40.

72. Daniel L. Overmeyer, *Folk Buddhist Religion*, 130-161.

73. Eliza A. Morrison, comp., *Memoirs of the Life and Labour of Robert Morrison, D. D.* (London: Longman, Orme, Brown, Green, and Longmans, 1839), vol. 1, 81-82.

74. "Pibo xieshuo" (Criticism on heterodoxy), in *Pixie jishi*, 18.

75. Laura M. White, "Maliya zhi yu Guanyin" (Mary and Guanyin) *NDB* 1/9 (December 1912): 3.

76. Zeng Baosun, "Christianity and Women as Seen at the Jerusalem Meeting," by P. S. Tseng, *CR* 59 (1928): 443.

77. Wing-hung Lam, *Chinese Theology in Construction* (Pasadena, Calif.: William Carey Library, 1983), 37-39.

78. In women's classes, the *Life of Christ* was frequently used as a reading text, A. M. Fielde of Shantou (Swatow) reported that the *Life of Christ*, a consolidated gospel, was taught to the Bible women; see her "The Training and Work of Native Female Evangelists," in *Records 1890*, 245.

79. Charles Gützlaff, *Jiushizhu Yesu Jidu xinglun zhi yaolüe zhuan* (A concise story of the life of Jesus Christ the savior) 9 juan (n.p., 1834); Charles Hartwell, *Zhengdao qimeng* (Enlightenment on truth) [Fuzhou colloquial] (Fuzhou: Taiping jie fuyin tang, 1871); Chester Holcomb, *Yesu yanxing lu* (The life of Jesus) (Beijing: Meihua shuguan, 1872); and Simeon Foster Woodin, *Jiuzhu xingzhuan* (The life of the savior) (Fuzhou: Meihua shuju, 1876).

80. Charles Gützlaff, *Jiushizhu Yesu*, 22b-23b, 54-55b.

81. Ibid., 33b-34, 56b-57.

82. Chester Holcomb, *Yesu yanxing lu*, 24, 45, 58.

83. Daniel H. Kulp, II, *Country Life in South China: The Sociology of Familism* (New York: Columbia University Press, 1925), 279.

84. Charles Hartwell's report of 1871, ABC 16.3.5 (1), no. 39.

85. Charles Hartwell, *Zhengdao qimeng*, 20b.

86. Ibid., 24.

87. *JHXB* 1 (1868-69): 6b, 21, 29, 37, 45, 130, 135, 140.

88. Yizhi zi, "Guanbao zhiyan" (Comments on reading the newspaper), *WGGB* 12 (19 June 1889): 396. The editor of *Wanguo gongbao* also encouraged women to buy and read the magazine; see Young J. Allen, "Wanguo gongbao gaobai" (*Wanguo gongbao* advertisement), *WGGB* 7 (7 August 1875): 670b.

89. Ada Haven, *Fuyin cuoyao* (Selections from the gospels) (n.p., 188?), illustrations opposite pages 2, 6, 10, 14, 20, 22, and 30.

90. Mary Martin Richard, "The Christian and the Chinese idea of Womanhood and How our Mission Schools May Help to Develop the Former Idea," by Mrs. Timothy Richard, *CR* 31 (1900): 11-12.

91. Zhang Zimou, "Jiaohui gaizao de wojian" (My opinion on church reform), *Shengming* (Life) 2/9-10 (June 1922): 5.

92. Peng Jinzhang, "Jidujiao shi mieshi nüxing mo?" 1.

93. W. H. Medhurst, *Sanzi jing*, 3.

94. Henry Blodget, *Sanzi jing*, 5.

95. W. H. Medhurst, *Sanzi jing*, 3b.

96. E. Doty, *Yesu zhengjiao wenda*, 6-6b; Henry Blodget, *Zhenli wenda*, 5b; and Otis Gibson, *Chuxue wenda*, 8.

97. Caleb C. Baldwin, *Shengxue wenda*, 15b; and Helen S. Nevius, *Yesujiao wenda*, 11.

98. John Roberts, "Shengshu tiwen" (An essay based on a biblical passage), *WGGB* 10 (10 November 1877): 177-178.

99. Charles Hartwell, *Wuzijing zhujie* (Five-character classic with commentary) (Fuzhou: Taiping jie fuyin tang, 1871), 12-12b.

100. Nancy F. Scott, *The Bonds of Womanhood: "Women's Sphere" in New England, 1780-1835* (New Haven: Yale University Press, 1977), 146-147.

101. Sidney A. Forsythe, *An American Missionary Community in China, 1895-1905* (Cambridge, Mass.: Harvard University Press, 1971), 88.

102. Young J. Allen, *Quandi wu dazhou nüsu tongkao;* and Arthur H. Smith, *Qingnian xingguo zhunfan* (Guidance on how young people can strengthen their country; a shortened translation of the author's *The Uplift of China*), (Shanghai: Christian Literature Society for China, 1913), 20-23.

103. Sidney A. Forsythe, *An American Missionary Community*, 28.

104. Huang Pinsan, "Da Lu Congzhou" (Reply to Lu Congzhou), *JHXB* 2 (25 September 1870): 20-20b.

105. Liang Fa, *Qiufu mianhuo yaolun*, 21-21b.

106. Charles Gützlaff, *Songyan zanyu*, 8b.

107. Chen Hongmou, *Jiaonü yigui zhaichao* (Selections from instructions

to girls) (Chongwen shuju, 1868), 65b-68.

108. Laura M. White, "Xiawa beiyou tu" (A portrait of the temptation of Eve), *NDB* 1/3 (June 1912): 24-25.

109. Young J. Allen et al., *Yesu shengjiao ruhua* (Memorial on the aims of Protestant mission in China) (n.p., 1895), 15.

110. Chiping sou, "Yesujiao yu Tianzhujiao yitong bian" (Differences and similarities in Protestantism and Roman Catholicism), *JHXB* 2 (29 January 1870): 109b.

111. Lu Shiqiang, *Zhongguo guanshen*, 36-37.

112. "Yesu zhi mu Maliya" (Jesus' mother, Mary), *Zhenguangbao* (True light magazine) 5/12 (February 1907): 17b-19.

113. "Maliya tu shuo" (A portrait of Mary), *NDB* 1/1 (April 1912): 21-23.

114. Laura M. White, "Maliya de muyi" (The motherhood of Mary), *NDB* 11/7 (December 1922): 1-4.

115. Paul Ricoeur, *Interpretation Theory: Discourse and the Surplus of Meaning* (Fort Worth, Texas: Texas Christian University Press, 1976).

116. For example, Caroline Walker Bynum, Steven Harrell, and Paula Richman, eds., *Gender and Religion: On the Complexity of Symbols* (Boston: Beacon Press, 1986).

117. See P. Steven Sangren, "Female Gender in Chinese Religious Symbols: Kuan Yin, Ma Tsu, and the 'Eternal Mother'," *Signs* 9/1 (1983): 4-25.

118. Caroline Walker Bynum, "'. . .And Woman His Humanity': Female Imagery in the Religious Writings of the Late Middle Ages," in *Gender and Religion*, ed., Caroline Walker Bynum, Steven Harrell, and Paula Richman, 257-288.

CHAPTER III

Women's Religious Participation and Leadership

When Chinese women became interested in Christianity, they would join the Sunday services and participate in other church activities for women, which included Sunday schools, Bible study classes, prayer meetings, catechism classes, and short term religious courses. In the beginning, these activities were led by women missionaries, but as time went by, Bible women and other female volunteers would share in the leadership. In the cities, women's religious meetings primarily took place at the church. In the country, where church members lived far away from the church, women gathered together at one of their homes.

Anti-Christian accusations of sexual impropriety in the church prompted Christian missions to think of special ways so that women could worship together with men. Many churches instituted a partition in the church, separating women from men in worship services. In other churches, women and men sat on opposite sides of the aisle. Segregation of the sexes took place not only in Sunday worship but also in other religious activities of the church.

Segregation of the sexes allowed women to form their own close personal bonding with one another and to cultivate their own leadership. The situation can be observed from a cross-cultural perspective. Historian Barbara Brown Zikmund has pointed out that in the latter half of the nineteenth century, women in the American churches formed their own mission societies and women's organizations sometimes to carve out a sphere of influence within the patriarchal church and sometimes out of "an ideology which argued that the uniqueness of female gifts required women's organizations."[1] In China, it was the historical and cultural situation that forced women to hold their own meetings and organize their own societies.

In both situations, the result was that women were able to gain some control and influence over their own religious lives.

Women's religious meetings served not only the spiritual needs of women but also provided fellowship and mutual support for women. As in the popular religious sects, women developed a sense of group identity and a supportive network in these women's groups at church. When women came together to sing and remember each other in prayers, they made new acquaintances, shared difficulties in their lives, and nurtured a sense of belonging. In times of crisis, they could find support in religious rituals and seek help from one another.

In nineteenth-century China where women had few chances to organize themselves, religious groupings provided an opportunity for women to step outside the family and experiment with new roles. They learned to be teachers, evangelists, leaders of religious rituals, and counselors in the local congregations. Some of the women got their first paid job serving as Bible women for the church. Other volunteers offered their help in teaching Sunday schools, organizing prayer meetings, visiting the sick, and providing comfort for women in need. Women's religious groups, therefore, became training grounds for women to develop their own leadership.

While women might be able to exercise considerable leadership in women's religious communities and meetings, their participation in the broader church setting was usually limited by their lower education and the male-dominance that prevailed both in the church hierarchy and in Chinese cultural values. However, as more educated women began to join the church, they did not want to circumscribe their leadership in the women's sphere, but wished to extend their influence in the whole church community. The feminist movement, which emerged in the early twentieth century, further provided the challenge and impetus for church women to seek equality in the Christian community.

In what follows, I shall discuss the procedure of women joining the church and how the segregation of the sexes affected church life. I shall then turn my attention to the religious activities of the women themselves and patterns of female leadership both in the women's communities and in the church as a whole. In the final section, I shall trace the struggle of women for equal recognition and representation in the male-dominated church. While general observations will also be made, the differences between city churches and rural parishes will be highlighted, and pertinent information on women's position in the major denominations will be provided.

Women Joining the Church

As we have discussed in chapter one, women had to overcome many social and cultural barriers in order to join the church. During the initial stage of a mission, it often took quite a while for the first woman to come to church, as W. E. Soothill, a missionary at Wenzhou, observed: "It is generally a severe ordeal in a newly established station for the first woman to begin to attend service. Sometimes the men are quite a numerous body before ever a woman is induced to come, and she, practically always, is one whose husband is a Christian."[2] The early female church members were drawn from among the relatives of the Chinese helpers and converts, as well as the domestic servants of missionary households.

When mission work began to grow, the city mission would form outstations in the outskirts of the city. At these rural outstations, country women joined the worship services and other religious activities much more readily. An American Presbyterian missionary John L. Nevius, for example, noted that the number of women increased quickly in the rural outstations to the extent that women sometimes predominated over men.[3] The American Board missionaries working at the rural parish at Pangzhuang, Shandong, also reported that women were active in church life from the beginning.[4] Country women were attracted by the church because they were less secluded and opportunities to attend other activities were limited.

After women had attended church services for some time, they would be encouraged to receive baptism to become full members of the church. If their family members were not yet converted, the decision to be baptized often involved prolonged personal struggle and conflict with the family. When they finally decided to receive baptism, women first became probationers. The period of probation varied according to different denominations, ranging from six to twelve months; in some instances, the missionaries required the candidates to wait for a longer time to observe their sincerity and faith.[5] The basic requirements of baptism included: (1) the knowledge of the basic tenets of Christianity, which usually consisted of the Ten Commandments, the Lord's Prayer, and the life and passion of

Jesus, (2) the confession of sin and the rejection of non-Christian forms of worship, and (3) observance of the Sabbath and other institutions of the church.[6] Although these requirements were not particularly harsh, women would find it more difficult to fulfill them than men. Evelyn S. Rawski's study shows that Chinese men in general had opportunities to receive some basic education,[7] but the majority of women were illiterate.

Since most missions required some knowledge of the Bible as a prerequisite for baptism, the churches were heavily involved in teaching women how to read. The centenary report of 1907 estimated that nearly half of the female communicants and one-fourth of regular attendants of worship were able to read.[8] Considering that about eighty or ninety percent of Chinese women were illiterate, the literacy rate among Christian women was exceptionally high. The method of preparing women for baptism varied from mission to mission. Some required prospective women to enter a school, while others only required a week of meetings. Usually there were regular catechumen's classes, which all candidates were expected to attend. In the city churches, these classes were conducted most often by women missionaries, although in some cases, they were under the charge of the Chinese clergy. In rural areas, the candidates were instructed by the preachers.[9]

It remains doubtful whether the requirements for baptism could be strictly adhered to, especially in rural areas where the standard of women's education was so low. Emma D. Smith, the wife of Arthur H. Smith, lamented that it took a full six months for the "oldest and stupidest" rural women to learn just seven verses from the first chapter of the gospel of Matthew.[10] In such cases, it could be expected that the missionaries had to be more lenient with these slow learners. The lowering of standards and the relaxation of rules for female candidates, however, was a concern of the women missionaries attending the centenary conference of 1907, who proposed stricter preparation for female candidates and an extension of the period of probation to one year.[11]

Although details of the baptismal ceremony varied considerably from denomination to denomination, the liturgy usually included the basic elements of examining the faith of the candidate, baptism, and admission to the church community. In the churches of the American Board, a church covenant was pledged between the candidates and the congregation. The candidates had to vow to accept Jesus as Savior, obey the Ten Commandments, help to propagate Christianity, lead a virtuous life, and love other church members as their family before they would be accepted into the church as "brothers and sisters."[12]

Initiation through baptism was something new to many Chinese, since no parallels could be found in the Chinese religious context. In the initiation ceremony of some Chinese religious sects, the candidates would burn incense, *koutou* before their teacher and important religious images, and recite some chants.[13] In contrast, baptism by immersion was so foreign that it was considered a "most unusual rite in China." Before a certain Mrs. Yee received baptism in 1855 from T. P. Crawford of the American Southern Baptist Mission, her friend asked her, "Are you not afraid? You have never taken a cold bath in your life." Mrs. Yee, the first woman to receive baptism in Shanghai, replied, "No, not even washed my face in cold water, but I am not afraid."[14] Timothy Richard baptized his first two converts, a silk-weaver and his wife, in a clear stream, borrowing a few rooms in a Buddhist temple as dressing rooms. Later, a baptistry was built in his courtyard, and to avoid evil reports and rumors, he invited his friend, the treasurer of the prefecture to witness to the "propriety of the ceremony."[15] In some denominations, women had to come forward to confess their faith and to answer questions before baptism or confirmation. Bishop Alford of the Anglican Church noted that this involved a "breach almost of propriety on their part, according to Chinese notions, that they should appear, or even speak in public."[16]

It is difficult to generalize the class and social background of female Christians, because information is scanty and statistics are not complete. We have little information concerning women who joined the church in the 1860's and 1870's, except from a few obituaries of Christian women in *Jiaohui xinbao* and *Wanguo gongbao*.[17] Most of them were converted either through proselytism by women missionaries or through persuasion of relatives and friends who had become Christians. Conversion stories of early female Christians showed that they often decided to become Christians during personal crises, such as disruption of family ties and other trying moments of life. A certain Mrs. Ma of Xiamen, for instance, abandoned her traditional religion and accepted Jesus after the death of her husband. Mrs. Yao of Shanghai was forbidden by her relatives to join the church until her impending death changed their minds.[18]

Obituaries of Christian women who lived at the turn of the century are included in the *Zhonghua Jidu jiaohui nianjian* (Chinese Christian church year book). Among the seventy-three obituaries published between 1916 and 1927,[19] one-third consist of members of Christian families or relatives of pastors and presbyters. About forty percent graduated from mission girls' schools or Bible schools for women, some serving as teachers in the schools or as female evangelists. The majority of these church women came from the lower and middle-class backgrounds, with the exception of a few who belonged to richer families and even donated property to the church. Quite a large number were older widowed women, including several former devout Buddhist vegetarians.

From missionary reports and the obituaries of Christian women, we can see that in China Christianity attracted particular groups of women. In general, rural women responded more readily than women in the cities, since rural populations tended to be less influenced by the dominant Confucian tradition and rural women were less secluded. Furthermore, young girls and older women, especially widows, who were not so tied up with family responsibilities, could participate more actively in church. They enjoyed relatively more freedom to search for new identities and possibilities, because they were situated somewhat at the margin of the family system. Just as popular religious sects provided an alternative in Chinese society, the Christian church offered a chance for women to come together to learn to read, to make new friends, and to explore new roles apart from familial ones.

The Segregation of the Sexes and Church Life

Although the missionaries preached that all human beings are the children of God and that Christians are "brothers" and "sisters" to one another, this did not imply that men and women could mix freely in church, nor could they enjoy the same status and privileges. As a social institution, the Christian church in China took root in a cultural setting that assigned distinct roles for women and men. Girls and boys had separate spheres of activities, and sisters and brothers were not supposed to intermingle once they had reached puberty. In a society with rather strict segregation of the sexes, women worshipping publicly with men evoked wide-spread rumors and suspicions.

The taboo against "women mixing with men" in Christian assemblies must be seen in the wider cultural and religious context. Chinese folk beliefs comprised a long tradition linking longevity with certain forms of sexual practice, and some popular religious sects, such as the White Lotus, permitted a certain degree of sexual permissiveness among members.[20] In the nineteenth century, these popular sects were frequently suppressed by the government, and some local officials even issued edicts, in the name of preventing sexual impropriety, banning women from going to the temples.[21] In the Chinese temples, women burned incense and offered prayers separately from men, although no formal partitions separated the sexes. Even in the religious meetings of some sectarian groups that accorded women a higher degree of participation, women worshipped the Buddha or other religious figures apart from the men and farther away from the altar. During the vegetarian meal after the religious ceremony, women would sit at separate tables, and if the tables were insufficient, they would sit on the floor.[22]

Since the 1860's, when women began to join the church in increasing numbers, the relations between male and female church members became an issue in the Christian community. Partly to avoid criticism and partly to encourage respectable women to come, the church adopted three strategies to safeguard itself from indiscriminate criticism: the prescription of codes of behavior, the institution of some form of partition during worship services, and the organization of separate religious meetings for women.

In his reply to queries about indecency among Christians, Zheng Yuren of a Baptist church in Shandong provided some rare information on rules of conduct adopted by his church. He wrote that men and women were not allowed to tease or joke with each other; should such incidences occur, the church would admonish or expel those violating the rules. When a woman came to attend a worship service, the wife of the missionary would invite her to stay and talk with her afterwards. Neither the priest nor the parishioners should interfere. If the woman had any language problem, the older women of the congregation would offer help and guidance.[23] Although such rules existed for some churches, others seemed to have allowed more interaction between men and women. Some missionaries reported that women and men could mingle together before and after worship.[24]

In order to attract women to worship, A. P. Happer suggested at the 1877 missionary conference to have separate chapels set apart for female converts. His proposal was rejected by others, however, who thought that the church should not "perpetuate the injurious distinction between men and women in public worship."[25] Instead, many churches instituted partitions separating the sexes during worship services. In 1849, when the first Chinese church was erected in Xiamen by the American Reformed Church, the interior was arranged like a Quaker meeting house, with a screen to separate the women and the men.[26] According to Soothill, this practice of setting up a screen or partition in church continued in central China where the seclusion of women was strongest. In the south, Soothill observed, most churches did not institute such a barrier; women and children just sat on one side, and men sat on the other.[27] However, other reports indicated that even in Guangzhou, the Wesleyan, the Presbyterian, and the London Mission all had partitions in their churches.[28] It seemed that the institution of some form of partition during worship was quite common in the Chinese churches until the early twentieth century.[29]

Although some missionaries felt that a partition was necessary to avoid courting trouble, others expressed reservations about its continued use. Soothill, for instance, maintained that even the Chinese temples did not install screens separating the sexes, and that it was regrettable that Christian churches found it necessary to do so.[30] Other missionaries pointed out that partitions in the churches hindered women from participating fully in worship services. J. V. N. Talmage of Xiamen said: "There are defects in the arrangement of many of our chapels. Screens are used to separate the women from the men. Often they are so arranged as to place women behind the preacher. This interferes greatly with their understanding of the preaching."[31] Women missionaries were also aware of the shortcomings of having partitions, for example, Elizabeth M. Fisher stated: "The partitions in many of our chapels are a bane to the women of those congregations. They sit in many instances at the back of the stand or in a little side room, where they are not a part of the congregation to whom the preacher is talking."[32]

Some missionaries had initially hoped that the partitions would be abandoned once there were more women in the pews, but the opposite turned out to be the case. After the destruction of church properties by the Boxers, when many churches had to be rebuilt in northern China, the issue of the segregation of the sexes was raised once again. At that time, more people had come to the conclusion that the removal of barriers would be the ideal. Some Chinese Christians in Guangzhou, who had long hoped for their removal, even wondered if this was a "foreign prejudice in favor of the symbol of separation."[33] Since the society had become more open to the mixing of the two sexes, many churches decided to give up the partitions.

Women and men both participated in Holy Communion after they were baptized and had become church members. In some churches where the congregation took communion at the altar, women and men would come separately to receive the bread and the wine from the priest. In other denominations, small pieces of bread and cups were distributed to the congregation by elders or senior members of the church. Harriet Newell Noyes, an American Presbyterian missionary at Guangzhou, recounted that men were not supposed to pass the bread and the wine to the women. At her Guangzhou church, the Bible woman had to be asked to offer female members communion prior to the election of deaconesses.[34]

Separation of women and men was enacted not only in public worship but extended also to other aspects of congregational life. As mentioned already, "woman's work" became a distinct component of mission work as women formed their own Bible study groups, prayer meetings, reading classes, and sometimes women's chapel services. Although some male missionaries observed that men were able to work among women in Shandong, Guangdong, and Fujian, all agreed that women missionaries and the Bible women could reach and influence women more effectively.[35] The division of mission work along gender lines allowed women missionaries to claim the results of their efforts more easily. On the other hand, once the "woman's domain" was established, the male missionaries tended to pay less attention to it, and women missionaries complained sometimes that their male colleagues overlooked women's issues.

Segregation of the sexes in church life affected women's participation and leadership in the Christian community as a whole. Even if they were accepted as full members of the church, women were treated differently and separately, not as integral parts of the body of Christ. The physical partition in churches limited the ritual roles women could perform and reestablished the gender distinction in society. Female religious leadership could be exercised more freely in women's meetings, less so in the larger church. On the other hand, segregation of the sexes allowed women to carve out their own sphere so that they could build up their own network and exert their influence.

Women's Religious Activities

The religious activities open to women differed according to individual social status and the geographical location of the congregation. The social grip was much tighter on the higher and richer classes of women than on those of the impoverished and lower classes, who had nothing to lose by joining a foreign religion. Religious activities at the city stations, usually under the more direct supervision of missionaries, centered around the mission compound. In the rural parishes, church members were scattered throughout numerous villages, and religious leadership depended more on the lay people. Women in coastal provinces had more exposure to mission activities, since mission work commenced early in the treaty ports, and missionary presence was always stronger along the coast than in the hinterland.

To gain a more comprehensive view of women's religious activities at the local level, I shall compare church life as it was found in the city and in the country. The following account is based on mission reports and papers of the American Board, one of the major mission boards of the United States. Although the work of this organization may not be taken as stereotypical in such a vast mission field as China, it gives a fairly representative picture of the types of religious activities going on. Special references will be made to the city station at Fuzhou, the capital of Fujian, and to the country station at Pangzhuang in Shandong, drawing also upon pertinent information from other sources.[36]

The station at Fuzhou was first opened in 1862, and the Taiping jie fuyin tang (Peace street church), completed in 1868, was under the supervision of Charles Hartwell. While men could be reached by religious literature and street preaching, women needed to be approached through house-to-house visitations. In 1867, Lucy E. Hartwell began to visit women in her neighborhood and to read to them lessons drawn from the scripture.[37] The girls' school provided an additional channel to reach women as Lucy E. Hartwell encouraged the children to teach their mothers the Bible and hymns, paying them each a small sum of money as teachers.[38] Small companies of three or four women would be invited to read to her at her house, while others would come to listen for half an hour or for as long as they could stay. In 1869, about thirty women, a few in their sixties or even eighties, read to her, and some began to attend church worship regularly.[39]

Work among women in the city stations was an uphill struggle. It often took a long time before women in the cities would show any receptivity to mission work. In the late 1870's, Caleb C. Baldwin, a senior missionary at Fuzhou, observed: "The work among women is difficult, but growing work, as the heathen homes are more accessible than in early years. In some parts of our field, the signs are hopeful, and occasionally women are found who ask for instruction."[40]

In contrast, the initial stage might not have been so difficult for the country stations or outstations, because they usually grew out of established city stations. The work at Pangzhuang, a village of more than 110 families located near the northwestern corner of Shandong Province, was originally an extension of the Tianjin station. Famine relief and church work had begun in Pangzhuang for some time before the station was opened in 1880 by Arthur H. Smith and the missionary doctor Henry D. Porter.[41] At that time, Pangzhuang already had a church membership of over three hundred scattered throughout many villages.[42] Woman's work, under the care of Smith's wife, Emma D. Smith, and Mary H. Porter, who was unmarried, was an integral part of the mission from the beginning. Missionaries at Pangzhuang reported that, "the women of Shantung [Shandong] in their native homes live a larger freer life than in many parts of the Empire."[43]

With Pangzhuang as the center, village work began in many neighboring villages; for example, the women missionaries visited 34 villages and established regular weekly or monthly meetings in some 14 villages in 1883. After the church building was completed in 1882, it served as the nucleus of religious activities for women. Small companies of women who lived farther away were invited to spend Saturday night and the Sabbath at Pangzhuang, so that they could have direct acquaintance with the women missionaries and other church members.[44] In the early 1880's the congregation at Pangzhuang had an average attendance of about fifty people.

On Sundays, the city stations usually held one or two worship services. Missionaries frequently reported that Chinese women enjoyed singing in church, although they were often out of tune.

Mary Porter, a Methodist missionary in Beijing, commented that the "hymn book is the most popular in the church."[45] Emily S. Hartwell, the daughter of Charles and Lucy E. Hartwell, confirmed that the hymns were "the most popular way of introducing the doctrine," because even the illiterate could memorize them easily. At one point, she recommended that the mission open an "organ manufactory" to provide cheap baby organs, so that women could be taught to play music in their homes.[46] Before or after the services, Sabbath school for girls and women was a common feature, and in some stations, women's meetings were held after the Sabbath service to help them understand the meaning of the sermon and the religious lesson of the day.[47]

Religious activities at the country station had to occur on weekends, since some women had to travel from afar. At Pangzhuang, a women's prayer meeting, well attended by church members, took place on Saturdays.[48] Two worship services took place on Sundays, and before each there was a rudimentary Sabbath school. A group of non-Christian girls received religious instruction from Emma D. Smith, and another class of Christian women read Chinese characters with Mary H. Porter. After the service, a simple meal of millet was provided for the women who came from other villages. In the afternoon, there were a class for Christian girls and a service for women attended by some forty to seventy women.[49] When the twin sisters, Grace and Gertrude Wyckoff, joined the station in 1887, they added Sunday morning music in the chapel[50] and started a Sabbath afternoon meeting "to make the Sunday services of greater benefit to the women, and also help them in forming habits of closer attention, to improve their power of expression, and to aid them in the study of the Word."[51]

During the week, some city churches opened a woman's chapel or a guest room in the mission compound, so that women could drop by in a free and casual way to listen to the gospel message. In the evenings, "magic lantern shows" were occasionally held, using slides and pictures to illustrate the life of Jesus or other biblical stories.[52] Christian women held prayer meetings during the week, either in their homes or in the church. They took turns as hostess and invited their relatives and friends to come. When the Christian Endeavor Society was first organized in the Fuzhou station, women could join as associate members; later, women of other stations, such as Beijing, established their own societies, parallel to those of men.[53] Many city stations opened women's dispensaries or hospitals sooner or later. The patients were encouraged to attend worship services led by the medical missionaries and to receive religious literature and instruction from the Bible women.

In the country, weekdays were spent visiting church women who lived far away from the stations and holding religious meetings in the villages. Occasional tours to the farthest villages would also be undertaken, during which the missionaries would stay for one week to ten days. The women missionaries at Pangzhuang were thoroughly committed to village tours, sometimes traveling more than 2,300 miles in one year and visiting some twenty to thirty villages. In the beginning, large crowds of village women and children came out of curiosity to listen to them, but as the initial interest subsided, only small groups of Christian women and children would come. During these village visits, a prepared lesson would be taught and the women would be drilled so as to memorize it along with prayers and hymns. A homily focusing on Christian discipleship and ethics would be presented, followed by a prayer meeting to close the day.[54]

At the turn of the century, opportunities for reaching women in the cities rapidly increased as China became more open to the West. Caroline E. Chittenden reported that women missionaries in the Fuzhou station had been preoccupied with educational work, and now the door for dealing more directly with the women had been thrown wide open.[55] In northern China, the Boxer incident struck a heavy blow to the work of the mission, but this did not dampen the enthusiasm of women missionaries to rebuild the Christian congregation. Many missions organized station classes for illiterate women, providing religious instruction and preparing candidates for baptism. In places like Fuzhou and Guangzhou, where people spoke a dialect different from the written language, it became an issue which language to use for teaching purpose. The majority of missionaries preferred the romanized local dialect, since it could be learned within a short period of time. In fact, some women could read intelligently after three months. Others still preferred to learn Chinese characters because of their familiarity and because of the scarcity of reading materials in romanization.[56]

In the Fuzhou station, station classes for women began in 1899 and lasted for one month at a time, usually with two sessions in a year. The class ran from one to six in the afternoon, with an hour each day devoted to Bible reading, prayer, and learning the Ten

Commandments.[57] Some of the women learned the three-, four-, and five-character books, and the more advanced class studied the *Life of Christ*. In the 1910's, there were both boarding station classes as well as the day schools.[58]

Station classes were a significant feature of the Pangzhuang station, which had grown to a scale much larger than that of many city stations sponsored by the American Board. In 1885, Mary H. Porter started a one-month writing class for village women, and subsequent station classes, each lasting for one month, were held after the autumn harvest and during the New Year season, when women were less engaged working in the fields. Women who lived far away had to stay in Pangzhuang with the missionaries and the teachers, while others came to class just for the day. The former women brought their own bedding and found their own means of transportation, while the mission provided food and fuel as means of inducement and encouragement.[59] The student body was very diverse, the ages ranging anywhere from eight to eighty-eight. The older and slower students were taught to read a primer consisting of the Lord's Prayer, the Ten Commandments in abridged form, the Beatitudes, and the Creed, while the advanced learners studied the catechism, the gospel of Matthew, *Pilgrim's Progress*, and Christian hymns.[60] From a small beginning, the number of station classes grew to 18 at Pangzhuang and the nearby villages, and these were attended by 280 women from 80 villages in 1904.[61]

Religious participation at the local level was affected by changing political circumstances in the wider society. For example, anti-missionary rumors during the poison scare of 1871 deterred women from attending church. When in August, the rumors reached Fuzhou, many women were afraid to entertain missionaries in their homes, and on one Sunday, only five women came to church, none of whom were members of the church.[62] In northern China, the Boxers destroyed many mission properties: all the churches sponsored by the American Board north of the Yellow River, except the one in Pangzhuang, were pulled down in the craze. In Pangzhuang, some of the Christians were forced to recant their faith, and women were no longer so enthusiastic to attend station classes as before. When the Smiths returned to Pangzhuang after the turbulence subsided, Emma D. Smith organized revival meetings for church women and students, which succeeded in rekindling the religious fervor in some women.[63]

Several observations can be made regarding religious activities at the local level. When compared to the religious activities of men, women's meetings were more involved in the teaching of characters and functioned almost like a literacy campaign. This new opportunity broadened the horizons of women, as observed by Caroline E. Chittenden of Fuzhou: "For such women, the quiet hours of study are a new experience, a revelation of a life such as they never dreamt of attaining."[64] Moreover, women's willingness to participate in religious meetings depended more on personal relationships than men. They would come to prayer meetings or station classes if they knew the women missionaries or the Bible woman. Finally, women's religious classes were less well structured and often run on a short-term basis since women could not come regularly because of household duties.

Women who could afford the time to participate in religious activities were those relatively free of household duties. Older women could come to religious meetings and even accompany missionaries on itinerations; young girls before the age of puberty would join the Sabbath schools and station classes. Nineteenth-century missionary reports often lamented that married women would not afford the time to attend religious activities or to come to station classes. Women missionaries in Fuzhou gave twenty-five cents to women each morning when they attended station class. In order to appease her husband at home, the station in Pangzhuang offered a pound of bread to each woman who came to station class.[65]

Women's religious activities not only allowed women to gather together to sing and to learn but provided also a training ground for female leadership. Local leadership was especially crucial in the countryside, since the majority of the missionaries and Chinese clergy resided in the cities. With church members scattered over a vast area, the country parishes depended on local women to lead religious meetings and prayer groups in the villages. The Pangzhuang station adopted a policy of not hiring full-time Bible women at the beginning, so that the work could be shared by many volunteers.[66] In the early twentieth century, more than thirty women and girls at Pangzhuang were involved in teaching the station classes and in village visits. The work of these volunteers were very significant as "they did the teaching of characters, gave daily Bible lessons, to the class and to the children, and had prayer meetings and helpful talks for the duller and more ignorant women."[67]

To cope with the rapidly expanding field of woman's work and the demand for more qualified female church workers, the mission stations had to provide leadership training for local women. Special advanced classes on Chinese characters and the scriptures were offered to future teachers of station classes and female workers in Pangzhuang.[68] In the bigger city stations, such as Fuzhou and Beijing, the mission boards opened women's schools or Bible schools for women, to train Bible women and female church workers. Thus, the women's religious communities allowed women not only to form personal bonds but also to develop their potential as teachers, counselors, leaders of worship, and evangelists.

Female Religious Leadership

Segregation of the sexes in church life and the organization of religious meetings for women by women provided the context for the emergence of female religious leaders. Bible women, or female evangelists, were employed full time or for several months a year, and there were other volunteers, who did not receive a regular salary. In the church hierarchy, the position of female evangelists was much lower than that of ordained pastors or other unordained male evangelists, who could preach from the pulpit and take charge of the church. But in the women's communities, these female evangelists were role models for women and assumed a variety of leadership roles.

Inspired by the work of female evangelists in London, R. H. Graves, an American Southern Baptist missionary in Guangzhou, was among the first to introduce Bible women to China.[69] The early Bible women were recruited from employees of missionary households, preachers' mothers or wives, patients of the hospitals, and other women who had acquired some education.[70] A large proportion of the Bible women were middle-aged or older women, as one missionary observed: "It is not considered just the proper thing for young women to go about alone in such a way even if married. Hence it is sometimes necessary to have on older woman, also, associated when younger women are employed."[71] Widows who had no children or other persons dependent upon them were most desirable because they could be sent away for days on village tours.[72] The following table illustrates the growth in the numbers of Bible women during the different periods of mission history:[73]

	Missionary wives	Single women missionaries	Bible women
1876	172	63	90
1890	391	316	180
1907	1148	1081	894
1917	1819	1818	2579

The chief responsibility of a Bible woman was to visit the homes of women and schoolgirls to teach them the Bible and to encourage them to attend Sunday worship. In some missions, such as the Methodist Episcopal Mission in Fuzhou, the Bible women did visitations rather extensively, reaching a large audience. In 1894, for example, the four Bible women made 600 visits reaching an audience of 7,000; and in 1909, the sixteen Bible women made 3,141 visits, teaching 899 women regularly and reaching more than 20,000 altogether.[74] In the country outstations, the Bible women accompanied women missionaries on their itinerations and went on village tours by themselves. Generally, two Bible women would go out together,[75] and during the home visits and itinerations, they did not just teach women and children but reached out indirectly to men as well.[76]

Many Bible women assumed important teaching roles in the women's communities, serving as instructors in Sunday schools, women's prayer groups, and station classes. Teaching in those days involved helping the class to recognize Chinese characters, explaining the text, and drilling students to memorize the lesson. Some missionaries noticed that the older Bible women were more patient to "prod and encourage and fix in memory by much repetition."[77] In bigger stations, where there was a dispensary or a hospital for women, the Bible woman would preach the Gospel to the women patients while they were waiting for consultation or for medicine.[78] She would also visit in-patients, teaching them the Christian Primer, the Ten Commandments, the Lord's Prayer, Christian hymns, and prayers. The healing ministry often elicited expressions of gratitude and appreciation from patients; the work of Bible women in hospitals was in general favorably received.

During the early stages, Bible women were supervised by women missionaries and trained on an individual basis, for example, Mary H. Porter of Pangzhuang gave daily lessons to a Bible woman, and

Hannah C. Woodhull of Fuzhou trained a Bible woman in romanization.[79] As the number of Bible women grew, many large missions formed special committees to supervise the work, laying down rules for qualifications and training. In the beginning, these committees consisted of missionaries only. Later, some missions invited Chinese Christians, both men and women, to join.[80]

Over the years, the work of Bible women, or female evangelists, expanded to encompass many forms of ministry, as one missioanry noted:

> She does house-to-house visiting, teaches Sunday School classes, leads meetings for the Christians and outside women, holds station classes for teaching the women to read, takes long country trips either with or without the foreign missionary, chaperones the young day-school teachers, visits the sick, helps bury the dead, is active in relief work, and often is one of the wise counsellors in the station.[81]

In some cases, where there were no male preachers, the Bible woman would even take charge of the church, discharging the duties of a pastor except for some special rites.[82] The celebrated lives of some female evangelists were cherished by the church members, and their obituaries appeared in the *Zhonghua Jidu jiaohui nianjian*. These include Ni Suen of Huanggang, Hubei, Ma Yana of Changsha, Hunan, and Ye Cai shi of Lantian County in Fujian.[83]

Employed Bible women or female church workers, however, comprised only a tiny portion of the female Christian population. In 1920, there was one female worker to every fifty-five female communicants, as compared to one male worker to twenty-four male communicants.[84] The work among women was shared by volunteers, consisting of the wives of Chinese evangelists, gate-keepers, dispensary assistants, and other female leaders in the local parish, such as the hospital matrons, teachers and graduates of girls' schools, and educated church members. As volunteers, they were only given food and a small compensation for expenses on the road.

The work of volunteers did not differ significantly from that of Bible women, especially in mission stations where the Bible women were employed only on a part-time basis. In country stations where lay leadership was more significant, volunteers accompanied missionaries on village tours, led prayer groups in their own villages, taught Sunday school and station classes. In special circumstances, the volunteers might be involved in a certain kind of relief work. After the Boxer incident, for example, church women at Pangzhuang took care of the children of the refugees, and during the revolution of 1911, women at Fuzhou assisted the missionaries providing relief for the refugees.[85]

At the turn of the century, women began to explore other religious and ritual roles in addition to those connected with the women's meetings. Reminiscent of some wealthy women who were founders of house churches in the early church,[86] several Chinese women invited their relatives and neighbors to their homes for religious activities. In Fuzhou, Mrs. Zhang (known as Mrs. Ahok in Fuzhou dialect), who became well known for her trip to England where she solicited support for missions in China, welcomed her relatives and friends to her house at Fuzhou where they were taught the "Jesus doctrine."[87] Other examples include Mrs. Zaw of Suzhou, who had a company of some thirty women reading and singing hymns in her house, and Mrs. Hwan of Nanjing, who opened her house to all her neighbors, rich and poor.[88]

In most other cases, it was women in the rural areas who after their conversion set up prayer groups or small religious communities in their own villages. John L. Nevius of Yantai (Chefoo) told the 1890 missionary conference that a certain rural woman had established a church in her village and had served now as its head for ten years.[89] Sociologist Martin Yang recorded a striking case in his native village near Qingdao. A certain woman was the first convert, who then became the only literate woman in her village after she attended a Bible school in the city. As a leader in her own community, she "formed prayer groups, taught inquirers, and supervised the building of a village church."[90]

As the participation of women increased in the church, the question surfaced whether women should be allowed to speak and preach in public. In the late 1890's, the *Chinese Recorder* published several articles supporting both sides of the debate. Some of the arguments closely resembled those raised in American churches at that time.[91] Those missionaries, who believed that the Christian home was "woman's God-appointed sphere," hastened to cite Paul's prohibition against women speaking in church (I Cor. 14:37, I Tim. 2:11-15).[92] Their opponents, on the other hand, contended that the Holy Spirit had given women the gift of prophesy, making references

to prophetesses and female apostles in the Bible, such as Deborah
(Judg. 4:4), Miriam (Exod. 15:20), Prisca (Rom. 16:3), and Junia
(Rom. 16:7).[93] Alluding to Paul's Greek text, they argued that his
admonition was directed only at "wives," who should be submissive
to their husbands, but not to "women" in general. Hence, Paul might
not have ruled out single women, widows, and virgins speaking and
prophesying in church.[94]

During the first decade of the twentieth century, the involvement
of women in radical revolutionary activities and the spreading of
feminist ideas by women's journals aroused the consciousness of some
church women, who began to demand the right to preach in church.
Zhang Zhujun, a medical doctor trained by John Kerr in Guangzhou,
was reported by a Chinese newspapers in 1906 to have preached in
her church. The article refers to Zhang as the first Chinese woman
to preach from the pulpit, but we have no other evidence to verify
this claim. In her sermon, Zhang boldly denounced Paul's injunc-
tion that women should not preach in church as faulty and illogical.
Employing the rhetoric of the feminist movement, she argued,
"Women and men have equal right; there is no reason why women
should not preach in church."[95]

In addition to preaching, a number of Chinese women served
as deacons, assuming leadership responsibilities in local congregations. A female missionary reported to the 1907 centenary conference:
"Already we hear of a few women-deacons, meeting with the men
to discuss the affairs of the church; it may in some cases be possible
to get our leading women to act on the board of management of
the girls' schools, to take counsel with us as to the appointment of
Bible-women, and the recommendation of candidates for baptism."[96]
Some of the women deacons exercised tremendous influence. For
example, Mrs. Hsu of Taiyuan, a deacon of the British Baptist
Mission, was the joint treasurer of her church and chairperson of
the Provincial Conference of the Mission in Shanxi.[97]

Women deacons, however, were considered by some denominations only as lay leaders, and not belonging to the Holy Order of
priests. The struggle for ecclesiastical power by Western women
benefitted their Chinese sisters in certain cases.[98] For instance, the
highly structured American Methodist Episcopal Church approved
the ordination of women in 1924. As a first stride towards recognizing women's pastoral leadership, the Methodist Episcopal Mission
(North) approved the appointment of female licensed preachers in

China. The Fuzhou Conference licensed Janet Ho as a local preacher in 1923, and in the next several years, four other women were licensed in the Jiangxi Conference.[99]

When we compare leadership roles of women in Christian communities to those of women in the popular religious sects during the same period of this study, we can discern many similarities. Women could be teachers of religious literature, founders of congregations, and leaders of local communities in either religious context. In fact, female leaders drawn from the popular religious sects could easily adapt their roles to the Christian setting after their conversion. Emma D. Smith gave an interesting example of Mrs. Liu K'o Chih of Pangzhuang, who had been an adherent of a Chinese sect and the head of a circle of women. Following her conversion, she taught the Bible to a dozen or so women in her village who had been following her in the religious sect.[100] On the other hand, however, the power of female religious leaders seemed to be more limited in Christian congregations, since church structure was generally more defined and hierarchical than in the religious sects, and women were barred from performing certain rites.

When we consider female religious leadership in the church as a whole, it is evident that women were not given the same recognition and opportunities as men. The London Mission took the lead to ordain Liang Fa in the 1820's, while other major denominations started to ordain Chinese men in the 1860's and 1870's. The number of ordained Chinese pastors reached 73 in 1877.[101] Bible women, on the other hand, were often employed on a temporary basis and their position was much lower than that of the male church workers. A survey of the stipends of Chinese workers in 1909 indicated that female church workers earned much less, sometimes less than half the salary of the male workers. Although female religious leaders could sometimes be founders of local congregations, preachers, and deacons, their number was extremely small.

On the other hand, if we look at female religious leadership in the women's communities, we see quite a different picture. Performing many pastoral functions, Bible women served as role models for women, demonstrating that women could dedicate themselves in service to the church and find fulfillment in serving other women. As Bible women were not ordained or set apart for special ritual duties, they shared tasks similar to those of other church volunteers. Female religious leadership expressed itself in more communal and less structured or hierarchical forms than that of male leadership. Relationships between teachers and pupils, leaders and followers, were more reciprocal and non-hierarchical. It was quite possible for younger women to teach the older women; and for those who had already learned, to instruct others.

Most female religious leaders in the nineteenth century received minimal education and were generally unskilled. Working as Bible women provided some means of self-support for destitute widows, who often found themselves dependent on the charity of relatives and benevolent institutions.[102] As time went by, when more women received higher training in secondary schools and colleges, the need to raise the qualifications required of female leaders increased. Many denominations started providing formal training for their female evangelists, and in 1923, there were altogether fifty-two Bible schools for women in China.[103] But the work of female evangelists lost its appeal when educated women could find other jobs as teachers, nurses, and shopkeepers. One missionary reported that women preferred to teach in mission or government girls' schools, because they offered better remuneration than the church.[104] In the 1920's, Chinese women made up twenty-eight percent of the Chinese Christian educational force, but only twenty percent of the Chinese evangelistic force.[105] The low position of female leaders in the church became an embarrassment when the secular feminist movement demanded economic justice and social equality. In the wake of the May Fourth movement, Christian women raised the issue of women's ordination and openly criticized the patriarchal church structure, demanding fuller participation and representation in the church.

The Struggle for Recognition in the Church

The growing participation of women on the local level laid the foundation for women to seek greater recognition and leadership in the wider church community. The first step was to organize women's meetings and conferences within the male hierarchical structure. The women missionaries of the Methodist Episcopal Mission (North) at Fuzhou organized annual women's conferences beginning in 1885. Members included all women missionaries at Fuzhou station and Chinese representatives from each of the districts having mission activities. The aim of the conference was to provide an occasion for women to come together to discuss issues pertaining to woman's work. The conference of several days' duration was well structured, and from the beginning, Chinese women were appointed to various offices and invited to present reports of their work and papers on numerous subjects, such as "The Importance of Having Jesus Constantly with Us in Our Work," "What Are We Doing for Heathen Women?" and "The Duties and Responsibilities of Christian Mothers."[106] Other Methodist Conferences in China—such as North China, Central China, Xinghua, and Jiangxi—followed suit and held annual women's meetings and issued annual conference reports.[107]

Women in other denominations similarly organized their own conferences, although the conferences were not as well structured as the Methodists'. In 1887, the annual meeting of the Congregationalist Church in Fuzhou devoted two extra sessions to women and decided that women should meet together each year.[108] These women's meetings were open to female church workers, preachers' wives, and female students, addressing a wide range of subjects such as ways to read the Bible, family management, moral reforms, and the anti-footbinding movement. Bible women were invited to give short accounts of their work.[109] In other stations, such as Pangzhuang, women gathered at their quarterly meetings, and joint women's conferences were held occasionally for women at Pangzhuang and Beijing.

The latter half of the nineteenth century saw the proliferation of women's mission societies as well as temperance and reform groups in American churches. Some of these women's organizations established branches in China. Women of the American Episcopal Church formed the Woman's Auxiliary in 1871 to raise funds to support mission work in foreign and domestic fields, and the secretary visited Shanghai in 1893, helping to found the first branch of the Woman's Auxiliary in China.[110] Other denominations in China also formed women's mission societies, raising funds to support the work of Bible women and local activities. For example, Congregationalist women in Fuzhou formed a Chinese Woman's Home Missionary Society in 1893 for the promotion of evangelism among women. The society was under Chinese control, although advice was sought from the women missionaries and a foreign woman served as treasurer. In Tongzhou, Congregationalist women and children formed a mission society called the Tongzhou Volunteers, each saving several cents a month for mission work.[111]

Apart from these mission societies, other women's organizations were formed specifically for moral and social reform purposes. The anti-footbinding movement initiated by Alicia Little gained widespread support in churches and schools in the cities. The Woman's Christian Temperance Union, under the outstanding leadership of Frances Willard of the United States, introduced its work to China in 1886. The Young Women's Christian Association also established a chapter in Hangzhou in 1890. In the early stages, these reform groups and women's organizations were under the leadership of foreign women, but Chinese gradually took over the work in the twentieth century. The details of these organizations will be discussed in the next chapter.

The experiences of women organizing among themselves and the elevation of women's educational standards encouraged church women to seek greater representation in church structure. In the Congregationalist and Baptist churches, women were eligible to be both members and officers on different committees. The position of women in Presbyterian churches seemed to be lower in some quarters, but the possibility of appointing women as elders was also considered. Women of the Methodist Episcopal Church could serve on committees and could be appointed as exhorters and licensed preachers. In the Anglican church, women could serve on the vestry and in diocesan council in some cases.[112] Luella Miner, the principal of the North China Union College for Women, observed: "The trend is certainly toward closer unity and truer democracy, wherein women can claim a place, not on the plea that she is a woman with a woman's 'right,' but on the nobler basis of having the ability and the spirit to fill a needed place in service."[113]

The growing openness of society toward social intercourse between the sexes allowed women to participate with men in Christian organizations. Assuming a greater share in propagating the Gospel, Chinese Christians founded the Chinese Missionary Society in 1918 to send Chinese missionaries under the sponsorship of Chinese churches. As a self-supporting society, the founding members consisted of four women and three men, including the medical doctor Shi Meiyu (Mary Stone), the evangelist Cai Sujuan (Christiana Tsai), Kate Woo, and the wife of F. H. Sung.[114] Shi Meiyu and Fan Yurong (Fan Yu Jung) of the Y.W.C.A. served on the executive committee at various times, and Chen Yuling was commissioned to work as a home missionary in Yunnan.

Around the same time, another influential organization, *Shengming she* (Life fellowship), was founded by some liberal Chinese and Western faculty members of Yenching University. The members were interested in such issues as Christianity and social change and the indigenization of the church in China.[115] The fellowship published a journal called *Shengming* (Life), which served as an important organ for intellectual exchange among Chinese Christians. Cheng Guanyi (Ruth Cheng) was on the editorial committee of the journal,[116] and Ding Shujing (Ting Shu Ching), general secretary of the Beijing Y.W.C.A. at that time, was one of the fellowship's members.[117] Xie Wanging (Ping Hsin), a student of Yenching Women's college, published early pieces of her Christian poetry in the journal.[118]

The growing participation of women in the wider Christian community can also be seen in a review of successive national conferences. At the first missionary conference of 1877, there was no Chinese woman present, and women missionaries were not expected to address the assembly although four prepared papers.[119] At the second conference of 1890, women missionaries prepared papers on women's evangelistic and educational work, but they held separate meetings to discuss women's issues among themselves.[120] There was no Chinese delegate, although the wife of Y. K. Yen attended the conference with her husband, who was an ordained pastor of the American Episcopal Church working at St. John's College, Shanghai.[121] Even in the centenary conference of 1907, where 94 out of 367 delegates were women missionaries, Chinese women were not represented, although some attended as visitors.[122] It was not until the establishment of the China Continuation Committee in 1913, formed after the Edinburgh Mission Conference of 1910, that the door was finally open to Chinese women. Among the 121 delegates, three were Chinese women, compared to 32 Chinese men. These three women leaders were Shi Meiyu, Cao Fangyun of the Shanghai Y.W.C.A., and Yu Cidu (Dora Yu) of the Methodist Episcopal Mission (South). [123] Under Shi Meiyu's leadership, the so-called woman's work made its last appearance in these meetings, and no special women's subcommittee was appointed. Instead, it was argued that women should be integrated in the whole mission of the church and they should serve on most of the subcommittees to represent their views.[124]

Before the National Christian Conference took place in Shanghai in May 1922, women missionaries contributed articles to the *Chinese Recorder*, urging the churches to elect more women delegates to represent Chinese female Christians, who made up more than one-third of church membership.[125] As it turned out, there were only 74 female delegates among a total of 564 Chinese delegates.[126] Although the number of women delegates was small, they represented a wide spectrum of women leaders, including "principals of schools, teachers, doctors, nurses, evangelists, home missionaries, deaconesses, Y.W.C.A. secretaries, church secretaries, editors, members of missionary boards, and women of wealth who are giving their leisure to some form of Christian work."[127] The conference brought together eminent women leaders in China, such as Cheng Guanyi representing Christian schools, Ding Shujing and Cheng Wanzhen (Zung Wei Tsung) of the Y.W.C.A., Mei Yunying of the Woman's Christian Temperance Union, Yu Cidu, a successful evangelist, and Chen Yuling, a home missionary of the Chinese Missionary Society.[128]

Unlike the previous conferences, the National Conference did not schedule a session for "woman's work"; instead, Chinese women were invited to address the assembly as a whole.[129] Jiang Hezhen (Anna Kong Mei), chairperson of the National Committee of the Y.W.C.A., gave an address on "Making the Home Christian." The daughter of a Chinese pastor, Jiang was brought up in Hawaii, and she was the first Chinese woman to graduate from Barnard College, Columbia University.[130] Cheng Guanyi, the sister of the prominent Chinese Christian leader Cheng Jingyi, presented an important paper on "Women and the Church." A graduate of the Bridgman Academy and North China Union College for Women, Cheng Guanyi later did graduate work in England.[131] Fan Yurong, a secretary of the National Committee of the Y.W.C.A., gave a short speech and strongly urged the conference to fully recognize the importance of women leaders. Also a graduate of North China Union College for Women, Fan Yurong was later appointed to the important position of one of the four secretaries of the National Christian Council.[132] When the National Christian Council was formed during the conference, about nine women, including Cheng Guanyi, Fan Yurong, Kang Cheng (Ida Kahn), and Zeng Baosun (Tseng Pao Suen), were elected as representatives of their denominations and as members-at-large.[133]

We can discern an evolving pattern of women claiming leadership in the church and in Christian organizations. In most cases, the initial impetus for women to organize came from the women missionaries who provided organizational and financial support. Gradually, however, Chinese women assumed greater responsibilities in raising funds, in managing their activities, and in leadership. At first, women organized their caucuses and meeting alongside regular church meetings and assemblies; subsequently, they formed alternative and separate women's bodies. At a later stage, they participated to a greater extent with men in joint activities, and they demanded greater representation in church bodies and at national Christian conferences.

Women's struggle for recognition climaxed in the 1920's, partly because of changing circumstances in the Chinese church and partly because of the challenge of the feminist movement. The number of Chinese Christians increased fourfold between 1900 and 1920, and Chinese Christians were aware that a strong Chinese church could not depend on the efforts of missionaries alone. During this transitional period when Chinese Christians came to shoulder greater responsibilities in building their own church, women likewise demanded their rightful place. At the same time, the growing number of educated women and the raising of women's consciousness during the first two decades of the twentieth century contributed to church women's quest for a more egalitarian church structure.

Our analysis indicates that women's religious participation and leadership must be interpreted from a dual perspective: from the vantage points of their own communities and from that of the church as a whole. The appeal of Christianity for women, apart from the symbolic resources it offered, lay in the local religious groups women formed among themselves. In these gatherings, women learned to read Chinese characters, to sing hymns, to offer prayers, and to meet new friends. Just like the popular Chinese religious sects, the communities of Christian women created an alternative structure in society, providing channels to meet the personal religious needs of women and to offer group support through ritual and mutual aid in times of family and social crises. Anthropologists, who have studied women's religious communities and their ritual roles in cross-cultural context, point out that the reciprocal relationship these women create forms a kind of "horizontal affective association," which cuts across the hierarchical roles in society.[134]

Because of the opposition of the gentry and the literati, Christianity in nineteenth-century China attracted women who were marginal to society: poor and illiterate women, widows, and women belonging to the sectarian tradition. The communities of these Christian women allowed them to explore new identities and to experiment with new roles. The bonding that women formed with one another together with their exposure to foreign missionaries and Christian values allowed them to look at themselves and their society from new perspectives. The women's religious communities served thus as bridges for women to move from the family into society, addressing the issues that women faced and bringing about social changes.

Contrasting Christianity with the Chinese sects, historian Daniel H. Bays emphasizes the commonalities of the two in terms of religious and value content, organizational structure, and general social roles.[135] He further suggests that Christianity, similar to the popular sects, accorded women a higher status: that a "greater and equal role for women as an important factor in the appeal of Christianity is evident in the relatively large percentage of Chinese girls and women in mission schools, working as 'Bible women,' and in the significant proportion of church members who were women."[136] Our discussion shows that women exercised more leadership in the women's groups and less so in mixed groups of men and women. Some denominations had a clearly male-dominated church polity, barring women from preaching, celebrating Holy Communion, or serving as elders or deacons. Yet, the changing circumstances of China also presented challenges and even forced the church to reconsider the relation between the sexes in the twentieth century. Women's participation in revolutionary movements and articles on sexual equality in women's journals stimulated church women to struggle for equal status in the church.

Since women missionaries played no small part in helping church women to organize, the struggle of Chinese women for ecclesiastical power resembled in certain aspects the claiming of leadership by Western women in their churches. Women formed their own meetings and organizations to train leaders and to consolidate their power base before seeking greater participation in the broader church. Demanding to be recognized as full members of the church, they sought representation in local church government. From there, they moved on to demand the same right to represent local congregations in church committees, diocesan councils, and national conferences. Once they had established themselves as lay leaders, they began to address the questions of preaching from the pulpit and women's ordination, maintaining that women could exercise pastoral leadership on the same footing as men. Women's critique of the patriarchal church structure would eventually lead them to question some basic teachings of the church and to reexamine Christian faith from their own experience.[137]

Notes

1. Barbara Brown Zikmund, "Attacking the Male Power Structure in American Protestantism," Paper presented at the Fourth Annual Berkshire Women's History Conference, Mount Holyoke College, South Hadley, Massachusetts, 1978.

2. W. E. Soothill, *A Typical Mission in China* (New York: Fleming H. Revell Co., 1906), 137.

3. John L. Nevius observed that women would predominate over men in a rural outstation, as soon as a Chinese preacher with his wife commenced work there. See his *China and the Chinese: A General Description of the Country and Its Inhabitants; Its Civilization and Form of Government; Its Religious and Social Institutions; Its Intercourse with Other Nations; and Its Present Conditions and Prospects* (New York: Harper and Brothers, Publishers, 1869), 373.

4. "Annual Report of the Shangtung Station, April 1, 1883—April 1, 1884," ABC 16.3.12 (8), no. 33.

5. J. W. Lambuth, "Standard of Admission to Full Church Membership," in *Records 1877*, 243; see also the discussion by J. V. N. Talmage on 253 and R. Lechler on 254.

6. J. W. Lambuth, "Standard of Admission," 242; see also *Records 1890*, 376-379.

7. Evelyn S. Rawski, *Education and Popular Literacy in Ch'ing China* (Ann Arbor: University of Michigan Press, 1979).

8. Edith Benham, "Women's Work: General," in *Records 1907*, 140.

9. Ibid.

10. Emma D. Smith, Pangzhuang Women, 1887-1888, ABC 16.3.12 (7), no. 36.

11. See Resolution No. 2 as presented to the centenary conference in *Records 1907*, 552.

12. Charles Hartwell, *Jianhui xinlu* (Church creed) (Fuzhou: Taiping jie fuyin tang, 1870), 4b-6.

13. J. J. M. DeGroot, *Sectarianism and Religious Persecution in China* (Amsterdam: Johannes Muller, 1903), vol. 1, 204-220, and Susan Naquin, *Millenarian Rebellion in China*, 33-35.

14. L. S. Foster, *Fifty Years in China: An Eventful Memoir of Tarleton Parry Crawford, D.D.* (Nashville: Bayless-Pullen Co., 1909), 87.

15. Timothy Richard, *Forty-five Years in China*, 95-96; and E. W. Burt, *After Sixty Years: The Story of the Church Founded by the Baptist Missionary Society in North China* (London: Carey Press, 1937), 12-13.

16. Bishop Alford was officiating at a confirmation in Fuzhou in 1868 when he made the observation quoted by Eugene Stock, *The Story of the Fuh-kien Mission of the Church Missionary Society* (London: Seeley, Jackson, and Halliday, 1890), 44.

17. See *JHXB* 1 (3 July 1869): 197b; 1 (24 July 1869): 212; 2 (20 August 1870): 242b; 4 (30 September 1871): 25b, 5 (5 April 1875): 212b; and *WGGB* 11 (7 December 1878): 230-230b; 12 (23 August 1879): 17b. Adrian A. Bennett draws my attention to these obituaries; see his *Missionary Journalist in China: Young J. Allen and His Magazines, 1860-1883* (Athens, Georgia: University of Georgia Press, 1983), 144.

18. W. P. Bentley, *Illustrious Chinese Christians* (Cincinnati: Standard Publishing Co., 1906), 197-201; and Huang Pinsan, "Xinnü Yao shi ji" (On a Christian woman, Mrs. Yao) *WGGB* 11 (7 December 1878): 230-230b.

19. *Nianjian* 3 (1916): section wei, 139-146; 4 (1917): 219-231; 5 (1918): 227-245; 6 (1921): 254-273; 7 (1924): 150-163; 8 (1925): 269-285; 9 (1927): 253-283.

20. Susan Naquin, *Millenarian Rebellion in China*, 48-49.

21. See, for example, "Ningbo Yinxian gaoshi" (Proclamation prohibiting females from entering Buddhist temples), *JHXB* 6 (14 March 1874): 190; and "Dezheng kechuan" (Guangdong officials assist a woman in Buddhist rites), *WGGB* 14 (17 December 1881): 171-171b.

22. J. J. M. DeGroot, *Sectarianism and Religious Persecution in China*, vol. 1, 221-222.

23. Zheng Yuren, "Yintai jinhui da Jueyi zi" (Reply to Jueyi zi concerning a misunderstanding of mission work), *JHXB* 1 (6 February 1869): 96b.

24. For example, see Elizabeth M. Fisher, "The Enlightenment of Our Native Christian Women. How Can It Be Accomplished?" *CR* 21 (1890): 392-393.

25. A. P. Happer, "Woman's Work for Woman," in *Records 1877*, 145, and the discussion by Carstairs Douglas on 155.

26. P. W. Pitcher, *A History of the Amoy Mission* (New York: Board of Publications of the Reformed Church in America, 1893), 105.

27. W. E. Soothill, *A Typical Mission*, 137.

28. J. A. Turner reported on the Wesleyan chapel in *Kwang Tung, or Five Years in South China* (London: S. W. Partridge, 1894?), 38. Andrew Beattie reported that the Presbyterian Mission and the London Mission began to abolish the partitions in 1903; see "Partitions," *CR* 34 (1903): 95.

29. Other denominations also mentioned having partitions in church: for the American Episcopal Church, see Arthur R. Gray and Arthur M. Sherman, *The Story of the Church in China* (New York: The Domestic and Foreign Missionary Society of the Protestant Episcopal Church in the U.S.A., 1913), 180; for the Methodist Free Church Mission, see W. E. Soothill, *A Typical Mission*, 137; and for the American Reformed Church, see *Records 1877*, 155.

30. W. E. Soothill, *A Typical Mission*, 137.

31. See J. V. N. Talmage's remarks in *Records 1877*, 155.

32. Elizabeth M. Fisher, "The Enlightenment of Our Native Christian Women," 392.

33. A. R. Crawford, "Shall Men and Women Be Separated in Our Public Chinese Services?" *CR* 34 (1903): 382.

34. Harriet Newell Noyes, *A Light in the Land of Sinim: Forty-five Years in the True Light Seminary, 1872-1917* (New York: Fleming H. Revell Co., 1919), 56-57.

35. *Records 1877*, 154, see also *Records 1890*, 261-262.

36. The American Board established stations in the cities of Fuzhou, Tianjin, Beijing, Zhuangjiakou (Kalgan), Tongzhou, Baoding, and Linqing, and a country station at Pangzhuang. (Pangzhuang was also rendered as P'ang Chuang, Pangkiachwang or P'angkiachuang in mission reports.) For a brief history of the American Board, see Henry Blodget and Caleb C. Baldwin, *Sketches of the Missions of the American Board in China* (Boston: American Board of Commissioners for Foreign Missions, 1896).

37. Charles Hartwell's letter of 9 November 1867, ABC 16.3.5 (1), no. 132.

38. Fuzhou Report, 1868, ABC 16.3.5. (1), no. 33.

39. Lucy E. Hartwell's letter of 7 December 1869, ABC 16.3.5. (1), no. 165; see also her letter of December, 1869, in *Missionary Herald* 66 (1870): 165-166.

40. Fuzhou Report, 1878, ABC 16.3.5. (2), no. 14.

41. Arthur H. Smith, "Sketches of a Parish Church," *CR* 12 (1881): 245-266, 316-344.

42. Arthur H. Smith, "Shantung Station Report, 1880-1881," ABC 16.3.12 (8), no. 24.

43. "Annual Report of the Shangtung Station, April 1, 1883—April 1, 1884," ABC 16.3.12 (8), no. 33.

44. Ibid.

45. A. H. Tuttle, *Mary Porter Gamewell*, 86.

46. Emily S. Hartwell's letter of 18 November 1885, ABC 16.3.5 (3), no. 219.

47. For instance, see Mary P. Ament and Ada Haven, "Work for Women and Children in Peking for the Year Ending April 30, 1889," ABC 16.3.12 (8), no. 22.

48. Henry D. Porter, "Sixth Annual Report of the P'ang Chuang Station, April 30, 1886," ABC 16.3.12 (7), no. 30.

49. "Annual Report of the Shantung Station, April 1, 1883—April 1, 1884," ABC 16.3.12 (8), no. 33.

50. Pangzhuang Women, 1887-1888, ABC 16.3.12 (7), no. 36.

51. Pangzhuang Women, 1889-1890, ABC 16.3.12 (14), no. 10.

52. Edith Benham, "Women's Work: General," 247.

53. Fuzhou Report, 1886-1887, ABC 16.3.5 (3), no. 7; and "Woman's Work, Peking and Outstations, 1903-1904," ABC 16.3.12 (24), no. 44.

54. Henry D. Porter, "Sixth Annual Report of the P'ang Chuang Station," ABC 16.3.12 (7), no. 30.

55. Caroline E. Chittenden's letter, n.d., ABC 16.3.6 (1).

56. Martha Wiley, "Report of Work for Women at An-Haeng Church, Foochow City, from January—June 1901," ABC 16.3.6 (1).

57. Ibid.

58. Emily S. Hartwell, "Foochow City Woman's Work, 1910," ABC 16.3.6 (4).

59. Pangzhuang Women, 1888-1889, ABC 16.3.12 (7), no. 37.

60. Ibid.

61. Pangzhuang Women, 1903-1904, ABC 16.3.12 (23), no. 288.

62. Lucy E. Hartwell's letter of 30 December 1871, ABC 16.3.5 (1), no. 167.

63. Pangzhuang Women, 1901-1902. ABC 16.3.12 (23), no. 284.

64. Caroline E. Chittenden's letter of 29 July 1898, ABC 16.3.5 (6), no. 209.

65. Ibid.; and Pangzhuang Women, 1891-1892, ABC 16.3.12 (14), no. 66.

66. Pangzhuang Women, 1889-1890, ABC 16.3.12 (14), no. 10.

67. Pangzhuang Women, 1902-1903, ABC 16.3.12 (23), no. 286.

68. Pangzhuang Women, 1903-1904, ABC 16.3.12 (23), no. 288.

69. R. H. Graves, "Fifty Years Service in South China," *CR* 38 (1907): 88.

70. Charles Hartwell's report for 1873, ABC 16.3.5 (2), no. 11; Henry D. Porter, "Sixth Annual Report of the P'ang Chuang Station," ABC 16.3.12 (7), no. 30; Pangzhuang Women, 1890-1891, ABC 16.3.12 (14), no. 33; and Harriet Newell Noyes, *History of the South China Mission of the American Presbyterian Church, 1845-1920* (Shanghai: Presbyterian Mission Press, 1927), 34.

71. H. T. Whitney's letter of 28 February 1905, ABC, 16.3.6 (2).

72. *Records 1877*, 143-144, and *Records 1907*, 155.

73. Luella Miner, "The Place of Woman," 341. She did not indicate her

sources. It should be noted that the centenary conference record gives the number of Bible women as 887 in 1905, see *Records 1907*, 782. The 1922 national report states the number of female evangelists as 2,341, see M. T. Stauffer, ed., *The Christian Occupation*, 290.

74. *Report of the Tenth Session of the Foochow Woman's Conference of the Methodist Episcopal Church* (n.p., 1894), 44; and *Report of the Twenty-fifth Session of the Foochow Woman's Conference of the Methodist Episcopal Church* (n.p., 1909), 109.

75. Pangzhuang Women, 1897-1898, ABC 16.3.12 (15), no. 86; and H. T. Whitney's letter of 28 February 1905, ABC 16.3.6 (2).

76. C. E. Chittenden, "Mrs. Diong Cing-hoing, Bible Woman," *Life and Light* 32 (1902): 212.

77. H. T. Whitney's letter of 28 February 1905, ABC 16.3.6 (2).

78. Mrs. R. Smyth, "C.M.S Women's Hospital, Ningpo," *WWFE* 21/2 (November 1900): 101; and Katherine C. Woodhull, "A.B.C.F.M. Hospital for Women and Children, Foochow City," *WWFE* 21/2 (November 1900): 95.

79. Henry D. Porter, "Sixth Annual Report of the P'ang Chuang Station," ABC 16.3.12 (7), no. 30; and Martha Wiley, "Report of Work for Women at An-Haeng Church," ABC 16.3.6 (1).

80. M. C. White, "Evangelistic Work among Women," *Year Book* 11 (1923): 148-150.

81. Ella C. Shaw, "The Work of Bible Women in China," *Year Book* 6 (1915): 344.

82. "Report of Woman's Work for Peking Station, May 1904-1905," ABC 16.3.12 (24), no. 47.

83. "Ni Suen" (Obituary of Ni Suen), *Nianjian* 5 (1918): 228; "Liu Ma Yana" (Obituary of Liu Ma Yana), *Nianjian* 5 (1918): 230; and "Ye Cai shi" (Obituary of Ye Cai shi), *Nianjian* 9 (1927): 278-279.

84. M. T. Stauffer, ed., *The Christian Occupation*, 290, 293.

85. Pangzhuang Women, 1901-1902, ABC 16.3.12 (24), no. 284; and Emily S. Hartwell, "Foochow City Woman's Work, 1910," ABC 16.3.6 (4).

86. Elisabeth Schüssler Fiorenza, "Word, Spirit, and Power: Women in Early Christian Communities," in *Women of Spirit: Female Leadership in the Jewish and Christian Traditions*, ed., Rosemary Radford Ruether and Eleanor McLaughlin (New York: Simon and Schuster, 1979), 32-39.

87. Irene H. Barnes, *Behind the Great Wall: The Story of the C.E.Z.M.S. Work and Workers in China* (London: Marshall Brothers, 1896), 63-64. (C.E.Z.M.S. stands for Church of England Zenana Missionary Society.)

88. "A Letter from Mrs. Zaw, a Native Christian Woman, to Mrs. Lambuth," *Woman's Work in China* 8/1 (November 1884): 65; and

Mary Kelly, "A Consecrated, Capable Chinese Woman," *WWFE* 22/2 (November 1901): 86.

89. *Records 1890*, 262.
90. See Irwin T. Hyatt, Jr., *Our Ordered Lives Confess*, 88.
91. Barbara Brown Zikmund, "The Struggle for the Right to Preach," in *Women and Religion in America*, vol. 1, *The Nineteenth Century*, ed., Rosemary Radford Ruether and Rosemary Skinner Keller (San Francisco: Harper and Row, Publishers, 1981), 193-205.
92. H. M. Woods, "Woman's God-Appointed Sphere as Set Forth in Scripture," *CR* 27 (1896): 468-469.
93. C. H. Judd, "Woman's Place in the Church as Taught in Holy Scripture," *CR* 27 (1896): 261-266.
94. Ibid., 265; and M. H. Houston, "Woman Speaking in the Church," *CR* 28 (1897): 58-59.
95. "Zhang Zhujun nüshi lishi," (History of Miss Zhang Zhujun), in vol. 2 of *Jindai Zhongguo nüquan yundong shiliao, 1842-1911* (Documents on the feminist movement in modern China, 1842-1911), ed., Li Youning and Zhang Yufa, (Taibei: Zhuanji wenxue she, 1975), 1380.
96. Edith Benham, "Women's Work: General," 144-145.
97. E. W. Burt, *After Sixty Years*, 137.
98. See Virginia Lieson Brereton and Christa Ressmeyer Klein, "American Women in Ministry: A History of Beginning Points," in *Women of Spirit: Female Leadership in the Jewish and Christian Traditions*, ed., Rosemary Radford Ruether and Eleanor McLaughlin, 301-332.
99. Walter N. Lacy, *A Hundred Years of China Methodism* (New York: Abingdon-Cokesbury Press, 1948), 230-231; and "The Hwangmei and North Kiangsi Districts Conference," *The China Christian Advocate* 12/5 (June 1925): 19-20.
100. Pangzhuang Women, 1890-1891, ABC 16.3.12 (14), no. 33.
101. *Records 1877*, 486.
102. For the life-style and status of widows in the Qing Dynasty, refer to Susan Mann, "Widows in the Kinship, Class, and Community Structure of Qing Dynasty China," *Journal of Asian Studies* 46/1 (February 1987): 37-55
103. M. C. White, "Evangelistic Work among Women," 147.
104. Kate L. Ogborn, "A Self-Propagating Church, the Goal of All Mission Work," *CR* 45 (1914): 277.
105. M. T. Stauffer, ed., *The Christian Occupation*, 297.
106. "Woman's Conference of the M. E. Church in the Fuhkien Province," *CR* 20 (1889): 88.
107. The General Commission on Archives and History, United Methodist Church at Madison, New Jersey, holds annual reports for the woman's conferences of Fuzhou 1896-1931, North China 1892-1939, Central

China 1903-1940, Xinghua 1899-1910, and Jiangxi 1913-1935. However, the reports are imcomplete, except for the Jiangxi conference.

108. George Hubbard, "Report for Our Mission Ending March 31, 1888," ABC 16.3.5 (3), no. 8.

109. Ella J. Newton, "Women's Meetings in Foochow," *Life and Light* 22 (1892): 162-164.

110. Arthur R. Gray and Arthur M. Sherman, *The Story of the Church in China*, 185-186; see also Mary Sudman Donavan, "Zealous Evangelists: The Woman's Auxiliary to the Board of Missions," *Historical Magazine of the Protestant Episcopal Church* 51 (1982): 371-383.

111. Ella J. Newton's report in *Life and Light* 27 (1897): 263-264; and Mrs. D. E. Sheffield, "Missionary Societies among Native Christians," *Woman's Work in China* 6/1 (November 1882): 3-9.

112. "Women's Work at the National Conference," *CR* 53 (1922): 268-269.

113. Luella Miner, "The Place of Woman," 340.

114. T. E. Tong, "The Chinese Missionary Society," *CR* 68 (1937): 691.

115. Philip West, *Yenching University and Sino-Western Relations, 1916-1952* (Cambridge, Mass.: Harvard University Press, 1976), 17-18.

116. *Shengming* 1/4 (15 November 1920), back page of front cover.

117. *Shengming* 6/5 (1926): 6. The publication date cannot be identified.

118. *Shengming* 1/8 (15 March 1921): poetry 1-3; 2/1 (15 June 1921): poetry 1-4; and 2/2 (15 September 1921): poetry 1.

119. A. M. Fielde created quite a flutter when she rose to speak, and one delegate even quoted Paul's directions to the Corinthian churches; see Arthur H. Smith, "How Mission Work Looked When I Came to China," *CR* 55 (1924): 92.

120. *Records 1890*, 509-513.

121. Kenneth S. Latourette, *A History of Christian Missions*, 414.

122. Luella Miner, "The Place of Woman," 340.

123. "List of Delegates to the Conference" *CR* 44 (1913): 237-239.

124. Luella Miner, "The Place of Woman," 340.

125. For example, Myfanwy Wood, "Women at the National Christian Conference," *CR* 53 (1922): 195-196.

126. The number of women delegates was cited in M. C. White, "Evangelistic Work among Women," 146; and the composition of the National Conference can be found discussed in *NCC 1922*, 21.

127. M. C. White, "Evangelistic Work among Women," 146.

128. *NCC 1922*, 3-7.

129. The content of these speeches will be discussed in chapter five.

130. "Contemporaneous Chinese Leaders: Mrs. H. C. Mei," *CR* 58 (1927): 576-577.

131. *Nianjian* 6 (1921): preface, 12.

132. "In Remembrance: Miss Fan Yu-jung," *CR* 58 (1927): 55-56; and *Nianjian* 6 (1921): preface, 13.
133. *NCC 1922*, 700-702.
134. Judith Hoch-Smith and Anita Spring, eds., *Women in Ritual and Symbolic Roles* (New York: Plenum Press, 1978), 14.
135. Daniel H. Bays, "Christianity and the Chinese Sectarian Tradition," *Ch'ing-shih wen-ti* (Issues in Qing history), 4/7 (1982): 35-55.
136. Daniel H. Bays, "Christianity and Chinese Sects: Religious Tracts in the Late Nineteenth Century," in *Christianity in China*, ed., Suzanne Wilson Barnett and John King Fairbank, 128.
137. Barbara Brown Zikmund discusses the different steps of women claiming leadership in the American churches; see "Attacking the Male Power Structure in American Protestantism."

CHAPTER IV

Christian Women and
Social Reform

The evolving leadership of Christian women both in the local congregations and at the national level served as a basis for their increasing participation in society. Beginning in the last decades of the nineteenth century, women in the Christian community organized themselves to address issues of footbinding, concubinage, health care, and family reform. In most of these reform movements, the initial stimulus came from the missionaries, but Chinese women made significant contributions both in terms of leadership and action. To understand the cross-cultural nature of the reform impulse, we have to pay attention to women's reform movements both abroad and in China.

The women's reform movement in the United States can be traced back to the 1830's and 1840's when the Female Moral Reform Society was formed to rescue prostitutes in the cities. During the American Civil War, women who participated in the abolitionist movement gained both organizational skills and fresh insights into the forms of their own bondage, which was more subtle than black slavery. After the Civil War, more radical reformers moved on to fight for women's rights and suffrage, while others organized reform societies, combining their evangelical fervor with the urge to change society. The most spectacular crusade was the temperance movement, which succeeded in enlisting thousands of church women to march in the streets. The reform activities trained women to do fund-raising, to speak in public, to petition the government, to publish literature, and to build their own network, enhancing their sense of power.[1]

Some of the women missionaries brought with them knowledge and experience of women's reform activities from back home, which they were eager to introduce in China. Moreover, Ernst Faber, in his book *Zixi cudong* (From the West to the East) published in 1884, gave a short description of women's benevolent societies in the West, urging Chinese women to form similar societies to provide free education for children, shelter for orphans, and care for the sick.[2] Under the auspices of the missionaries, Christian women were the first group of women in China to denounce footbinding and other forms of social and cultural bondage. During the last decades of the nineteenth century, women in the church and mission schools participated in social reforms to improve the physical and social conditions of women.

The initiation of social reforms by the Christian community reflects a shift of emphasis in terms of mission ideology. While earlier missionaries committed themselves primarily to saving the souls of "heathens," missionaries at the turn of the century eagerly sought opportunities to regenerate "heathen" culture and society under the influence of the currently popular Social Gospel.[3] It is ironic that women missionaries, who were generally considered to be rather conservative at home, took upon themselves the responsibility of emancipating the women in the mission field. Trying to supply a plausible explanation, historian Alison R. Drucker suggests: "it was less disturbing to criticize another culture for injustice to women than to castigate one's own; religious women frequently avowed that introducing Christianity to the heathen world raise the status of women abroad."[4] In the strange juxtaposition of missionary ethnocentrism and the rising consciousness of Chinese women, Christian women sought to reform society by denouncing the practice of footbinding and by supporting efforts toward greater self-improvement, education, temperance, and social services.

It is important to bear in mind that Christian women's reform activities took place in the larger context of the socioeconomic change of women's status in China. Beginning in the mid-nineteenth century, women gained access to modern education, first in mission schools and subsequently in the government and private schools for girls. A small number of women went to Japan, Europe, and the United States to study, bringing back new ideas and new images of womanhood. In the urban cities, the early phase of industrialization created a new class of working women who were employed by the cotton mills, silk, tobacco, and hairnet industries. In the early twentieth century, women with feminist consciousness began to publish women's journals, advocating equality of the sexes. Some radical women took part in the revolutionary struggles to bring about the downfall of the Qing regime. The reform activities of Christian women were a part of this multi-faceted women's movement in China. Christian women tended to opt for a more gradual approach to social change rather than an abrupt and radical one like some of the secular feminists.

To fully comprehend the dynamics of the reform activities, I shall first outline the changing religious and social context that made these reform activities possible. Afterwards, four areas of social reform initiated and led by Christian women will be analyzed, focusing on specifics of organization and action. Finally, the Christian reform impulse will be evaluated and interpreted within the larger framework of Chinese politics during this era.

From Conversion to Social Reform

With an evangelical passion, missionaries in the nineteenth century devoted themselves to bring the Gospel to all men and women who had not heard of Jesus Christ. "Heathen" women, described in missionary literature and propaganda as illiterate, secluded, and idolatrous, were perceived to be in dire need of the Gospel, which would bring light into their lives of darkness. A. P. Happer, for example, told the 1877 missionary conference that "the condition of women in heathen lands presents the most pressing and urgent calls to Christian women to use their most strenuous efforts to communicate to them the knowledge of the blessed Gospel of our Lord."[5] Salvation of the soul, rather than improvement of women's lot on earth, was the chief goal of the missionary effort.

In the mid-nineteenth-century missionary ideology, conversion of "heathen" mothers was commonly held as a key to Christianizing the "heathen" nation.[6] Although Chinese women were subordinated to men both in the family and the society, missionaries recognized their enormous influence on their children and at home. William Muirhead of the London Mission once referred to the mothers in China as the chief upholders of so-called idolatrous practices in the household. The idolatrous system would become "effete and powerless," he declared, without their patronage.[7] According to his colleague Griffith John, China would not be brought to Christ without first winning over women: "Give us the mothers and daughters of China, and China must soon become Christ's; without them we shall never feel that an impression has been made on the nation."[8] It was hoped that once they were converted, women would learn to read the Bible, educate the young, and influence their family members and neighbors.

Finding it difficult to directly approach adult women, Christian missions set up schools for young girls, trying to reach their mothers indirectly. The early schools were not meant to develop the girls' intellects nor to enlighten their minds but to provide wives for Chinese helpers and to train female church workers. Thus, when during the 1877 missionary conference C. W. Mateer stirred up a controversy over the relationship between education and evangelism in Christian mission,[9] nobody seemed to have objected to opening girls' schools as part of an evangelizing strategy. Martha F. Crawford concurred with this view: "Though secular education and many other blessings follow in its train, yet let it be ever present before our minds, that the *chief want* of this people is the Gospel. . . . Let no side issues hide this from our view—no cultivating of the physical, social, or intellectual ever cause us to throw into the back ground the moral and religious."[10] The training provided in the schools neither challenged the traditional roles of women nor threatened the established Chinese ideal of womanhood. In fact, mission schools in the 1880's widely adopted the Chinese female classics, such as *Nü xiaojing* (Female classic on filial piety), to teach pupils the Chinese idea of propriety, preparing them before and after marriage to be good wives.[11]

As women joined the church in increasing numbers, articles appeared in the *Chinese Recorder* during the late 1860's, discussing how Christian churches should handle the issues of footbinding and concubinage. The missionaries held no consensus opinion on the peculiar Chinese custom of footbinding, since neither the Bible nor Christian morality offered straightforward advice on the subject. Although missionaries generally denounced the practice as cruel and injurious to the health of women, they were shrewd enough to recognize the sensitive nature of the subject, and the potential trouble that would arise if they were to confront it head-on. The discussion on concubinage demonstrated similar ambivalent attitudes, since some condemned the practice as contrary to Jesus' teaching on marriage, while others pleaded tolerance, citing cases of polygamy in the Old Testament as their support.[12] Some of the missionaries probably realized that only those from families of some means could afford having several wives, and they did not wish to offend them. Others were careful to point out that concubinage was not merely a question of sexual appetite but was rooted in the culturally informed need to have a male heir in order to continue the patrilineal line.

The last decade of the nineteenth century saw the "feminization of the mission force" in China.[13] Working daily among girls in the schools and women at church, female missionaries became more sensitive to the suffering caused by footbinding and arranged marriages. As advocates of woman's work, they often criticized the male missionaries who did not pay sufficient attention to women's needs. Women missionaries who attended the 1890 missionary conference held a session of their own to discuss issues pertinent to their work, such as how to teach women to read, the value of romanized Chinese writing, and the relation of health care to evangelism.[14] The composition of the female missionary force also shifted during this period, as more single women were commissioned to be professional teachers and physicians who sought to regenerate non-Christian cultures and not just win "feminine souls."[15]

The different outlooks of earlier and more recent women missionaries can be illustrated with reference to two papers on "Girls' Schools," presented at the 1890 missionary conference. Hattie Newell Noyes, belonging to the older generation, still believed that "a mission shool should always be regarded as an evangelistic rather than an educational agency," and "the instruction given in mission schools should resemble that of Sabbath schools."[16] But Laura A. Haygood, who arrived in China sixteen years later than Noyes, argued for a more liberal, Western style of learning for girls.

> But with the study of Chinese classics there must go hand in hand the study of Western science, made more and more thorough, more and more extensive, as the years go on, giving to them broader and broader vision, making their hands stronger and yet more strong to help in uplifting the daughters of China.[17]

Haygood's concern to uplift the women of China was shared by some of her more liberal-minded male colleagues, notably Young J. Allen and Timothy Richard. Through their writings on social reforms, Allen and Richard popularized "educated motherhood" as an ideal for Chinese women. Comparing the position of women in China to women in the West, Allen argued that Christianity had led

the Western countries to adopt the notion of equality of the sexes,
the prohibition of divorce, and the establishment of female education. In contrast, the Chinese customs of footbinding and female
illiteracy rendered half of the Chinese population useless, producing
inadequate mothers who could not properly educate the young.[18]
Timothy Richard, secretary of the influential Society for the Diffu-
sion of Christian and General Knowledge among the Chinese,
published numerous articles and books on reform, praising the contributions of Western women in China and recommending schools
for girls.[19] The prevalence of footbinding, concubinage, and female
infanticide were taken as signs and symptoms of the inferiority of
the Chinese culture. In his *Quandi wu dazhou nüsu tongkao* (Women
in all lands) published in 1903, Allen said that the best single test
of the civilization of any people is the degree to which their women
are free and educated.[20] If China wished to win a place in the
family of nations, declared Allen, she had to take heed of the benefits
of Christian civilization to transform her culture and society.

The idea of educated motherhood found some resonance among
Chinese reformers. Both Kang Youwei and his disciple Liang Qichao
were enthusiastic audiences of missionary writings and had a personal acquaintance with Timothy Richard. In his influential writings
on social reform, Liang advocated abolition of footbinding and the
establishment of schools for girls. Condemning footbinding as cruel
and inhumane, Liang charged further that female illiteracy causes
women to be dependent on men and affects the quality of
motherhood, weakening thereby the Chinese people.[21] In his reform
programs submitted to the throne, Kang criticized footbinding for
crippling women and leading to the production of feeble offspring,
and he proposed turning Chinese temples into classrooms for boys
and girls.[22] Like the missionaries, Kang and Liang tried to inject new
meanings onto the traditional conception of motherhood, but unlike
their foreign counterparts, Kang and Liang spoke out of intense
patriotism, without assuming that China needed to be Christianized
to save herself.

As the Chinese began to open schools for girls in the 1890's,
the idea of female education became more acceptable even among
the rich and the literati. Some of these families sent their daughters
to famous Christian girls' schools which offered courses in English
and other Western sciences in addition to Chinese subjects. Haygood's
McTyeire School opened in 1891 in Shanghai and was quickly filled

to its capacity, with a reputation as one of the best schools for girls. With a larger student enrollment and fewer drop outs than former periods, the mission schools could develop a full eight-year program. The curricula of five representative schools in 1900 included Bible and Christian books, Chinese classics, mathematics, history and geography, and subjects in the sciences such as physics, chemistry, biology, and geology. Music and singing were taught in four schools, and two schools offered English as an optional subject.[23] The schools aimed at training future teachers and educated mothers who could fulfill their duties "more intelligently, more willingly, and more efficiently."[24]

During this period, female missionaries in China displayed less tolerance toward the Chinese ideals of womanhood; for example, Mary Porter, later the wife of Frank D. Gamewell, told a conference of women missionaries: "The Christian world recognizes woman as a responsible personality, as a power in the intellectual, moral and spiritual worlds. . . . The Chinese idea of women is the negative of all this."[25] Women missionaries spoke of their responsibility to impart the "Christian ideal of womanhood" through Christian schools and the example of missionary households. With an unshakable belief in their own cultural superiority, these women missionaries perceived the "Christian ideal of womanhood" as not much different from their own Victorian values of womanliness. For example, they prescribed that women should have "refined and womanly qualities," keeping their homes comfortable and clean. Wives should win respect from their husbands through their intelligence and learning, and they should handle relations with in-laws to the satifaction of all. As enlightened mothers, they would treat their children conscientiously, judiciously, and with self-control, and they should be ready to extend charity to all those in need.[26] In short, women missionaries increasingly found footbinding, concubinage, and arranged marriage unacceptable, and they wished to transmit their own life style, social manners, and cultural values onto their sisters in China.

In *Woman's Work in the Far East*, a journal published by women missionaries, contributors began to discuss the roles of women in areas of self-improvement, development of moral character, temperance, child welfare, health, and the Y.W.C.A. The writers argued that women could use traditional feminine virtues, such as self-sacrifice, caring for the young, and protection of the home, in a new way to serve society.[27] The conventional role of a woman as housekeeper could be extended to keep society free of drugs and alcohol, to provide shelter for young women and school children, and to care for factory girls, who were vulnerable to all kinds of temptations in the modern world. This new image of women as "social housekeeper," current in the United Stated at the turn of the century, was popularized in China, although the social settings and the strategies adopted were very different. Political scientist Ethel Klein elucidates what "social housekeeping" meant:

> According to this expanded vision of women, they thought
> of themselves as the housekeeper not merely of the home
> but also of society. The nation was seen as a macrocosm
> of the home that needed women's special abilities to cope
> with human problems.[28]

This conception of womanhood not only recognized women's past domestic roles but justified also women's entrance into the public realm. Middle-class women found moderate reform especially attractive, because they did not wish to upset the status quo nor court public disapproval.

At the turn of the century, a self-consciousness feminist movement began to emerge in China, with the publication of women's journals and the formation of women's groups. The first of these women's journals appeared in 1902, and by 1911, there were at least sixteen more periodicals for women. Feminist ideas were introduced by female students who had studied overseas, and they were quickly spread among urban women, who shared a more cosmopolitan worldview. Nationalistic in tone, these feminist publications advocated a drastic change of society and promoted an image of women beyond the domestic confines. Historian Charlotte L. Beahan observes:

> the new women's journals now addressed themselves to
> women as an integral part of society, giving them infor-
> mation about the world beyond the "baton doors" of the
> women's quarters, promoting a feeling of group identifica-
> tion and providing new alternatives to a physically and
> mentally confined life dictated by social custom.[29]

The ideal of womanhood presented at this time was much more radical than that embraced by evangelical Christianity, and the concomitant demand for a new kind of relationship between the sexes went far beyond the Victorian concepts of gender introduced by the missionaries.

During the revolution of 1911, radical feminists organized women's corps and battalions, assuming titles such as the Women's National Army, the Women's Suicide Army, the Women's Murder Squad, and the Women's Military Squad.[30] After the revolution, the woman's suffrage societies demanded equal political rights from the national assembly of the new republic. The Christian community, both missionaries and Chinese, opposed generally the militant revolutionary activities of the radicals. Luella Miner accused the military squads and the suffragists of "offending against the laws of the land and human nature, and betraying womanly virtues."[31] The editor of *Woman's Work in the Far East* asked her readers to pray for these Chinese Amazons, who, she felt, were "plastic in mind, meeting the flaunting emptiness of agnosticism, whose unmeasured social power waits to be moulded."[32] Even Zhang Zhujun, the daring medical doctor, opposed the idea of military bands, feeling that women were not "physical strong" or "courageous" enough to go into battle.[33] For the majority of missionaries and Christian women, there was a better way for women to contribute to their county—through gradual reform and social service. Christian social reform in the urban areas provided an alternative for women who were not quite ready to enter into intense political and revolutionary activities to contribute to society in this period.

Social Reform in Action

We shall discuss four areas of reform activities in which Chinese Christian women participated beginning in the last several decades of the nineteenth century: the anti-footbinding movement, the introduction of Western medicine and health campaigns, the woman's Christian temperance movement, and various reforms sponsored by the Y.W.C.A. in China. The anti-footbinding movement and health reforms concerned the well-being of women's bodies and their strength to fulfill maternal roles; the temperance movement was waged in the name of "home protection," and the Y.W.C.A. sought to extend women's influence in society. The social reforms will be discussed according to the sequence of their occurrence but their activities overlapped in the early twentieth century.

The Anti-Footbinding Movement

The origin of footbinding is a mystery, and scholars generally believe that it originated in the Chinese court and gradually spread to the populace. In the Qing Dynasty, even though the Manchu government had issued an edict prohibiting the practice, it was tenaciously followed in many parts of the empire, especially in northern China. The custom was prevalent, because the three-inch "lily feet" had become a class symbol, signifying good breeding and beauty, while natural feet were looked down upon as a sign of humble origin or of disreputable character. Even the poorer families insisted on binding their daughters' feet and making them as small as possible, in an attempt to marry them into rich families. In southern China where women had to work in the rice fields, footbinding was less prevalent; also among ethnic peoples, such as the Manchus, Mongols, Hakkas, and Tibetans, women were allowed to keep their feet natural.[34]

In 1874, a ground-breaking event happened in Xiamen, when some sixty Chinese Christian women gathered in a church to discuss the issue of footbinding and to organize the *Jie chanzu hui* (Anti-footbinding society) under the auspices of John Macgowan of the London Mission and his wife. Several women, including a seventy-year old grandmother, addressed the assembly, condemning the evil custom that crippled women. One speaker, in particular, criticized the church's ambivalent attitude toward the subject:

> my conscience has been greatly troubled at the attitude that the Church has taken towards footbinding. Your efforts to arouse a conscience on the subject have made me think very seriously upon the wrong that we Christians have been doing in consenting to carry on a custom that is inflicting such sorrow upon ourselves and on the women of this city.[35]

The church at the time was quite reluctant to touch on this sensitive subject, which might alienate the literati and enrage the populace. Furthermore, the medical missionaries, who generally held that footbinding was detrimental to women's health, were divided on what strategy would best serve to deal with the issue. Two of the most respected members of the medical community held opposing views: J. Dudgeon of Beijing did not deem the practice as "morally wrong,'' and he warned against making unbound feet a requirement for admission to the schools. In contrast, John Kerr of the Canton Hospital indicted the practice as "a sin against God, and a sin against man" that Christians should condemn.[36] When the custom of footbinding was discussed at the missionary conference of 1877, the majority of members agreed to discourage the practice without making it a priority issue. Alexander Williamson's attitude was fairly representative, at least of the male missionaries: "We should be extremely careful about interfering with the customs of the country when no moral question is involved. We have plenty to do without exciting a new opposition among the Literati and mercantile class."[37]

Since there was no general agreement among the Christian missions, measures against footbinding remained a localized effort, depending on the inclination of specific missionaries and the consciousness of specific women. The anti-footbinding society in Xiamen continued to hold semi-annual meetings, encouraging members not to bind their daughters' feet, and later the society requested that adult women unbind their feet. Some progress had been made in Fuzhou, since two of the three missions demanded their preachers and church members to stop footbinding.[38] In northern China, where the possession of small feet was the definitive norm of femininity and beauty, the churches faced an uphill battle to modify both women's feet and people's minds. T. P. Crawford reported that his church at Dengzhou, Shandong, relied on moral persuasion rather than on church discipline, hoping that Christian women would set the first examples by unbinding themselves.[39]

Women missionaries, working closely with Chinese women and children, were more likely to see the need to abolish footbinding, and they pushed harder than the male missionaries to make unbinding a requirement for admission to the schools. In spite of the reservations of some other missionaries, Mary Porter and Maria Brown when they opened a girls' school in Beijing in 1872 insisted on admitting only those girls whose parents consented to the unbinding.[40] The Bridgman Academy, also in Beijing, did not make such a requirement during the 1870's, because the male missionaries were more hesitant to adopt such a policy.[41] In Fuzhou, the schools seemed to be more ready to support unbinding: the schools supported by the American Board used a primary reading text that included a chapter on the harmful effects of footbinding, and the Methodist schools

supported anti-footbinding from the beginning.[42] Harriet Newell
Noyes's True Light Seminary in Guangzhou did not require
unbinding for admission, but she used her personal influence to
encourage students to remove their bandages.[43]

Strong institutional support was indispensable in motivating
girls to rebel against the social norm and to undertake the painful
process of unbinding. Many girls needed to put their feet in warm
water when the bandages were removed, and some even had to stay
in bed for days. Without peer support and personal encouragement
from teachers, the girls would have felt very isolated and powerless
to face the harsh criticism of relatives and neighbors. After
unbinding, the girls and their parents faced the haunting fear of how
to find a good husband who would not mind a pair of large feet.
But as we have mentioned, the early schools were set up to provide
wives for Chinese helpers, and when they offered to defray all of the
child's educational and living expenses, some schools required that
parents give up all control over the choice of the girl's husband.[44]
Often the missionaries helped to arrange marriages for the girls with
Christian helpers and teachers, but some Christian men also
preferred a wife with small feet.

During the 1870's, a number of Chinese evangelists and pastors
wrote articles condemning the practice of footbinding. In support
of their position they gave religious reasons based on biblical teachings
in addition to the harmful effects footbinding had on women's health.
An evangelist from Beijing, Cao Jingrong, argued that God had
created both men and women perfect and complete and that it was
unnatural to alter the shape of a girl's feet to make them more
beautiful. Referring to Paul's teaching that fathers should not
provoke their children to anger, he charged that footbinding inflicted
pain and suffering on little girls, in contradiction to the benevolence
and love required of parents.[45] Another pastor from Yaoyu, Bao
Guangxi, also condemned footbinding as sinful, because it deform-
ed God's created work, injured human conscience, evoked lust and
desire in men, and instilled anger in women.[46] The body was the
"temple of the Lord," another wrote, and Christians should use it
for Christian service to the glory of God.

In the Christian community, most of the adult women who first
unbound their feet were either preachers' wives, Bible women, or
teachers at girls' schools. The public act of defiance, requiring

willpower and courage, often led to a new awareness of self, as demonstrated by the moving testimony of Mrs. Ding Si-ngok, the matron of the Fuzhou Girls' Boarding School:

> I remember, when a child, how I suffered while my mother was binding my feet.
> I could neither eat nor sleep, so I sat in one position all the day long and cried. . . .
> When I was first spoken to on the subject it seemed I could not unbind my feet. Few people had yet unbound, and those who had taken such a step had become the talk of the neighborhood. . . . I had been a Christian for years, but could see no advantage in unbinding my feet.
> Now I want to say that I have not words to express the good resulting. Not only has my body been greatly benefited, but also my soul. . . .
> Before I unbound a step an inch long was attended with pain, so no matter how many open doors there might be for the gospel, I could not enter them.
> Now I can go wherever I want to go.
> I can now present my "body a living sacrifice, holy and acceptable," something I could not do when I had bound feet.[47]

In 1895, a more organized anti-footbinding movement was launched when Alicia Little, the wife of an English merchant, founded the *Tianzuhui* (Natural foot society) in Shanghai. At a time when both Chinese reformers and missionaries had a new ideal for women, Little received enthusiastic support from churches and schools as well as from enlightened governor-generals such as Zhang Zhidong. Branch societies were organized in many cities, as she traveled and spoke in Hankou, Wuchang, Hengyang, Guangzhou, Shantou, Xiamen, Hong Kong, and Macao. Women listened attentively to her speech, some publicly testified to their own suffering, and quite a number agreed never again to bind the feet of their daughters.[48]

At this time, more schools made unbinding a definite requirement for admission. In 1896, the Bridgman Academy referred to footbinding as a "thing of the past" when the last student with bound feet had left.[49] Julia Bonafield of the Methodist Episcopal Mission in Fuzhou reported that in their Fuzhou and Xinghua boarding schools, not one of over one-hundred boarders had bound feet. Some mission schools also exerted economic sanctions by refusing to employ women with bound feet as teachers.[50] The mission schools helped to generate a social climate wherein the old custom of footbinding was incompatible with educated womanhood. Thus, when in the early twentieth century the Chinese opened girls' schools in Shanghai, some schools also made unbound feet a condition for entrance.[51]

At the local level, some churches began to mount an attack on the entrenched custom with unwavering zeal, and we can cite Pangzhuang station as an example. In 1892, women missionaries gathered some forty mothers and grandmothers as well as twenty-four little girls in the chapel to listen to an anti-footbinding talk by the Chinese teachers. The women were told that a girls' boarding school would soon be opened for girls with unbound feet, who would also receive new stockings and shoes.[52]

The anti-footbinding effort was temporarily halted, however, when the Boxers searched out Christians for persecution, and the large feet of Christian girls made it more difficult for them to hide. Most of them had to rebind for a time to avoid the hunt of the fanatics, unbinding them again after they returned to school.[53] In the early twentieth century, female church workers who urged women to unbind their feet whenever they visited the outstations set an example by unbinding their own. Despite continued opposition from relatives, more women responded to the call, including a few elderly women, and sometimes mothers and daughters unbound their feet together. One woman walking freely in her new shoes, said: "I feel as if I had added two pounds to my Christian weight since I unbound my feet."[54]

At the turn of the century, educated Chinese women contributed their efforts to propagate the anti-footbinding movement among a wider sector of the population. While studying medicine, Shi Meiyu, the first girl in Jiujiang, Jiangxi, to have natural feet, became more convinced of the evils of footbinding. With Meiyu's encouragement, her mother announced during a well-attended church gathering her plan to unbind her feet, creating quite an impact on the audience.[55] Some wealthy Christian women used their personal influence to affect relatives and friends; for instance, Mrs. Zhang of Fuzhou, hosted an anti-footbinding meeting for upper class women, distributing literature of the Natural Foot Society and new patterns for shoes.[56] Other educated women contributed articles to *Wanguo gongbao*, discussing the social consequences of footbinding on women's lives, such as limiting the mobility of women and making them dependent on their husbands.[57] In an article in *Nüduobao*, Yuan Yuying wrote that women were created by God and that the human body should by presented as a "living sacrifice" to the Lord. She highlighted also the relationship between nationalism and the liberation of women's bodies, arguing that feeble mothers endangered the Chinese species.[58]

In response to mounting social pressure both from the Chinese literati and the foreign community, the Empress Dowager promulgated an edict banning footbinding in 1902. In the big cities, footbinding became less fashionable, especially among the educated, but in rural areas, the practice still prevailed. In 1907, when Alicia Little returned with her husband to England, leadership of the Natural Foot Society passed on to a Chinese man. As a nation-wide movement, it lost its momentum in the 1910's, but individual efforts were continued by Chinese women and open-minded officials.[59]

In previous studies on the anti-footbinding movement, Western scholars have tended to emphasize the contribution of Western women, while Chinese scholars focused on the work of Kang Youwei and Liang Qichao in popularizing the idea.[60] Ironically, the courageous women who challenged the custom by removing their bandages were seldom named or mentioned. The anti-footbinding society formed in 1874 represented the first organized effort of Chinese women to challenge the patriarchal system. Christian women played an important role, and female religious leaders led the fight in their local communities. Beginning in 1895, Kang Youwei and others formed anti-footbinding societies in Shanghai and Guangzhou, recruiting mostly men as members. In contrast, the Natural Foot Society was an organized women's movement, arousing women's consciousness of their own situations in many cities. It is not surprising that the first women's movement in China took the form of an anti-footbinding movement, because small feet symbolized the oppression of women in a most dramatic and concrete way. While male supporters focused more on the effects that footbinding has on national strength, women themselves began to explore how physical bondage was inseparably linked to other forms of bondage affecting their lives.

Western Medicine and Health Campaigns

In traditional Chinese folk beliefs, the normal functions of the female body, such as menstruation and pregnancy, were associated with pollution and marked by taboos. During the days of her period, a woman could not worship the gods, because she was considered unclean and hence dangerous.[61] A pregnant woman had to take extreme caution not to violate certain taboos, lest she had a difficult delivery; for example, she should not rearrange her room, lift heavy objects, enter a construction site, or eat any food with a strong flavor.[62] Before the advent of Western medicine, Chinese women consulted traditional medical practitioners, took herbal medicine, and resorted to various kinds of religious healing when they fell sick. During childbirth, most women sought help from older neighbors and relatives, while women of the nobility turned to midwives, who typically were illiterate women with little or no medical training.[63] The lack of adequate scientific knowledge of anatomy, hygiene, and anaesthesia often caused unnecessary complications and suffering during childbirth.

Western medicine was introduced in China to relieve the "bodily affliction of the people" and to serve as a "handmaid to the gospel."[64] Development of Western medicine in nineteenth-century China gave birth to a class of male medical professionals, but unlike their Western counterparts, they did not replace the midwives and the female support systems, because the population was so large and the doctors were so few in number. On the contrary, missionary medicine produced the unintended result of training Chinese women in medicine, and they became ardent reformers in health and in other areas related to the welfare of women.

Although women would consult a male physician for certain diseases, social propriety made it embarrassing for them to see a man when they had obstetrical and gynecological problems. Many medical doctors regretted that it was often "too late" when during a medical emergency women were rushed to the hospital only as a last resort. The situation called for women medical missionaries, but since the number of available female doctors was very small, Chinese women had to be trained to take care of women patients.

Medical education for women began when two young women from the True Light Seminary requested that John Kerr admit them to his medical class at the Canton Hospital in 1879. Harriet Newell Noyes recorded this historical beginning as follows:

> This was an entirely new idea for a Chinese woman, and the pros and cons were discussed at length, but their request was finally presented to Dr. Kerr who encouraged them to make the attempt, and gave them a place in his class of medical students, promising them the same advantages and instruction that the young men received.[65]

A small number of women also received informal training as medical assistants from female missionary doctors, although the hospitals were poorly equipped for medical training and the teaching was rudimentary. Angie M. Myers, a medical missionary in Xiamen, described her situation: "Anatomy with no dissecting, chemistry with no laboratory, pathology with no microscope are all difficult subjects to teach. All the teaching was done in Chinese, and was by lectures and recitations, with occasional written examinations."[66] At the turn of the century, the growth towards professionalism of Western medicine in China prompted the establishment of medical schools for women, including the Women's Medical College at Suzhou, the Hackett Medical College for Women at Guangzhou, and the most advanced of these, the China Union Medical College for Women in Beijing.[67]

A few Chinese women, mostly daughters of Chinese pastors or adopted daughters of foreign missionaries, were sent abroad to receive formal medical education. The first was Jin Yunmei, the orphan daughter of a Chinese pastor, who was adopted by Divie Bethune McCartee and his wife. Graduating with high honors from the Woman's Medical College in New York, she was sent back to China under the auspices of the Woman's Board of the Dutch Reformed Church in 1888. Hu Jinying, the daughter of one of the first Methodist pastors in Fuzhou, followed suit and graduated from the Woman's Medical College of Philadelphia. Among the several foreign-trained doctors, the best known were Kang Cheng and Shi Meiyu, who were brought to the University of Michigan by the Methodist missionary Gertrude Howe. Upon completion of their studies in 1896, they returned to work in the mission hospital in Jiujiang, and they were warmly welcomed by the local people, who were so overwhelmed with joy that they fired 40,000 fire-crackers in celebration of the homecoming. Later, Li Bi Cu from Fuzhou went to Philadelphia to study medicine and returned to China in 1905.[68]

Working in mission hospitals, these women doctors treated out-patients in the dispensary, cared for in-patients in the small hospital, and made house calls. Most of the mission hospitals in those days were poorly equipped, many without running water, microscope, laboratory, or operating room. Despite such limitations, the women doctors attracted a large number of women patients and won their respect. During the first year of their service, Kang Cheng and Shi Meiyu treated 2,352 dispensary patients, made 343 house calls, and treated 13 patients in their small hospital.[69] Many of these doctors combined their medical expertise with evangelical zeal, trying their best to explain to the illiterate women why their diseases had nothing to do with evil spirits. For example, Kang Cheng once had to convince a young woman that burning incense in the temple would not cure her mother's sickness.[70]

Although few in number, the women doctors made a significant impact on the growing acceptance of Western medicine by Chinese women. The number of Hu Jinying's out-patients grew from 1,837 in 1895 to 24,091 in 1910. Her Woolston Memorial Hospital in Fuzhou attracted the largest number of women patients, much to the envy of the foreign medical missionaries there.[71] At Jiujiang, the peasants also confided to Kang Cheng and Shi Meiyu with admiration and appreciation: "We are afraid of foreigners, but you can understand our nature."[72] The changing attitude of Chinese women toward Western medicine was discerned by Mary Fulton, a medical doctor who had worked for many years in Guangzhou. In 1900, she noted that whereas fifteen years earlier, there were scarcely a score of calls to women in their homes during the year, now the women physicians were kept busy day and night answering such calls. With pride and pleasure, she added: "the native public are putting confidence in our graduates [of the medical school], and two now have an excellent reputation as obstetricians. They are sent for not only throughout Canton City but in the region round about."[73]

In 1920, Chinese women comprised twelve percent of the physicians in China,[74] but they exercised considerable influence on the welfare of women and children. The medical profession placed them at a strategic position to wage war on footbinding. For example, Hu Jinying, the first girl to have natural feet in the Fuzhou neighborhood, earnestly persuaded other women to unbind, citing her own experience as model for others to follow.[75] In addition to hospital duties and training nurses, the women doctors offered public lectures on physiology, hygiene, child care, and first aid.[76] Shi Meiyu was a leader of the woman's Christian temperance movement, and she drew attention to eugenics and birth control at the National Christian Conference.[77] Highly respected in the medical community, Kang Cheng and Shi Meiyu were invited to address health care for women at the Conference of the China Medical Missionary Association.[78] In Guangzhou and Shanghai, the daring doctor Zhang Zhujun initiated various projects for women and child welfare, including a women's medical school, industrial training for women, public seminars on hygiene, and an orphanage.[79]

Nursing, usually considered a feminine profession nowadays, was carried out mostly by men when it was introduced in China with Western medicine and hospitals. Many Chinese had a low esteem for nurses, regarding them as "a rather peculiar mixture of an unqualified doctor and a ward coolie."[80] Because menial duties were considered dirty and degrading in the society, nursing did not appeal to women in the beginning, attracting only young widows, deserted wives, and women of the lower classes. But with the passing away of many superstitions and the gradual acceptance of nursing as a profession, an increasing number, many from the mission schools, enrolled in nursing schools in cities such as Hong Kong, Fuzhou, Shanghai, Changsha, and Beijing.[81] According to Cora E. Simpson, later the general secretary of the Nurses' Association, the nursing schools trained students to serve in hospitals, enter into private practice, and to be better wives and mothers since many left their jobs after marriage.[82] The senior class of female nursing students were also given one additional year's training in midwifery. As late as 1918, female nurses had the primary duty of taking care of women patients and children, since it was considered improper to employ them in the treatment of men, except in the big cities.[83] In addition to their regular duties, the nurses also taught patients about personal hygiene, child care, and public sanitation.

Apart from the efforts of medical professionals, Christian women organized health campaigns on the community level to teach the public about disease and basic health care. The students of the Ginling College at Nanjing held public lectures for women on how to prevent and treat consumption, colds, and malaria.[84] During summer vacations, pupils of the North China Union College for Women at Beijing devoted themselves to health education, helping to explain the causes of diseases and social hygiene during public health exhibitions.[85] As a member of Shanghai's National Council of Health Education, the Y.W.C.A. sponsored health campaigns in local communities and issued and distributed literature and charts on health care to the public. Through a health secretary, the Y.W.C.A. initiated a health campaign for the people in Shanxi, promoting better hygiene and child welfare in many cities through the provision of public lectures, pamphlets, and movies.[86] Beginning in 1917, the Y.W.C.A. sponsored Better Baby Contests, illustrating improved methods of infant care through demonstrations of baths, diets, and clothes. In 1924, the Beijing chapter opened its first child clinic and began an experimental station for feeding babies and distributed bean-curd milk for infants.[87]

The contribution of Christian women in Western medicine and health reform was widely recognized both among the Chinese and among the missionaries. Women who suffered from a difficult delivery, fractured bones, or life-threatening tumors appreciated, naturally, what the doctors did for them. Further, Liang Qichao exalted Kang Cheng and Shi Meiyu as new models for Chinese women to emulate.[88] The general acceptance of women in medicine, which was a novelty in Chinese society, revealed some interesting cultural dynamics at work. Sara Waitstill Tucker has pointed out that Western medicine, unlike the Christian churches or the mission schools that were also products of Western culture introduced into China at the same time, carried less obvious Western cultural baggage, and therefore, it was less threatening to the Chinese.[89] Social propriety justified the need to have women doctors taking care of women patients, and the work of the female doctors and nurses centered around pregnancy, childbirth, and the welfare of women and children, all of which could be seen as an extension of traditional midwifery and nursing roles. On the other hand, the practice of Western medicine and health campaigns introduced scientific knowledge about the body, helping to shatter some of the centuries-old myths regarding women's bodily functions and creating a new awareness of women's identity, freedom, and responsibility.

The Woman's Christian Temperance Movement

The Woman's Christian Temperance Union (W.C.T.U.) was formed in 1874 in the United States, as American women organized themselves to battle against Demon Rum, which was then identified as the chief cause of social evils and broken families. Under the motto "For God and Home and Native Land," Frances Willard, the national president, mobilized several hundred thousand women in this nation-wide crusade.[90] Women crusaders, most of them church women, marched down the streets, held prayer meetings in saloons, confronted liquor dealers, and picketed liquor establishments. Assuming that women, by nature, were more pious, pure, and faithful, these temperance champions felt that God had ordained them to elevate society according to the values of the home. As Susan Dye Lee reports: "The crusaders believed that the world could be made perfect through the redemptive power of women. Emboldened by the strong feelings of moral superiority that these convictions encouraged, the crusaders went out into the community as evangelists for the home."[91]

In 1886, the W.C.T.U. sent representatives to China, but temperance work among the Chinese had already begun three years earlier when Frances Willard stopped over in San Francisco during her national circuit and decided to begin a chapter for drunkards and prostitutes in China Town. In Shanghai and Zhenjiang, the W.C.T.U. established two branches with the support of women missionaries, reaching out to a small number of school girls and church women.[92] The movement did not expand until Sarah Goodrich, the wife of Chauncey Goodrich, took up the position of general secretary in 1909. The aim of the W.C.T.U. was explained in this way: "The organization of women for the protection and betterment of their homes with the ultimate aim of abolishing those evils which blight Society, ruin homes and weaken the empire."[93] Sarah Goodrich shared the conviction of W.C.T.U. leaders in America that the temperance movement was a kind of "organized mother-love," committed to saving the home from any evils whatsoever.[94]

Since the situation in China during the early twentieth century was quite different from that in the United States, the Chinese W.C.T.U. had to map out the battlefront and develop strategies that were acceptable to society. The rampant use of opium, together with alcohol drinking and cigarette smoking, were targeted as major evils affecting social morale and the health of the nation. Although the government stepped up its opium suppression campaigns since 1906, opium smokers could find ways to get around the law because of the corrupted government bureaucracy.[95] The majority of the opium smokers were men, but women could also become addicted "by following the prescription of a doctor for some painful disease," by "smoking to keep one's husband company," or in the attempt to "drown sorrow arising from the loss of a near relative, or from domestic unhappiness," writes one women missionary.[96] Cigarette smoking had increased to such proportions that early in the 1910's one writer noted: "It is estimated that one-half the cigarette consumption of the world is in China." The British-American Tobacco Company opened a factory in Hankou, employing over 1,500 Chinese workers, with an output of two hundred million cigarettes per month.[97] Although foreign liquor was expensive and its use restricted to the rich, the import of wine, whisky, and bottled beer was rising.

The W.C.T.U. worked primarily among women and children, since there was a Christian Endeavor movement campaigning for a similar cause among men. Issues threatening the home, such as polygamy, footbinding, prostitution, and the selling of daughters as domestic maids, were also identified as special concerns. In 1916, there were altogether forty Women's Unions and Young People's and Loyal Temperance Legions, scattered in seven different provinces.[98] During temperance meetings, mothers and children were taught to revere their bodies as the temples of God and to dissuade their fathers, husbands, and brothers from opium, alcohol, and tobacco consumption. Each wore a white ribbon, symbolizing purity, following the practice of the American temperance societies.

Lacking organizational strength and the support of public religious sentiment, marching and singing down the streets or praying in the saloons was quite unthinkable in China at the time. The W.C.T.U. resorted to strategies of a less dramatic nature, which would not arose public disapproval. In addition to holding regular temperance meetings in local and youth chapters, public lectures on social morality were presented in schools and churches, with the aids of charts, posters, and slide shows. Participants were encouraged to make pledges to refrain from smoking or drinking. Through the distribution of temperance leaflets, charts on eugenics, and physiological diagrams on the effects of alcohol and cigarettes on the organs of the body, the movement hoped to reach a wider audience.[99]

The W.C.T.U. maintained a regular column in *Nüduobao* and frequently published on "temperance and reform" in the pages of

Woman's Work in the Far East. These articles quoted and discussed scientific studies done on cigarettes and alcohol and on their effects on the human body and mind.[100] Examples of how foreign governments legislated against the excessive use of alcohol and prohibited minors from smoking cigarettes were also reported.[101] Several leaflets on temperance, a book on the life and career of Frances Willard, and a story book promoting temperance among school children were published.[102] If Mary Wollstonecraft was adored by the Chinese suffragists, Frances Willard was the most popular woman in church circles; her picture and story appeared in both *Wanguo gongbao* and *Nüduobao.*[103]

To further promote their cause, the W.C.T.U. worked through other women's associations and extended its appeal to international organizations. Temperance committees were set up in some student branches of the Y.W.C.A. to draw attention to temperance work. In Beijing, the W.C.T.U. worked with the Anti-Cigarette Society, which had over 1,000 members, largely students and teachers from the government and mission schools. Large rallies were held to stir up public opinion against the use of opium and cigarettes. Occasionally, international help was solicited: a petition signed by over thirty-five hundred women and girls was sent to the Anti-Opium Society of England, asking them to continue their efforts to fight the opium traffic between England and China.[104] A similar appeal was addressed to the W.C.T.U. of England, requesting English women to use their influence to have the trade discontinued.[105]

During the middle of the 1910's, leadership of the movement passed into the hands of Chinese women: Chen Yuling, a graduate of the North China Union College for Women, joined the staff in 1916, later to be joined by Yuan Yuying as secretary. At the first national convention in 1922 held in Shanghai, Shi Meiyu was elected president, Mei Yunying appointed general secretary, Wang Liming secretary of the young people's branch, and Faith Liu secretary of the editorial department. At that time, the organization had 6,300 members in all branches, established in eleven provinces.[106] Although the purpose of the movement was still to promote the betterment of the home, it was broadened to include: (1) good life habits, (2) higher moral standards for men and women, (3) protection of motherhood, (4) child education and welfare, and (5) world peace and goodwill among all peoples.[107]

The ideology of "home protection" had not changed, but the Chinese leadership expanded and modified its meaning according to the needs of the Chinese family. Wang Liming, who served as the national president of the W.C.T.U. in the 1920's, graduated from a mission school in Jiujiang and subsequently attended Northwestern University in Illinois, where Frances Willard had once been in charge of the Ladies' College.[108] Her articles published in *Jiezhi yuekan* (Temperance monthly) espouse the idea of reforming society by improving its families, since "no nation can rise above its homes." In her view, women are by nature morally superior to men, even though they may not receive as much education. She asserts further that women are more merciful and compassionate and have contributed a great deal to society through their unselfish care of the young and by acting as the anchor of family relationships.[109] Happily married to Herman C. E. Liu, Wang Liming believed that arranged marriages should be abolished to allow women and men to choose their own spouses. She suggested that the traditional extended family be replaced by the small nuclear family, and that the family be ruled by love instead of authority. Once families were improved, they could in turn contribute to society by providing recreation for children, helping the poor, and by sponsoring social services such as public sanitation, the literacy campaign, and village self-government.[110]

As the organization came to employ more staff, the work was divided into four departments. The adult department worked chiefly with Christian women, although non-Christians could sign a pledge and become associate members. Sponsoring annual oratorical and written contests, the youth department also organized volunteer temperance lectures and social service. The official organ, *Jiezhi jikan* (Temperance quarterly) began its publication in 1922, and shortly turned into a monthly, publishing articles on temperance lessons, songs, moral and physiological issues, home economics, and scientific investigations.[111] The scientific temperance instruction department was under the direction of Christiane I. Tinling, an experienced temperance teacher sponsored by the American W.C.T.U.[112] Additional books on temperance, such as *The Life of Frances Willard, Some Truths about Alcohol, Victory from Defeat* by Yuan Yuying, *A Temperance Hygiene, Why America Went Dry*, and *Temperance Tales* by Tinling were published.[113]

The feminist movement in China made W.C.T.U. leaders more aware of the needs of the women themselves, instead of focusing simply on drinking and smoking. Wang Liming wrote:

> The W.C.T.U. realizes that poverty and illiteracy are just as much enemies of the country as drinking, smoking and gambling. This organization therefore advocates and promotes education, child welfare, and woman's economic independence as necessary lines of work.[114]

The W.C.T.U. began to provide services catering to the needs of working mothers, such as nurseries during the day and night shifts. Student members in Shanghai planned a settlement house to take care of women beggars in the poorest section of the city as well as a free day school for their children.

Learning from the political demonstrations of students and workers during the early 1920's, the W.C.T.U. adopted strategies such as marching in the streets and holding big rallies. During the national anti-opium campaign sponsored in cooperation with the National Anti-Opium Association, the student chapter in Xiamen, for example, marched in the streets, holding public meetings with farmers, construction workers, and businessmen. In Pingding, Shanxi, the W.C.T.U. of a local girls' school joined with groups of male students and church members to demonstrate on the national anti-opium day. These demonstrations and rallies were aimed at exerting pressure on the government and fanning public sentiment against opium, marihuana, and other drugs.[115]

As we have seen, the woman's Christian temperance movement, originating as a middle-class American women's movement targeted at alcohol consumption, had to broaden its appeal when transplanted in China. As Chinese staff assumed leadership positions, they brought with them the awareness that the evils of society could not be attributed to opium, alcohol, and cigarettes alone but were connected also to poverty, illiteracy, and the economic dependence of women. In the name of "home protection," the W.C.T.U. succeeded to organize mothers to emerge from their homes and to express concern about social problems. Its impact, however, was limited by its allegiance to traditional feminine roles and its failure to explore new conceptions of womanhood in a rapidly changing society. In the United States, the W.C.T.U. did not move beyond the conventional roles of women to effect changes in the political realm, although their activities had become increasingly political.[116] In China, the issues of opium and cigarettes were intricately related to corruption of government and foreign domination, which could not be solved either through moral influence or personal temperance alone. Most of the members of temperance groups were middle-class women or girls in the schools, who failed to comprehend that the problems China faced were much more systemic. The "orgainzed mother-love" strategy lost its attraction, becoming almost anachronistic, as radical students advocated a more fundamental and drastic change of society.

The Young Women's Christian Association

The Y.W.C.A. was introduced into China four years later than the W.C.T.U., but it grew to be the largest women's organization in China. The work of the Y.W.C.A. originated in England and the United States in the latter half of the nineteenth century when industrialization brought many women to work in the factories, and male academic institutions began to admit women students. Combining religious revivalism and zeal for social service, the Y.W.C.A. provided boarding houses, vocational training, and prayer groups for working class women, as well as hostels and recreation for students.[117] At the turn of the century, when Christian missions in China attempted to enlarge their influences through Christian education and social service, the Y.W.C.A. and the Y.M.C.A. represented cooperative efforts between the Chinese and foreigners to provide a wide range of programs and activities.

The first branch of the Y.W.C.A. was established in 1890 in the Hongdao girls' school of the American Southern Presbyterian Mission in Hangzhou, but the national committee was not formed until 1899. Working primarily in major cities, the Y.W.C.A. appealed to a broad constituency, including students at mission and government schools, working class women employed in the cotton, silk, matches, and tobacco industries, as well as a new class of urban women, the wives of educators, businessmen, and government officials. After the revolution of 1911, its work expanded very rapidly, reaching a climax with the first national convention in 1923. Its goal as set out in 1919 was as follows:

> to unite Chinese girls and women for advancement along
> spiritual, mental, physical and social lines, and for

service to God and country—according to the teachings
of Jesus Christ.[118]

The Y.W.C.A. was first staffed by foreign secretaries supported
by their own associations abroad. However, it made a definite
commitment to increase Chinese participation both in terms of staff
and policy making. From 1911 to 1923, the number of foreign
secretaries increased from 8 to 87; the majority came from the United
States, while others came from England, Sweden, Canada, Australia,
and Norway. Ding Mingyu (Mary Ting), general secretary of the
Shanghai branch in 1906, was the first Chinese staff member. Since
then, the number increased from 8 in 1915 to 51 by 1924.[119] The
Y.W.C.A. provided attractive opportunities for the young women who
graduated from China's newly established women's colleges. Some
of the Chinese staff such as Ding Shujing, Fan Yurong, and Deng
Yuzhi were graduates of North China Union College for Women and
Ginling College. A number of foreign-trained Chinese women serv-
ed also as staff or officers of the association, including Ding Mingyu,
Chen Yingmei, Jiang Hezhen, and Hu Binxia.

The organization of the Y.W.C.A. consisted of a national committee and boards of directors of both city and student associations.
V. Y. Tsao and Julia Yen were among the early officers, and by 1920,
the ratio of Chinese to foreigners on the national committee was
17 to 13.[120] Chinese participation in decision making was more
notable in the local chapters. For example, in Shanghai, eight out
of the nine board members in 1911 were Chinese, and the board was
made up entirely of Chinese members by 1919. Similarly in Guangzhou, the students and graduates of the True Light Seminary
formed the basis of the Guangzhou chapter, and Luo Youjie served
as its general secretary.[121] Membership in the Y.W.C.A. was not
limited to Christians, and non-Christians also could serve on the
committees.[122]

Student work, the vanguard of the organization, enjoyed
phenomenal growth during the first two decades of the twentieth
century. In the beginning, student chapters were formed in the
mission schools, but when government and private schools were
opened for girls, the 1907 China centenary conference resolved that
the Y.W.C.A. should also initiate work in government and non-
Christian schools. Both in mission and government schools, a
student branch could be formed only at the invitation of teachers and
administrators. Student chapters increased from 10 in 1903 to 20 in

1907, more than doubled to 49 in 1915, reaching 91 in 1924. During the decade between 1915 to 1924, student membership rose from 2,824 to 6,000.[123] The majority of the student members were middle-school girls, since there were only three women's colleges with less than 100 students. To reach girls younger than those in middle schools as well as those who were not attending schools, three kinds of clubs—the Rainbow, Pioneer, and *Hua Guang* (Light of glorious Chinese youth)—were formed. Activities for the students included Bible study, prayer meetings, Christian fellowship, and providing social services such as hospital visitation and summer schools for children. In the women's colleges, the Y.W.C.A. held Bible-study meetings and Sunday evening services, and the organization contributed to society in general through community service. At Ginling College, the student chapter established a half-day free school staffed by students, and student members in the Yenching University Women's College opened a free day school, taught a children's class, and participated in social service and famine relief.[124]

The growth of chapters in cities was relatively slower: the first one was formed in Shanghai in 1908, followed by Guangzhou in 1912, Tianjin in 1913, Beijing in 1916, Changsha and Fuzhou in 1919. New chapters were opened subsequently in Hong Kong, Chengdu, Hangzhou, Mukden, Nanjing, Jinan, and Yantai during the 1920's. Membership in the bigger associations, such as those in Beijing, Guangzhou, and Shanghai, ranged from 300 to 500, while the smaller organizations in Tianjin, Changsha, and Hong Kong had between 100 and 200 members. In 1924, the total membership of city associations reached 3,000.[125] Unlike the student branches, the city chapters did not have a captive audience and had to attract members through social activities and special programs such as classes in Chinese cooking, sewing, and candy making, or English conversation, Mandarin, the domestic arts, typing, foreign cooking, first aid, and nursing.[126] Each local chapter had its own board of directors, from 10 to 15 persons elected by the members and serving for a term of three years. The board decided all questions of policy, finance, property, secretariat, and programs, independently of the national committee.

At the national level, the student secretariat, established first in 1914, coordinated the student branches and held conferences for students during their vacations. The work among students placed the Y.W.C.A. at the crosscurrents of rising student consciousness, nationalism, and social protest. The program and the topics discussed reflected the changing consciousness of female students during that period. During the late nineteenth century, students of girls' schools were concerned primarily with the spread of educational opportunities and the anti-footbinding movement. In the early twentieth century, students became more aware that freedom from bondage also entailed new responsibilities to serve society. The themes of the student conferences "Our Opportunity for Service," "Women and Society," or "Women and Social Work," suggest the change. The patriotic fervor of the May Fourth movement cast its influence on Y.W.C.A. activities, as issues such as "Christ and National Salvation" were brought up. The social teaching of Jesus received much attention during the student demonstrations of the 1920's.[127]

Influenced by the work of English and American Y.W.C.A.'s among working class women, the Chinese Y.W.C.A. early on initiated work among cotton-mill workers in Shanghai in 1906, renting a building in the cotton-mill district. In the sweatshops and the cotton mills female workers worked for almost twelve hours a day, six days a week, accompanied often by their nursing babies.[128] There were no official statistics of female workers, but one worker of the Y.W.C.A. estimated a number of roughly 200,000 in 1924.[129] When the first industrial secretary was appointed in 1921, the Y.W.C.A. had to decide between two lines of work: (1) providing recreational activities for workers, or (2) working toward changing public opinion and labor law. Opting for the latter course, the industrial secretariat made surveys on working conditions in typical centers as basis for recommending policy changes.[130] In order to arouse public concern, Cheng Wanzhen, who joined the industrial department, wrote many articles on the poor sanitation and crowded conditions of the mill floor, welfare work in the factories, and the apprenticeship system. The industrial department made an impact on the wider Christian community when it successfully urged the National Christian Council of China to establish an industrial commission to promote safe and humane working conditions and the elimination of child labor. The Y.W.C.A. cooperated also with the other women's clubs in Shanghai to promote interest in the Municipal Council of the International Settlement in order to stop child labor abuses.[131] The most significant contribution, however, was the establishment of literacy classes and the formation of leadership among female workers, which proved to have a long-lasting influence on workers' consciousness.

Concerned about women's personal and community health, the Y.W.C.A. recognized the need to cultivate a more positive evaluation of the female body and its vitality. Cai Kui (Tsai Kuei) and Lily K. Haass, historians of the Y.W.C.A., observed: "Quite apart from the incidence of sickness and the inability of many Chinese women to face the onset of disease, there remained the whole question of the need for the development of a new health outlook."[132] Through the activities of student chapters, playgrounds, talks, and demonstrations, the Y.W.C.A. promoted physical education for women and girls. Plans were made for the establishment of a Normal School for Physical Education to train qualified physical education directors to teach in the schools. Upon the return of Chen Yingmei, who studied physical education at Wellesley College in the United States, the first normal class began in 1915. Meant to teach "the gospel of the body," the Normal School offered a two-year training course and later incorporated with Ginling College to provide a full college course in 1925.

Apart from regular activities, the Y.W.C.A. cooperated with and supported other associations in carrying out social reforms and services. As a member of the National Anti-Opium Association, the Y.W.C.A. took part in anti-opium campaigns and temperance work. When the Mass Education Movement was launched in 1923, city associations ran day schools for rural and working women, using "the thousand characters" as a reading text. As mentioned already, the Y.W.C.A. worked with the Council of Health Education to promote baby welfare and social hygiene. Through the "social service league," or "community service group" organized by local chapters, members rendered social services such as flood and famine relief, shelter for the homeless, child welfare stations, maternity clinics, and orphanages. Hotels for young women in government schools for nursing and other professions were opened in Guangzhou, Changsha, Tianjin, Beijing, and Shanghai, providing cheap dormitories for those in need.[133]

In 1923, the Chinese Y.W.C.A. was sufficiently developed to call its first national convention in Shanghai, which was attended by representatives of local and student chapters. Choosing the theme "The Contribution of Y.W.C.A. to Today's Chinese Women," the national convention marked the emergence of a national organization, a new spirit, and a first step toward building a Chinese movement. Ding Shujing, secretary of the Beijing chapter, was the chief engineer of the convention, while Hu Binxia, the first Chinese chairperson of the national committee, and Cheng Guanyi presided over most of the meetings. Apart from business matters and reports from various departments, the plenaries discussed important topics of central importance to the Chinese Christian church, such as "The Christian Principle of Social Reform," "Christianity and China," and "International Relations."[134] After the convention, steps were taken to develop independence by planning a budget and administering funds entirely through the China Committee. Local chapters were also encouraged to raise their own funds.[135]

During the anti-Christian movement, churches, mission schools, and Christian organizations were attacked by radical students and accused of being the "running dogs" of imperialistic powers. These accusations together with general social unrest definitely turned students away from Christianity. The work of the Y.M.C.A. was seriously affected, with financial resources diminishing and membership declining during the mid-1920's.[136] The Y.W.C.A. was less hard hit, because the students in the girls' schools, on the whole, were "less likely to go to extremes" than those in the boys' schools.[137] Student membership, however, did not increase as rapidly as before. From 1920 to 1924, student membership increased from about 4,000 to 6,000, which was quite a remarkable achievement considering that there were altogether only 60,000 female students in primary and middle mission schools.[138] In 1926, however, the membership leveled off to only about 6,500.[139]

The radicalization of students made the Chinese Y.W.C.A. leaders more aware of the need to integrate the Y.W.C.A. with the national aspiration for self-determination and political independence. During the May Thirtieth Incident in 1925, when demonstrators were shot by police troops under English officers, the Y.W.C.A. joined other patriotic groups, workers, and students in demanding justice and international peace.[140] Under the leadership of Ding Shujing, who assumed the position of general secretary in 1926, the Y.W.C.A. moved towards expanding its coalition with the working classes and poorer women. This shift in orientation was evident at the second national convention in 1928, as stated in a booklet introducing the Y.W.C.A. at that time:

> Whereas the main field for some years tended to be students and educated women, the so-called "upper classes," the scene had already changed by 1928, the date of the Second National Convention. The horizon had

enlarged, thinking was in term of an all inclusive women's
movement. Rural women and industrial women became
more an integral part of the Association rather than the
groups singled out to be served.[141]

Following the model of Y.W.C.A. abroad, the Chinese Y.W.C.A. which
started out providing social service for students and urban women,
became more socially conscious in the changing circumstances of
China. Night schools, literacy classes, and leadership training among
cotton-mill workers in Shanghai had contributed to a rising political
consciousness among female workers, and some of them later became
leaders of the Chinese Communist Party. Although radical students
in the 1920's criticized the Y.M.C.A. and Y.W.C.A. as too
Westernized, the Chinese Communist Party later recognized the
contribution of the Y.W.C.A. for its pioneer work among women
workers.

The Reform Impulse and Chinese Politics

Christian women's reform activities took place in a changing
context of Christian mission when more and more missionaries
engaged in education and social reforms under the influence of
the Social Gospel. When Chinese women, encouraged by the missionaries, initiated various kinds of reform movements, they justified
their action by extending the maternal role of women beyond the
family to the society as a whole. The adaptation of the traditional
concept of motherhood to a new situation appealed to women,
because it was less unconventional. On the other hand, it corres-
ponded to the evangelical feminine ideals, which glorified women's
domestic roles and stressed the use of feminine virtues as leaven for
social change.

Chinese women embarked on an unprecedented journey beginning with the removal of foot bandages in the 1890's and resulting
with their entry into mass politics in the 1920's. Development of
women's consciousness depended on the formation of forums,
groups, and networks, in which issues of importance to women could
be articulated and publicly addressed. Christian girls' schools,
women's groups in churches, local chapters of the W.C.T.U. and
Y.W.C.A. provided channels for women to form peer groups and
to effect changes in ways acceptable to society. The Christian

organizations and networks must be seen as an integral part of the proliferation of women's groups and the birth of a new women's consciousness in twentieth-century China.

When we evaluate those women's reform activities that were closely related to mission schools and church organizations, we have to place them in historical perspective. First of all, Christian women leaders themselves affirmed that the reform movements made important contributions to the development of China. Writing in 1914, Shi Meiyu commended the work of Christian women in education, medicine, philanthropy, temperance, the anti-footbinding movement, and homemaking, saying: "Now Chinese womanhood has come to a new consciousness of itself."[142] Both the W.C.T.U. and the Y.W.C.A. reached a large number of women, attracting non-Christians as members, one noted example being the writer Ding Ling, who participated in temperance activities.[143] In 1922, membership of the W.C.T.U. reached 6,300 with branches in eleven provinces, while the Y.W.C.A. had 3,000 members in the city associations and another 6,000 in the student branches in the mid-1920's.

However, we have also seen that the ideology that portrayed women as having distinct roles based on their maternal function had its limiting effects. It reinforced the stereotypical sexual roles prescribed by society. The extent of women's reform activities were circumscribed further to those areas directly related to the home and child care. The Victorian concepts of womanhood introduced by the women missionaries might not be adequate for China, which was dominated by foreign powers and was on the point of a revolution. In fact, when the leadership of the W.C.T.U. and the Y.W.C.A. was passed onto Chinese hands, Chinese women leaders began to see that Christian reformist activities in Europe and America had their limitations when transplanted in China. They tried to broaden the scope of activities to address the changing demands of the day.

When we compare the reforms of Christian women to the activities of secular feminists, we can say that Christian women preferred moderate reform to radical revolution. But there were also marked exceptions because membership in women's groups was very fluid; one person could be a member in several groups of different orientations. For example, Hu Binxia, the first Chinese chairperson of the national Y.W.C.A., was a member of the *Gongaihui* (Common love society), a revolutionary organization to subvert the Manchu government. Stirring Chinese women to join the struggle

to build a new China and a new culture, her speeches for the
Gongaihui were just as patriotic as those of anybody else.[144]
During the revolution of 1911, some of the mission school girls, with
deep patriotic passion, enlisted in the Amazon Corps, volunteering
to go as nurses, or to throw bombs, and demonstrating a willingness
to die for their country.[145] After the revolution, when attention was
turned to the women's vote, the Christian schools provided forums
for discussion on women's suffrage. Wang Liming, president of the
W.C.T.U., served also as the chairperson of the Woman's Suffrage
Association at one time.[146] During and after the May Fourth
movement, patriotic students from Ginling College and the Yenching
University Women's College joined other students in demonstrating
against foreign aggression, in spite of the disapproval of their
missionary teachers.[147]

In the 1920's, the leaders of the Chinese Communist Party, which
was founded in 1921, criticized women's rights groups and their
reform activities as "bourgeois" and "reformist," heavily influenced by Western ideology. During the time of anti-Christian movement (1922-1927), students under Marxist influence attacked the
Y.M.C.A. and other Christian organizations as instruments of
imperialists to "poison the spirit and deceive the minds of the Chinese
youth."[148] One of the top party women leaders, Xiang Jingyu,
criticized the bourgeois women's movement for lacking a strong
organization and failing to integrate the poorer women and working
class. She accused the family reforms advocated by middle-class
women as too individualistic, covering up the systemic issues of
poverty and class oppression. Although she affirmed the Y.W.C.A.
as historically important, she charged that it was too tied to the West
and irrelevant for the 1920's. The reformist activities masked basic
class contradictions, Xiang said, by blaming men as the oppressor,
instead of the social structure that caused the oppression of both men
and women.[149]

Scholars who study Chinese women's history from a socialist
perspective tend to concur with Xiang Jingyu when evaluating
women's reformist activities between 1900 and 1920.[150] However,
recent studies on Chinese women have cautioned against a one-
dimensional approach leading to overly simplified generalizations.
For instance, Emily Honig's detailed reconstruction of the lives of
female mill workers in Shanghai has shown that the workers did not
automatically develop a proletariat consciousness nor readily embrace

the socialist cause.[151] Kay Ann Johnson's study of women in relation to the family and the peasant revolution demonstrates that the
Chinese Communist Party had often placed the interests of women
below that of male peasants, who were the backbone of the party.
Johnson suggests further that the early women leaders in the party,
such as Xiang Jingyu and Cai Chang, did not seem to have "any
tactical concern for specific women's issues."[152]

The evidence calls for a more comprehensive and refined analysis
of activities of women's groups in the same historical period. Christian reforms were more concerned with the immediate issues women
faced, such as footbinding, concubinage, women's health, family
reform, and child welfare. They articulated women's aspiration for
a less authoritarian family structure and a married life based on love
and respect. Current feminist theorists have coined the phrase
"relations of reproduction" to analyze the relationship between the
sexes in the domestic setting. They also indicate that Marxist theory
on women's oppression tends to overlook women's subordination at
home, focusing more on their exploitation in the economic realm.[153]
In fact, the two aspects must be taken into consideration together
in order to arrive at a more comprehensive analysis of women's
oppression in any given society. In the Chinese setting, the Marxist
feminists were concerned with women's economic and political
oppression, while the Christian feminists were more preoccupied with
women's domestic oppression. These two emphases were not mutually
exclusive, since women's economic dependence affected their position in the family, and family problems hindered women's participation in both production and revolution struggle.[154]

Moreover, the so-called reformist activities, such as literacy campaigns and leadership training, did contribute to the socialist struggle in unforeseeable ways. A concrete example is the work of the
Y.W.C.A. among cotton-mill workers in Shanghai. As Emily Honig
notes:

> Although the number of women who participated in
> YWCA programs was never more than a fraction of the
> female work force, an overwhelming majority of women
> workers who became active in the labor movement and
> in the CCP [Chinese Communist Party] after 1937
> attribute their initial "political awakening" to the
> night schools run by the YWCA for women workers.[155]

Deng Yuzhi, the industrial secretary of the Y.W.C.A., emerged as an important leader after 1949, and so did Song Qingling, the widow of Sun Yat Sen, Li Dequan, the wife of the "Christian General" Feng Yuxiang, and Wu Yifang, the president of Ginling College; all were related to Christian women's groups.

Finally, it should be stressed that student unrest, the labor movement, and Marxist criticism helped Christian women leaders to see the bourgeois nature of the Christian women's movement and the need to integrate their efforts with those of the poorer and working classes. Wang Liming, for instance, wrote in the 1930's that the work of the W.C.T.U. had been limited largely to urban women, and she urged others to be more concerned with rural women, who suffered most under the multiple oppressions.[156] Ding Shujing, the top Y.W.C.A. leader, also had her political consciousness sharpened during the turbulent years of the 1920's. In 1918, two years after joining the staff of the Beijing Y.W.C.A., she reported that religious activities and Bible studies constituted the major work of the Beijing chapter. In 1928, however, she clearly placed the mission of the Y.W.C.A. in the overall political context of China when addressing the second Y.W.C.A. national convention. Like Wang Liming, she saw the necessity of broadening the women's movement to include the poorer masses, especially rural women. The Y.W.C.A. should actively involve itself in national reconstruction, she said, and not simply do welfare work.[157]

Increased social participation and heightened political awareness provided an exciting context for deeper religious reflection. Indeed, the Christian women leaders, just like other members of the Christian community, were challenged to defend their Christian faith and to reveal its relevance for China. In the next chapter, we shall examine the writings of Christian women in this period to see how patriotism, feminism, and their own religious experiences interplayed in shaping their faith and consciousness.

Notes

1. Carolyn DeSwarte Gifford, "Women in Reform Movements," in *Women and Religion in America*, ed., Rosemary Radford Ruether and Rosemary Skinner Keller, vol. 1, 294-303.

2. Ernest Faber, juan 5 of *Zixi cudong* (From the West to the East), (N.p., 1884), 384-385.

3. See Paul A. Varg, *Missionaries, Chinese and Diplomats: The American Protestant Missionary Movement in China, 1890-1952* (Princeton: Princeton University Press, 1958), 86-104; and William R. Hutchison, *Errand to the World: American Protestant Thought and Foreign Mission* (Chicago: University of Chicago Press, 1987), 91-124.

4. Alison R. Drucker, "The Role of the Y.W.C.A. in the Development of the Chinese Women's Movement, 1890-1927," *Social Service Review* 53 (1979): 425.

5. A. P. Happer, "Woman's Work for Woman," 147.

6. Patricia R. Hill, *The World Their Household: The American Woman's Foreign Mission Movement and Cultural Transformation, 1870-1920* (Ann Arbor: University of Michigan Press, 1985), 5.

7. *Records 1877*, 72.

8. Griffith John, "The Chinese Circular on Mission," 150.

9. *Records 1877*, 171-180, 196-203.

10. Martha F. Crawford, "Woman's Work for Woman," 151-152.

11. Mrs. Foster, "The Nü Hiao King," *Woman's Work in China* 7/1 (November 1883): 69.

12. See for example, R. Nelson, "The Relation of Christianity to Polygamy." *CR* 1 (1869): 169-173; and Samuel Dodd, "The Relation of Christianity to Polygamy," *CR* 2 (1869): 31-35.

13. Jane Hunter used the term feminization to refer to the predominance of women over men in the missionary force; see her *Gospel of Gentility*, Preface xiii.

14. *Records 1890*, 509-513.

15. Patricia R. Hill, *The World Their Household*, 123-160.

16. Hattie Newell Noyes, "Girls' Schools," in *Records 1890*, 218-219.

17. Laura A. Haygood, "Girls' Schools," in *Records 1890*, 229.

18. Young J. Allen, "Xianyu dui xia" (Words of warning), part one, *WGGB* n.s. 8/86 (March 1896): 8-12.

19. Timothy Richard, "Xinü youyi Zhongguo shuo" (Western women are beneficial to China), trans., Cai Erkang, *WGGB* n.s. 8/129 (October 1899): 1-2; and *Jiushi jiaoyi* (Teachings to save the world) (Shanghai: Guangxue hui, 1899), 32.

20. Young J. Allen, *Quandi wu dazhou nüsu tongkao*, Preface.

21. Liang Qichao, "Changshe nü xuetang qi" (On establishing girls' schools) and "Shiban Buchanzu hui jianming zhangcheng" (Concise rules for founding an anti-footbinding society) in *Liang Rengong wenji* (Collected works of Liang Qichao) (Shanghai: Zhonghua shuju, 1936), vol. 2, 19-20, 20-30.

22. Kang Youwei, "Qingchi gesheng gai shuyuan yinci wei xuetang zhe" (Memorial on transforming Chinese academies and temples into modern schools) and "Qingjin funü guozu zhe" (Memorial on forbidding women to bind their feet) in *Wuxu bianfa* (Reform of 1898), ed., Jian Bozan, et al. (Shanghai: Shenzhou guoguang she, 1953), vol. 2, 219-222, 242-244.

23. M. Melvin, "The Curricula of Five Representative Mission Schools for Girls in China," *WWFE* 21/1 (May 1900): 5-16.

24. A. R. M., "Girls' Schools: Use Versus Ornament," *WWFE* 22/1 (May 1901): 21.

25. Mary Porter Gamewell, "The Christian and the Chinese Idea of Woman and How the Former Can Be Propagated in Our Girls Schools," *WWFE* 20/2 (November 1899): 132-133.

26. Mary Martin Richard, "The Christian and the Chinese Idea of Womanhood," 58-62; Mary Porter Gamewell, "The Christian and the Chinese Idea of Woman," 132-138; G. Newton, "What Our Girls' Schools Are Doing for Christian Womanhood?" *WWFE* 20/2 (November 1899): 138-141.

27. For example, Luella Miner, "Jidujiao nüzi jiaoyu" (Christian women's education), *Nianjian* 1 (1914): 80; M. Pearl Boggs, "The Nanking Woman's Christian Temperance Union," *WWFE* 32/2 (June 1911): 82-83; and Miss Liu, "How to Make the Girls Responsible for Social Service?" *WWFE* 38/3 (September 1917): 99.

28. Ethel Klein, *Gender Politics: From Consciousness to Mass Politics* (Cambridge, Mass.: Harvard University Press, 1984), 83.

29. Charlotte L. Beahan, "Feminism and Nationalism in the Chinese Women's Press, 1902-1922," *Modern China* 1 (1975): 380.

30. For a discussion on this topic, see Elisabeth Croll, *Feminism and Socialism in China* (London: Routledge and Kegan Paul, 1978), 64-65.

31. Luella Miner, "Jidujiao nüzi jiaoyu," 79.

32. "The 'Women's Army'—A Sequel," *WWFE* 34/1 (March 1913): 35.

33. Rong Tisheng, "The Women's Movement in China before and after the 1911 Revolution," *Chinese Studies in History* 16/3-4 (Spring-Summer 1983): 191.

34. Virginia Chui-tin Chau, "The Anti-Footbinding Movement in China (1850-1912)," (M.A. Thesis, Columbia University, 1965), 10-11.

35. John Macgowan, *How England Saved China*, 59.

36. J. Dudgeon, "The Small Feet of Chinese Women," *CR* 2 (1869): 93-96, 130-133; and J. G. Kerr, "Small Feet," *CR* 2 (1896): 169-170; 3 (1870): 22-23.

37. *Records 1877*, 138.

38. S. H. Woolston, "Feet Binding," in *Records 1877*, 136.

39. *Records 1877*, 137-138.

40. A. H. Tuttle, *Mary Porter Gamewell*, 62.

41. See Arthur H. Smith, D. Z. Sheffield, and Henry D. Porter, "Report of the Committee on Education, 1877-1878," ABC 16.3.12 (3), no. 107; and Jennie E. Chapin, "Report of Bridgman School, 1878-1879," ABC 16.3.12 (3), no. 117.

42. See Charles Hartwell, *Xiaoxue sizi jing* (Primary four-character classic) (Fuzhou: Meihua shuju, 1874), 9b-10b; and Julia Bonafield, "Some Observations on Foot-Binding," *WWFE* 13/2 (May 1893): 121.

43. Hattie Newell Noyes, *A Light in the Land of Sinim*, 151.

44. See Mary H. Porter, "Report of Bridgman School 1871-1872," ABC 16.3.12 (3), no. 109; Ellsworth C. Carlson, *The Foochow Missionaries*, 86; and D. MacGillivary, "Women's Work," *Year Book* 2 (1911): 433-434.

45. Cao Jingrong (Cao Ziyu) "Chanzu lun," and "Le chengrenmei lun" (The pleasure of helping others attack footbinding), *WGGB* 7 (24 April 1875): 456b-457b; 7 (1 May 1875): 474-474b; 7 (15 May 1875): 500-500b.

46. Bao Guangxi on anti-footbinding in *WWFE* 9/2 (May 1886): 121-124.

47. Mrs. Ding Ai-nyok, "Results of Unbinding My Feet," *WWFE* 17/2 (November 1896): 120-121.

48. Alicia Little, *In The Land of the Blue Gown* (London: T. Fisher Unwin, 1902), 305-370.

49. Ada Haven, Jennie E. Chapin, and Susan F. Hinnan, "Report of the Bridgman School for Year 1896," ABC 16.3.12 (15), no. 39.

50. Julia Bonafield, "Some Observations on Foot-Binding," 121-122.

51. Margaret Burton, *The Education of Women in China*, 121.

52. Pangzhuang Women, 1892-1893, ABC 16.3.12 (14), no. 91.

53. Pangzhuang Women, 1901-1902, ABC 16.3.12 (23), no. 284.

54. E. G. Wycloff, "Reform in Foot Binding," *Life and Light* 34 (1904): 576.

55. Margaret Burton, *Notable Women of China* (New York: Fleming H. Revell Co., 1912), 167.

56. M. Faith Davies, "Anti-Foot-Binding in Foochow City," *WWFE* 27/3 (September 1906): 116-119.

57. Jia Fu, "Chanzu lun' (On footbinding), *WGGB* n.s. 8/1 (August 1896): 4b-5b.

58. Yuan Yuying, "Chanzu lun" (On footbinding), *NDB* 8/11 (February 1920): 21-26.

59. Martha E. Pyle, "The Present Situation of the Anti-Foot-Binding Movement," *Year Book* 12 (1924): 419-421.

60. For example, Alison R. Drucker, "The Influence of Western Women on the Anti-Footbinding Movement, 1840-1911," 179-199; and Wang Ermin, "Jindai Hunan nüquan sichao xianqu" (Pioneers in Hunan feminist thought in the modern period), in *Zhongguo funü shi lunwen ji* (Collected essays on the history of Chinese women), ed., Li Youning

and Zhang Yufa (Taibei: Commercial Press, 1981), 115-128.

61. Emily M. Ahern, "The Power and Pollution of Chinese Women," in *Women in Chinese Society*, ed., Margery Wolf and Roxane Witke (Stanford: Stanford University Press, 1975), 195-196.

62. Gail Hershatter, *The Workers of Tianjin, 1900-1949* (Stanford: Stanford University Press, 1986), 205.

63. Charlotte Furth, "Concepts of Pregnancy, Childbirth, and Infancy in Ch'ing Dynasty China," *Journal of Asian Studies* 46/1 (1987): 15-17.

64. Sara Waitstill Tucker, "The Canton Hospital," 15.

65. Harriet Newell Noyes, *A Light in the Land of Sinim*, 85.

66. Angie M. Myers, "Medical Training in Amoy," *WWFE* 21/2 (November 1900): 152.

67. China Medical Commission of the Rockefeller Foundation, *Medicine in China* (New York: Rockefeller Foundation, 1914), 36-37; see also "Report on Medical Schools in China Connected with Christian Missions," *The China Medical Journal* 36/6 (November 1922): 522-524.

68. For the life of Jin Yunmei (also known as Yamei Kin, Y. May King or King Ya-mei), see Chimin K. Wong and Wu Lien-teh, *History of Chinese Medicine,* 333-334; and "Nü yishi Jin Yunmei jilue" (Biography of the woman doctor Jin Yunmei), in *Jindai Zhongguo nüquan yundong shiliao, 1842-1911* ed., Li Youning and Zhang Yufa, vol. 2, 1386-1388. The life stories of Hu Jinying, Kang Cheng, and Shi Meiyu can be found in Margaret Burton, *Notable Women of China*. For Li Bi Cu, see Margaret Burton, *Comrades in Service* (New York: Board of Foreign Missions of the Presbyterian Church in the U.S.A., 1915), 101-114.

69. Margaret Burton, *Notable Women of China*, 169.

70. Kang Cheng "The Doctor's Opportunity in Visiting Homes," by Ida Kahn, *WWFE* 35/4 (December 1914): 174.

71. H. N. Kinnear's letter of 22 May 1908, ABC 16.3.6 (2).

72. Gertrude Howe, "Danforth Memorial Hospital," *WWFE* 23/2 (June 1902): 59.

73. Mary Fulton, "Letter from Canton," *WWFE* 21/2 (November 1900): 115.

74. M. T. Stauffer, ed., *The Christian Occupation*, 297.

75. Margaret Burton, *Notable Women in China*, 50-51.

76. Shi Meiyu, "What Chinese Women Have Done and Are Doing for China," by Mary Stone, *Year Book* 5 (1914): 243. The Chinese version "Zhongguo xianjin funü jiaoyu shiye zhi jinbu" (The progress of Chinese women's educational enterprise) is found in *Nianjian* 1 (1914): 89-93.

77. "The W.C.T.U. in China," *CR* 55 (1923): 567-568; and *NCC 1922*, 473.

78. Harold Balme, "Medical Missionaries in Conference," *CR* 46 (1915): 184.

79. Ying Mei Chun, "The Place of Woman in Social Service," *Year Book* 5 (1914): 292; and Li Youning and Zhang Yufa eds., *Jindai Zhongguo nüquan yundong shiliao, 1842-1911*, vol. 2, 927-932, 1087-1088, 1290-1291.

80. Harold Balme, *China and Modern Medicine*, 136.

81. Alice Clark, "Training of Men and Women Nurses in China," *Year Book* 7 (1916): 326-327.

82. Cora E. Simpson, "The Training of the Chinese Pupil Nurse," *China Christian Advocate* 2/6 (July 1915): 4-5, 7.

83. Edith J. Howard, "Is China Ready for Women Nurses in Men's Hospital?" *The China Medical Journal* 33/2 (March 1919): 175.

84. "What Ginling Girls Do for Their Community?" *WWFE* 40/3 (September 1919): 95.

85. Luella Miner, "Extracts from the Report of the North China Union Woman's College for the Year July 1, 1915, to June 20, 1916," ABC 16.3.12 (31), no. 137.

86. Hu Binxia, *Zhongguo nü qingnianhui xiaoshi* (A short history of the Chinese Y.W.C.A.) (N.p., 1923), 11.

87. Alison R. Drucker, "The Role of the Y.W.C.A.," 431.

88. Liang Qichao, "Ji Jiangxi Kang nüshi" (On Miss Kang of Jiangxi), in *Liang Rengong wenji*, vol. 2, 119-120.

89. Sara Waitstill Tucker, "The Canton Hospital," 298.

90. Carolyn DeSwarte Gifford, "For God and Home and Native Land," in *Women in New Worlds*, vol. 1, *Historical Perspectives on the Wesleyan Tradition*, ed., Hilah F. Thomas and Rosemary Skinner Keller (Nashville: Abington Press, 1981), 310-311.

91. Susan Dye Lee, "Evangelical Domesticity," in *Women in New Worlds*, ed., Hilah F. Thomas and Rosemary Shinner Keller, vol. 1, 293.

92. Chen Yuling, "Wanguo funü jiezhi hui" (Woman's Christian Temperance Union), *Nianjian* 3 (1916): section wei, 87; and reports in *WWFE* 13/2 (May 1893): 159-160 and 21/1 (May 1900): 74-75.

93. Sara Goodrich, "Woman's Christian Temperance Union," *Year Book* 2 (1911): 452.

94. Sara Goodrich, "Woman's Christian Temperance Union of China," *Year Book* 7 (1916): 489.

95. Gu Ziren, "Yijiuersi nian zhi guoji jinyan huiyi ji woguo zhi judu wenti" (The 1924 international anti-opium conference and problems of opium suppression in China), *Nianjian* 8 (1925): 225; and Jonathan Spence, "Opium Smoking in Ch'ing China," in *Conflict and Control in Late Imperial China*, ed., Frederic Wakeman, Jr., and Carolyn Grant (Berkeley and Los Angeles: University of California Press, 1975), 173.

96. A. C. Safford, "Gleanings," *Woman's Work in China* 4/2 (May 1881): 148.

97. Mrs. W. S. Elliot's report in *WWFE* 33/3 (September 1912): 136-137.

98. Sara Goodrich, "Woman's Christian Temperance Union of China," 492.

99. Ibid., 489-491.

100. Grace Goodrich, "Cigarettes: Study Number One," *WWFE* 34/2 (June 1913): 88-91; and her "Beer: Study Number Three," *WWFE* 35/1 (March 1914): 42-46. See also "Zhiyan zhi mohai" (The harmful effects of cigarettes), *NDB* 4/4 (July 1915): 11-14; and "Pijiu zhi yanjiu" (Study on beer), *NDB* 4/10 (January 1914): 14-17.

101. Sara Goodrich, "Shall We Not Inaugurate a United and Earnest Anti-Cigarette Campaign," *WWFE* 34/1 (March 1913): 39-42; and her "The Anti-Alcohol Campaign," *WWFE* 35/4 (December 1914): 189-194.

102. See the advertisement in *CR* 46 (1915): 782-783.

103. For example, Mary Martin Richard, "Weiladi Falangshi nüshi zhuan" (Biography of Miss Frances Willard), *NDB* 4/5 (August 1915): 45-48; 4/6 (September 1915): 48-51; 4/7 (October 1915): 49-53.

104. Sara Goodrich, "Woman's Christian Temperance Union," 454-455.

105. L. Pearl Boggs's report in *WWFE* 32/3 (September 1911): 134-135.

106. "The W.C.T.U. in China," 567-568.

107. Wang Liming, "Funü jiezhi hui" (Woman's Christian Temperance Union), *Nianjian* 8 (1925): 243.

108. See the short biography of Wang Liming in *Jiezhi yuekan* (Temperance monthly) 5/4 (April 1926), n.p.

109. Wang Liming, "Funü wenti" (Women's problems), *Jiezhi yuekan* 5/10 (December 1926): 1-3.

110. Wang Liming, "Jiating wei shehui fuwu" (The family serving society), *Jiezhi yuekan* 5/3 (March 1926): 1-6.

111. At the Library of the National Committee of Chinese Christian Three-Self Patriotic Movement at Shanghai, only 3/1-4 (1924) and 5/2-10 (1926) were preserved.

112. Wang Liming, "The Woman's Christian Temperance Union," by Mrs. Herman C. E. Liu, *Year Book* 11 (1923): 257-258.

113. Laura M. White, "Temperance Literature," *WWFE* 42/1 (March 1921): 16-17.

114. Wang Liming, "The Woman's Christian Temperance Union," 258.

115. See the report in *Jiezhi jikan* (Temperance quarterly), 3/4 (Winter 1924): 39.

116. Susan Dye Lee, "Evangelical Domesticity," in *Women in New Worlds*, ed., Hilah F. Thomas and Rosemary Skinner Keller, vol. 1, 294.

117. Alison R. Drucker, "The Role of the Y.W.C.A.," 428.

118. Y.W.C.A. of China, *The Widening Circle: The Y.W.C.A. of China, 1919* (Shanghai: National Committee of the Y.W.C.A. of China, 1919), 11.

119. Alison R. Drucker, "The Role of the Y.W.C.A.," 429.

120. Tsai Kuei and Lily K. Haass, "A Study of the Young Women's

Christian Association of China, 1890-1930," *Chinese Studies in History* 10/3 (Spring 1977): 76.

121. Alison R. Drucker, "The Role of the Y.W.C.A.," 429; Tsai Kuei and Lily K. Haass, "A Study of the Young Women's Christian Association," 84.

122. Author's personal interview with Deng Yuzhi in Shanghai, November, 1987.

123. Tsai Kuei and Lily K. Haass, "A Study of the Young Women's Christian Association," 80; Y.W.C.A. of China, *A 1915 Message from the Young Women's Christian Associations of China* (Shanghai: Presbyterian Mission Press, 1916), 14; and Y.W.C.A. of China ed., *Chinese Triangles* (Shanghai: National Committee of the Y.W.C.A. of China, 1924), 3.

124. Liang Fen-siu, "The Y.W.C.A in Ginling College," *Ginling College Magazine* 1/1 (June 1924): 27-28; Xie Wanying, "Yanjing daxue" (Yenching University), *Shengming* 2/2 (September 1921): 3.

125. M. T. Stauffer, ed., *The Christian Occupation*, 375; and Y.W.C.A of China ed., *Chinese Triangles*, 3.

126. Y.W.C.A. of China, *Y.W.C.A.—China, 1917* (N.p., n.d.), 8.

127. Tsai Kuei and Lily K. Haass, "A Study of the Young Women's Christian Association," *Chinese Studies in History* 11/1 (Fall 1977): 30-31.

128. Emily Honig, *Sisters and Strangers: Women in the Shanghai Cotton Mills, 1919-1949* (Stanford: Stanford University Press, 1986), 132-165.

129. Elizabeth K. Morrison, "Women and Factories," in *Chinese Triangles*, 62.

130. Florence Sutton, "A History of Industrial Work in China to 1924," in *Chinese Triangles*, 56-57.

131. Tsai Kuei and Lily K. Haass, "A Study of the Young Women's Christian Association," *Chinese Studies in History* 11/1 (Fall 1977): 57.

132. Ibid., 37-38.

133. Ibid., 43-50.

134. National Committee of the Y.W.C.A. of China, *Diyici quanguo dahui jilu* (Report of the first national convention) (Shanghai: National Committee of the Y.W.C.A. in China, 1924).

135. Tsai Kuei and Lily K. Haass, "A Study of the Young Women's Christian Association," *Chinese Studies in History* 11/1 (Fall 1977): 21-22.

136. Shirley S. Garrett, *Social Reformers in Urban China: The Chinese Y.M.C.A., 1895-1926* (Cambridge, Mass.: Harvard University Press, 1970), 180.

137. Eleanor MacNeil, "Women Students in 1926, As Seen by a Y.W.C.A. Secretary," *CR* 57 (1926): 876-877.

138. M. T. Stauffer, ed., *Christian Occupation*, 376; Y.W.C.A. of China, *Chinese Triangles*, 3.

139. Eleanor MacNeil, "Women Students in 1926," 880.

140. *Shengming* 5/9 (1925): 44.

141. Y.W.C.A. of China, *Introduction to the Young Women's Christian Association of China, 1933-1947* (Shanghai: The National Committee of the Y.W.C.A. of China, n.d.), 1.

142. Shi Meiyu, "What Chinese Women Have Done," 240.

143. Frank Rawlinson, "Christian Co-operation for a National-Wide Task," *CR* 51 (1920): 424.

144. Hu Bingxia, "Zhu Gongaihui zhi qiantu" (Celebrating the future of the Common love society) in *Jiandai Zhongguo nüquan yundong shiliao, 1842-1911,* ed., Li Youning and Zhang Yufa, vol. 2, 916-917.

145. Elsie M. Garretson and Irene L. Dorublaser, "Foochow Girls College: Report for 1911," ABC 16.3.6 (3).

146. "Nüzi canzheng hui de zhiyuan hui" (Committee of the Woman's Suffrage Association), *NDB* 11/10 (January 1923): 57; and Helen F. Snow, *Women in Modern China* (The Hague: Mouton and Co., 1967), 79.

147. Yunying, "Guomin geming sheng zhong zhi Jin nüda" (Ginling College in the midst of national revolution), *Ginling College Magazine* 4/1 (December 1927): 39; Matilda C. Thurston (Mrs. Lawrence Thurston) and Ruth M. Chester, *Ginling College* (New York: United Board for Christian Colleges in China, 1955), 30, 49-52; and Luella Miner, "Peking University College of Arts and Sciences for Women, Peking, China: First Annual Report to the Board of Managers," ABC 16.3.12 (38), no. 42.

148. Shirley S. Garrett, *Social Reformers in Urban China*, 179.

149. Suzette Leith, "Chinese Women in the Early Communist Movement," in *Women in China: Studies in Social Change and Feminism*, ed., Marilyn Young (Ann Arbor: Center for Chinese Studies, University of Michigan, 1973), 50-51.

150. For example, Elisabeth Croll, *Feminism and Socialism in China*, 111-116.

151. Emily Honig, *Sisters and Strangers*, 202-243.

152. Kay Ann Johnson, *Women, the Family and Peasant Revolution in China* (Chicago: University of Chicago Press, 1983), 43.

153. See, for example, Alison M. Jaggar, *Feminist Politics and Human Nature* (Totowa, N. J.: Rowman and Allanheld, 1983); and Michèle Barrett, *Women's Oppression Today: Problems in Marxist Feminist Analysis* (London: NLB, 1980?).

154. Kay Ann Johnson, *Women, the Family and Peasant Revolution in China*; Judith Stacey, *Patriarchy and Social Revolution in China* (Berkeley and Los Angeles: University of California Press, 1983).

155. Emily Honig, *Sisters and Strangers*, 217.

156. Wang Liming, "Zhonghua funü jiezhi xiehui" (The Chinese Woman's Christian Temperance Union), *Nianjian* 12 (1933): 173. See also her

Zhongguo funü yundong (Chinese women's movement) (Shanghai: Commercial Press, 1934).

157. Ding Shujing, "Beijing Jidujiao nü qingnianhui" (Beijing Y.W.C.A.), *Nianjian* 5 (1918): 201-204; and her "Jinri Zhongguo Jidujiao nü qingnianhui de shiming" (Mission of the Chinese Y.W.C.A. today) *Nüqingnian* 7/7 (November 1928): 3-10.

CHAPTER V

Women's Consciousness and Faith

The previous chapters have outlined women as listeners to the Christian Gospel, integral partners in the Christian community, and historical participants of social reform. In this chapter, we will try to listen to the voices of Chinese women through their own writings. Treating women as historical subjects, scholars who are interested in women's consciousness and experiences pay special attention to women's own descriptions of their lives and the society of which they are a part, instead of just what others have written about them. Regarding the period under study, we can readily find numerous accounts of Chinese women given by missionaries, yet there has been no attempt, in Chinese or in Western languages, to gather together and document the writings of Chinese Christian women themselves.

The early twentieth century is marked by the emergence of a "discourse on women" by Chinese women. Although during the nineteenth century enlightened men such as Wang Tao, Zheng Guanying, Kang Youwei, and Liang Qichao had drawn public attention to women's issues, women as a group did not speak out on their own predicament. As we mentioned in chapter four, Chinese women published their journals at the turn of the century, articulating their views on a wide range of issues such as sex discrimination, female education, and patriotism. In Christian circles, most of the female converts in the nineteenth-century were either illiterate or received little education. Chinese Christian women only began to publish their writings in the early twentieth century as they recognized that women's journals and newspapers were influential instruments to spread new ideas and to provide informal education for women not attending schools.[1]

The women's writings I have located appear in many journals, such as *Nüduobao, Nüqingnian, Zhonghua Jidu jiaohui nianjian, Ginling College Magazine, The Chinese Recorder*, and others. Two Christian women's journals are worth special recognition. *Nüduobao* was first published in April, 1912, by Laura M. White.[2] The opening remarks in the first issue say, the newspaper wishes "to be the wooden *duo* ["bell"] for women, so that Chinese women, whether at home or in schools, whether they can read or they are illiterate, can hear the warning sound of the *duo* and be encouraged to follow good words and deeds."[3] As a monthly, *Nüduobao*, which continued to be published into the 1940's, is the most important resource of Chinese Christian women's earlier writings. Yuan Yuying helped in translating articles, and later, Li Guanfang served as the editor-in-chief. In 1918, it had a circulation of several thousand.[4] Further, the Y.W.C.A. began to publish its official organ in 1916, first as a quarterly entitled *Qingnian nübao* (The young women's quarterly). In 1922, its name was changed to *Nüqingnian bao* (The Y.W.C.A. Magazine). The title was subsequently shortened to *Nüqingnian*. The journal eventually became a monthly.[5] Qiu Liying, Fan Yurong, and Cheng Wanzhen were associated with the magazine in different stages.

The *Nüduobao* contains articles on women's issues, and short sections on education, domestic science, religion, students' essays, and poetry. The early Chinese contributors of *Nüduobao* were women affiliated with the mission schools. Their short articles addressed more immediate issues such as the importance of female education and women's role in the family. The *Nüqingnian*, however, encompasses a wider social perspective, probably due to the Y.W.C.A.'s involvement in social service and education for women factory workers. Leaders of the Y.W.C.A., such as Ding Shujing, Jiang Hezhen, and Cheng Wanzhen, demonstrated both a feminist consciousness and a Christian identity in their writings. Although these Christian women addressed the same problems that confronted their contemporaries in the May Fourth period, they also tried to look at these issues from a Christian perspective. During a period of anti-Christian sentiment they, like their male counterparts, had to defend their faith in addition to discussing the role of women in the church.

The purpose of this chapter is to reconstruct what Christian women said about women's identity, issues concerning women in the 1920's, women and social change, and women's relation to religious faith and the church.

Chinese Christian women wrote several autobiographies, but their letters, diaries, private papers, and other unpublished works, the study of which has become increasingly valued in the writing of women's history are scarce. The majority of the authors are students or graduates of mission schools, while a few have studied abroad. Their voices may not represent the vast majority of Chinese Christian women who have received far less education; nevertheless, they are significant in the reconstruction of women's self-awareness and religious faith. Although scholars in women's history are paying more attention to the lives of ordinary women, historian Hilda L. Smith has argued that we should not overlook the leaders. She said: "It is important to understand and appreciate the ideas and accomplishments of women leaders and to integrate them into our historical memories."[6]

Women's Identity and Consciousness

Ethel Klein, in her study of American gender politics, points out that feminist consciousness needs to be learned: "Women had to learn to reject traditional group definitions based on biological explanations and to accept new images of womanhood based on sex equality."[7] Traditionally, women's roles have centered around the family and the creation of a home, but at a different stage, women begin to challenge previous conceptions as new options and possibilities become available to them. Klein states that women's consciousness is not just a by-product of social and economic change, but periods of rapid change also facilitate the emergence of a new group definition and consciousness when altered social circumstances call for the adaptation of new behavior.[8] Klein's insight is helpful in the analysis of the development of women's consciousness in the midst of rapid social transformation in twentieth-century China.

The development of a feminist consciousness in China cannot be attributed, however, to any single cause, since many social and political factors contribute to it. Charlotte L. Beahan has documented that during the late Qing period nationalism was the most important driving force of the women's movement.[9] In addition, women were offered higher education first at the Christian women's colleges—North China Union College for Women, Ginling College, and Hwa Nan College—and subsequently at the Christian and national universities when coeducation became acceptable in the

1920's.[10] When the new Chinese republic founded in 1911 refused women the right to vote, the Woman's Suffrage Association and the Woman's Rights League were organized, with branches spreading throughout major cities, pushing for women's political rights. Industrialization drew rural women into the big cities, looking for jobs that did not exist in their mothers' generation. Margaret Sanger, an American pioneer of birth control, visited China to preach about family planning and new concepts of motherhood in the early 1920's. Roxane Heater Witke has shown that the May Fourth period was marked by the transformation of attitudes towards women.[11]

These rapid social changes caused social dislocation and loss of self-identity. Women found that the old conception of womanhood failed to help them cope with the new situation, so that it was necessary to "learn" to redefine what it means to be female. Many Christian women harshly evaluated the social system and cultural tradition that accorded women inferior status in the long Chinese history. They condemned the "three obediences" that a woman was supposed to follow, that is, to obey the father before marriage, to obey the husband after marriage, and to obey the son at the death of the husband. Hu Binxia emphatically stated, "This is the well-known doctrine of three-fold subordination, against which no woman in the past dared rebel, and with which she secured the necessary subsistence."[12] Cheng Wanzhen, the industrial secretary of the Y.W.C.A., noted that Chinese society set stringent limitations for women in addition to their status as dependents: "For centuries Chinese women were considered inferior to men. They were not given any opportunity for self-expression and self-development."[13]

Criticizing the past, Chinese Christian women found that it was necessary to search for new identity as modern Chinese women. They discussed women's appearance, such as hairstyle and fashion, women's role in the family, and the cultural construction of gender. Christian women, depending on their age and background, had different views on these subjects. These differences reflected both their divergent understanding of gender roles and their variant responses to the social changes occurring at the time.

With the founding of the Chinese republic and the beginning of a new era, modern Chinese women needed to create a new public image. Women in the Qing dynasty put on silk jackets and long gowns during formal gatherings, and they laboriously coiled and pinned their hair on their heads. At the other extreme, during the revolution

Qiu Jin and other radical women cut their hair, dressing like men when they pledged to join the Dare-to-Die Corps. Short hair thus replaced natural feet as an avant-garde symbol signifying nonconformity for women. Christian women had different opinions of short hair. Yuan Yuying of the W.C.T.U. was skeptical of those revolutionary women who cut their hair short, and she accused them of behaving like the Greek Amazons or the French Joan of Arc.[14] On the other hand, Cao Fangyun of the Y.W.C.A. wrote in favor of the new hairstyle, praising it for the fact that "it both saved time and made women look cleaner."[15] Among eminent Christian women, Shi Meiyu and Kang Cheng preferred to pin up their hair and dress in long gowns for formal meetings, whereas leaders of the younger generation, such as Ding Shujing and other Y.W.C.A. staff, generally wore short hair.

In the big coastal cities, fashionable women lost no time trying on lavish Western dresses and accessories as the out-dated Manchu gown lost its appeal. Christian women criticized women in the past for spending too much time and money on their clothing, cosmetics, and beauty needs.[16] However, they did not unconditionally advocate Western fashion. Cao Fangyun, for example, pointed out that Western gowns easily spread dirt on the ground, women's corsets were detrimental to health, and high-heeled shoes made walking difficult. She was especially scornful of those women who put on men's caps and clothing, saying that they looked "neither Chinese nor Western, male nor female." Other writers also cautioned that Chinese women should not imitate Western women, especially their low cut and sensuous dresses.[17] In general, these Christian writers felt that it was important to keep their Chinese identity while adopting new things from the West. To them, women should dress like women because the equality of the sexes did not mean the abolition of gender differences. Their evangelical upbringing also conditioned women to be modest and restrained in their demeanor, and not to show signs of sexual appeal.

Besides women's outward appearance, many Christian women discussed the most intimate and immediate subject that concerns women, that is, women's role in the family. The various points of view on this subject best exemplify the development of women's consciousness. From 1912 to 1913, several articles appearing in *Nüduobao* emphasized that a woman's chief responsibility was in the home, although she had other obligations toward society. Qiu Yinlan, for example, wrote, "Men work outside the home, and women are in charge of family, This is an unchanging principle from the past to the present. . . . to educate the young is the responsibility of women."[18] Xu Guifen, in her essay on women's patriotism, wrote: "The foundation of the country is the family, therefore, to govern the home is more important than to govern the country. Women are naturally ordained to be in charge of the family."[19] During this period, many writers still subscribed to the view that women's roles are biologically determined, that nurturing the young is their principal responsibility. Trying to adapt the traditional conception of motherhood to a new context, they insisted that good mothering is the foundation of a strong nation. In the previous chapter, we have shown how this expanded view of mothering and "social housekeeping" enabled some women to move from their domestic spheres into the social arena.

The May Fourth movement served as a springboard for women to challenge traditional images of women and to explore the possibility of transforming women's roles. In her article on "The Emancipation of Chinese Women," which appeared in the October issue of the *Chinese Recorder* in 1919, Hu Binxia maintained that married women should work outside the home: "Marriage is, of course, the career for most girls, but it is a sacred duty, not a means of winning men's favour, but an opportunity to live in a larger way. They must also be taught that to earn an honest living is much more honorable than to rely upon others; to work for dollars and pennies is better than to ask for help."[20] The increasing number of women entering the labor force raised questions about the old conception that a woman's career is confined to the home, as Jiang Hezhen noted:

> Other indications are not lacking that our modern women are resenting the old role of contented idleness or that of only rearing babies and mending socks. Women and girls in the cities are now filling business offices as bookkeepers, shop assistants, saleswomen, stenographers and even commission agents, while hundreds have become telephone operators and bank clerks.[21]

In 1923, *Nüqingnian* held an essay competition on "Women Leaders Who Transform Society." The tone of the essays was much more uncompromising, as the winners unreservedly denounced the feminine ideal of "good wife and virtuous mother." Guo Fangyun, comparing women to slaves who depend on others for their living, cried: "Our Chinese society is an abnormal society, for it is an androcentric, male dominated, and patriarchal society. The only natural role for women is to be a good wife and a virtuous mother. Women are dependent on men, relying on men's support for their living. Therefore, they cannot receive the same education as men, nor lead an independent life and enjoy the same privileges as men."[22] Another winner, Shen Caizhen, charged that a woman's sphere was limited to the home and that she had no share or influence in the social arena. Since her husband was the highest authority at home, a woman had no choice but to obey and depend on men.[23] Both writers espoused the idea that women should lead an independent life, struggle to be complete human beings, and not be satisfied with simply being "a good wife and a virtuous mother."

Recognizing that women are separate individuals independent of men, Christian women grounded their struggle for liberation on the belief in the equality of the sexes. In the 1920's, Wang Huiwu advocated that the basic principle of the feminist movement was to enable women to have the same social status as that of men, including educational opportunity, political rights, equal pay for equal work, and the right to inheritance.[24] Wang's view was echoed by a number of writers, who spelled out clearly that the real emancipation of women includes a constitutional guarantee of women's rights, the economic independence of women, equal opportunity in education, marriage laws based on the equality of the sexes, and the prohibition of licensed prostitution, slave trade, and foot-binding.[25]

Women's heightened consciousness led them to see that women are not biologically ordained to be inferior to men and that women's subordination is a "cultural construction." Zeng Baosun's article "The Chinese Woman Past and Present" published in 1931, can be seen as a good summary for women's quest for a positive identity and their liberation from social conditioning during this period.[26] As the great-granddaughter of Zeng Guofan, she came from a very prominent family in Hunan. In this article, Zeng tried to reclaim the past heritage of women and to suggest an explanation for the inferior status of women in the Chinese society.

Women were not always inferior, Zeng forcefully argued, for they occupied an important place in early Chinese history. Referring to Chinese classical texts, she pointed out that women in ancient China were founders of the family and inventors of many household things. For example, the queen of Huangdi reportedly discovered silk weaving, and women mentioned in the *Book of Odes* made garments, shoes, and practised the dyeing of colors. In the Spring and Autumn Period (722-481 B.C.) and during the Warring States (403-221 B.C.), women were not entirely barred from political activities, and in the Han Dynasty (206 B.C.-220 A.D.), there were eminent women scholars and literary figures such Ti Ying and Ban Zhao. But it was also in the Han Dynasty, when the state became more stable, that men's predominance over women began to be established. "It seems to be a universal rule that when men have established themselves as rulers, they proceed at once to make laws and evolve doctrines to limit the freedom and power of women," Zeng observed.[27]

Having rejected the assumption that women were subordinate to men throughout history, Zeng went on to explain why men devised plans to keep women in an inferior status. During the Tang Dynasty (618-907 A.D.), she pointed out, powerful empresses and consorts, such as the Empress Wei and Yang Guifei, caused great trouble to the country; Empress Wei even succeeded in usurping the throne. "The fear of women thirsting for power called forth men's theories which further restricted what was meant by maternal duty and feminine virtue."[28] For Zeng, the so-called women's virtues, such as absolute obedience to the husband, self-abandonment for sake of the family, and living an ignorant and limited life, were not rooted in women's natural endowment but were culturally constructed by men to reinforce and rationalize their superiority.

Zeng and other female writers blamed the introduction of Indian religion and civilization for its detrimental influence on women's development in China.[29] Zeng lamented that the cultural scaffolding circumscribing women's power became tightest during the Song Dynasty (960-1279 A.D.), that is, after Buddhism had been incorporated into Chinese culture. During this period, the Neo-Confucian masters singled out chastity and loyalty to one man as women's cardinal virtue, for "it is a small matter to die of starvation but a serious matter to lose her virtue."[30] Zeng warned that these cultural prescriptions for women were dangerous, because women have been socialized to a self-censorship that imprisons them in these social confines. "A woman under such hypnotic suggestion really does feel that only by striving after such an ideal can she find her true self."[31] Delighted by the tremendous change in social status of women in the modern period, Zeng envisioned a modern Chinese woman to be "free in mind and behaviour, eager to learn and to serve, seeking to work out the destiny of her people, and striving to set right the social and economic wrongs of her nation."[32]

During the first three decades of the twentieth century, the women's movement passed through several stages; first as a patriotic movement fighting the Manchus, then briefly as a suffragist movement when the Chinese republic was founded, and finally as a mass movement demanding an overall transformation of the family and society. The metamorphosis of the women's movement was integrally related to the process of women learning to reject old roles and to internalize new forms of self-identity. We have seen how some of the Christian women first adapted old conceptions of womanhood to changing circumstances. Later, they found the traditional image of womanhood no longer plausible and started to realize a transformation of sexual roles. They had finally come to the awareness that women's subordination was a cultural construction and not naturally ordained and that a belief in sexual equality was the basis for a women's movement.

Women's Issues and Problems

The development of a feminist consciousness enables Christian women to look at women's issues and problems from a new perspective. Some of the most urgent issues facing women at that time were problems surrounding love, marriage, and family life. Traditional Chinese marriage was arranged by parents through go-betweens. Sometimes, the young couple might not have seen each other before the marriage ceremony. Missionaries in the nineteenth century demanded that parents give up the right to arrange marriages for schoolgirls, hoping that they would not be married into non-Christian families after studying for a number of years. In the twentieth century, when Western marriage customs were introduced into China, progressive young intellectuals advocated that marriage should be based on love. As with all social changes, fundamental transformation in the marriage institution created new possibilities as well as chaos and confusion, especially when young people abused their freedom.

Christian women concurred that marriage should be decided by the induviduals concerned, because arranged marriages sometimes led to prolonged suffering and even women's suicide in extreme cases. Marriage should be based on love, and a woman should have the right to choose her future husband.[33] Some of the more liberal Christian men expressed sympathy for women in their plight, saying that traditional marriage customs treated women unfairly.[34] A group of Ginling college girls wrote in support of freer interaction between the sexes, for example, coeducation and social activities in both church and school that create opportunities for young people to become acquainted with each other before making further commitments.[35]

However, Christian women were also cautious of the risk that men could use "free love" as a facade for acts of seduction. They warned young women to be careful when selecting boy friends, lest they fall into a relationship that would ruin their lives.[36] In general, Christian women held more conservative attitudes towards romantic love and sexuality than the secular feminists because of the puritan teachings of many evangelical churches. Female sexual desire and needs were not subjects that could be publicly addressed and dealt with.

One unique problem facing Christian women during marriage was whether to adopt Christian or Chinese marriage rituals. Even in the nineteenth-century, missionary journals reported many incidents of Chinese Christian women refusing to follow traditional marriage rites.[37] The worship of heaven and earth, as well as the ritual *koutou* before the ancestors during the marriage ceremony, were condemned as idolatrous by missionaries in the missionary conference of 1877.[38] Since the wedding ceremony was a big social gathering joining two families and a festive event in the villages, women had to summon extreme courage to stand up against tradition. Deng Yuzhi, a Y.W.C.A. worker, said she consented to marry the man to whom she was betrothed since childhood, but she refused to *koutou* before the idols during marriage. Although her family agreed to her demands, she was forced to undergo the traditional ceremony as soon as she was brought into the groom's house.[39] In spite of great obstacles, Christian women's resistance to traditional wedding rituals demonstrated an awareness of their Christian identity and their attempt to gain some control over a marriage not of their choosing. In the twentieth century, Christian women's writings expressed the desire for a new marriage ritual, one that symbolizes the ideals of equality and mutuality in the marriage relationship. Incidents of *wenming jiehun* (civilized marriage) were reported in women's journals as encouragements for others to follow.[40]

In addition to love and marriage, Christian women voiced their opinions on concubinage and the keeping of domestic maids. After listing many reasons why she was against keeping concubines, one Christian woman also pointed out the social factors—such as poverty, the illiteracy of women, and young girls wishing to marry into rich families—that caused women to become concubines.[41] Ginling college students were also against polygamy, since it is based on a double moral standard treating women unfavorably.[42] Many representatives of the National Conference of the Y.W.C.A in 1923 proposed a rule forbidding concubines to join the Y.W.C.A in order to make a public statement against concubinage.[43] Y.W.C.A. leaders, including Jiang Hezhen, Ding Shujing, and others, expressed concern over the plight of domestic maids. Comparing the situation of domestics to that of slaves, Jiang Hezhen leveled her criticism specifically against those Christian owners whom she thought should be the first to denounce slavery as inhumane.[44] The Y.W.C.A. in South China organized a movement against keeping domestic maids, requesting the provincial government to outlaw the practice. Ding Shujing wrote that the institution of keeping domestic maids is inhumane because it degrades women and adversely affects the image of the nation and the spirit of the Chinese people.[45]

The authors of articles in women's journals also began to question the legitimacy of the extended family, since many generations living together creates unavoidable tension and conflict and encourages younger generation to depend on their parents.[46] Christian women envisaged a more egalitarian relationship between husband and wife, one that supports reciprocity and mutual respect in the nuclear family. According to one graduate of a mission school in Shandong, a modern Chinese family should also include shared recreation and the abolition of superstition, such as fortune-telling and going to temples.[47]

As a tiny minority living in Chinese society, Christian women saw the Christian family as a "light unto the nation." In her speech entitled "Making the Home Christian" before the National Christian Conference of 1922, Jiang Hezhen enumerated three characteristics of a Christian family. First, all family relationships—between in-laws, husband and wife, parents and children, and employers and servants—should be based on love and sympathy. Second, a Christian home should be a training school for Christian virtues, practising the Chrsitain customs of keeping the Sabbath, Bible reading, habitual prayer, moral education for children, and saying grace before meals. Third, a Christian home should avoid social vices such as gambling, ostentation, drinking, and gossip, devoting their time and energy instead to social service.[48]

Marrige between Christians and non-Christians became a more pressing issue once young people had more chances of making acquaintances with the opposite sex. A Christian man observed that church leaders taught that Christian women should not marry non-Christian men, but that Christian men could marry non-Christian women and bring them to church. He said this double standard limits the choices of marriage for Christian women, some of whom had to remain single.[49] The question of marrying non-Christians also puzzled female college students. They, too, advised Christian women not to marry non-Christians, because it was more difficult for wives to influence their husbands than vice versa.[50]

Besides the issues of love and marriage, Christian women were also concerned about the opportunities for women to receive education. Although female education had become more popular, Christian women demonstrated that the number of women in schools still lagged far behind, as sex discrimination continued to affect women's educational opportunities. Fang Suxin lamented that many parents sent their daughters only to primary school, for they expected girls to be able to "write and read letters, and know a few characters," never dreaming that their daughters would go to secondary school or find a job after graduation.[51] Christian women encouraged parents to send their daughters to secondary school or college so that they could find better jobs and develop themselves as leaders of society. Cheng Guanyi, one of the few women working in university, affirmed that higher education for women can "transform women's lives and elevate the status of women, so that women can receive the same education as men, enjoy the same happiness and shoulder the same responsibilities."[52]

A few writers criticized the liberal curriculum in girls' schools, which did not prepare students for the professions. A student from a mission school in Fuzhou said many girls' schools offered only painting, embroidery, and singing, without training the girls in some practical knowledge. She suggested the addition of practical courses, such as courses in the sciences, law, mathematics, electricity, biology, and zoology, to the curriculum.[53] Another author went even further to say that it was no use educating women in literature, foreign languages, or art because these subjects did not equip them for suitable jobs. Instead, she suggested the training of women in economics, mining, telecommunications, and education, so that they could put what they have learned into practice.[54]

Christian women recognized the significance of women's economic independence, attributing the low position of women to the fact that in the past they had to depend on men for their existence.[55] In 1918, Hu Shi published an article on "American Women," in which he wrote that a woman has to be first a human being before she can be a woman, urging women to go beyond "virtuous wife and good mother" to seek independence.[56] His idea was quoted by some Christian women who reiterated that only when a woman gets a job, can she exert her freedom and independence.[57] In this period when only a tiny proportion of women were employed in the professions, Christian writers did not talk about jobs as a means to develop a career or the full potential of women.

In the nineteenth century, when women first began to work as teachers and nurses, they frequently left their jobs once they got married. But in the 1920's, Christian writers encouraged women to continue working even after marriage. In a prize-winning essay, Li Zhezhen said educated women should not stop earning their living after marriage, because the presence of so many non-productive people leads to the poverty of the nation. She tried to persuade educated women to work outside the home in addition to taking care of the family, thus setting an example for less educated women to follow.[58] However, it was quite demanding for women to fulfil their dual roles; some of the major women leaders such as Ding Shujing, Zeng Baosun, and Fan Yurong opted to remain single.[59] Although Hu Binxia was married, she was most outspoken and declared that like men, single women could contribute to society, because they did not have the burden of caring for the family.[60]

Concerning women and work, some Christian women were aware of the segregation of sexes in the labor force. Shen Caizhen noted that the majority of working women worked in factories, some worked in schools and hospitals, but none occupied leadership positions in industry, commerce, news, or politics.[61] Hu Binxia was particularly enlightening in her observation that the Chinese have traditionally over-exalted mental work and despised manual labor; for example, the social status of scholars was much higher than that of farmers, workers, or businessmen. People's attitudes had changed in the twentieth century, such that businessmen and owners of big industries were respected, but the kinds of work open to women, such as shopkeeping, working in a mill, or cottage craft, were belittled by society. This cultural constraint restricted the job market for women:

> They are certainly not yet ready to be commercial and industrial leaders, having neither the education, ability, nor experience necessary. Yet to be stenographers in offices, clerks in stores, seamstresses, milliners, or the like is considered to be below the dignity of girls of well-to-do families. One who is skillful in teaching or writing may become a tutor or an author and one of very poor origin may work in a mill or factory. But for a girl of moderate means with average ability, there seems to be no suitable occupation; she dislikes to be ranked as a wage-earner and is afraid to let it be known that her family circumstances force her to do work.[62]

As we have already mentioned, the growing number of women working in the mill factories created new social problems. Some Christian women read the socialist writings of Ellen Key and learned that the Russian Revolution of 1917 had liberated women and the proletariat.[63] However, most writers did not seem to be interested in economic and political analyses but were more concerned with the improvement of inhumane working conditions. Cheng Wanzhen urged the Chinese church to stand up for working standards set by the International Labor Conference of the League of Nations, which included an eight-hour workday, one day's rest per week, no night work, a minimum working age of fourteen, maternity benefits, insurance against sickness and injury, and provision for unemployment. Although Cheng did not use Marxist rhetoric, she criticized the new industrial system that treated human lives as "of less value than soulless machinery." She was outspoken also against those foreign employers who came to China only to reap profits, disregarding the welfare of the workers. With a theological awareness ahead of her time, she wrote:

> If we wish to see the establishment of the Kingdom of God on earth, China included, we cannot allow the continuance of the miserable state of labor. It is true that the Church is ever ready to do any kind of charitable work

but the cry of these exploited poor is, "We want no charity—we want justice. . . . Will the Chinese Church again lay the foundation stone of standing for social justice and humanity as she did nobly for other causes in her earlier days?[64]

Traditionally denied political rights, women in the 1920's demanded more participation in decision making on both national and provincial levels. After the Chinese republic was founded in 1911, a small group of women had petitioned for woman's suffrage, and several women were elected representatives in the Provisional Legislature of Guangdong Province, although their term was cut short because of political changes. In 1922, women in Beijing formed a Woman's Suffrage Association and a Woman's Rights League; branches of these associations were formed in ten different provinces within one year.[65] Although most of the women in the church did not participate in any of these political activities, some women in Christian circles were awakened to the fact that women's issues must be addressed in a more systemic and political way. Wang Liming of the W.C.T.U., who also served as the chairperson of the Shanghai Woman's Suffrage Association, said in retrospect:

Although both the Y.W.C.A. and the W.C.T.U. were at work for the general welfare of women, children and the home, before the founding of the Republic, they did not touch upon current political and economic questions. It was not until the Woman's Suffrage Association and the Woman's Rights' League were organized that such problems as political equality, an equal chance to receive education and marriage based on love, and love only, received attention.[66]

Progressive leaders of the Y.W.C.A., such as Cheng Wanzhen, also wrote in support of the secular women's struggle for political rights, praising them for working for "the real emancipation of Chinese women."[67]

Female students who participated in the May Fourth student demonstrations learned the wisdom that political struggle requires collective power. A contributor to the *Ginling College Magazine* wrote that women needed both talented leaders and conscientious followers in order to fight for women's political rights. She saw the weakness of women coming together for just one particular issue, handing out propaganda and sending out a few telegrams. She urged women to form instead their own efficient and dynamic organizations, strengthen their networks, and educate female students in women's rights.[68]

As we have seen, Christian women's social and political awareness deepened as they were more socially involved. Their writings addressed a wide range of women's issues and problems, demonstrating that they fully participated in the discourse of the May Fourth period. They had come to appreciate that women's oppression could not be alleviated without changing basic social institutions such as the family, education, work, and politics. The liberation of women, for them, contributes directly to national survival and the building of a stronger nation. Christian women did not regard the women's movement as women fighting solely for their rights. They related their struggle to the liberation of the Chinese people. Their voices were heard and supported by open-minded Christian men, who saw women's liberation as integrally related to their liberation, especially on issues such as love and marriage. Realizing that women were faced with an enormous burden and limitations, Christian women discussed their role in the overall social transformation of China.

Women and Social Change

Women leaders in the Christian community affirmed the contribution of Christian women to social change in China. Shi Meiyu contributed an article "What Chinese Women Have Done and Are Doing for China" to the 1914 *China Missioin Year Book*, in which she listed different areas in which Christian women had acted as leaven for social change. The first was social service and free education provided by students in the mission schools; for example, Saint Mary's School founded a day school for the children of a village, and McTyeire School opened a Sunday school for street children. The second was women's contribution in their professions, especially medicine and nursing, teaching, and workers in church agencies and in the Y.W.C.A. The third included community services, such as philanthropy, famine relief, and orphanages, as well as social reforms, such as temperance and the abolition of footbinding.[69]

Kang Cheng, Shi's friend and colleague, shared her positive evaluation of Chinese Christian women: "Chinese Christian womanhood will be the most potent factor in the regeneration of China, for it will attain the strongest place in the fabric of Chinese society, and its function will be to lead other women in the march of progress."[70] Acknowledging women's influences in their homes, Kang said they help to nurture a Christ-like character in the children who will become pillars of the nation. She also affirmed the role of Bible women and day school teachers in enlightening their students and neighbors, reaching out to the less educated. Kang was optimistic that Christian women's influence would continue to grow: "Already many of the recent reforms such as anti-footbinding and anti-opium smoking have been largely brought about by the Christian women of China, and their influence will become more patent as their circle enlarges."[71]

Many Christian women believed Christianity to be a motivating force for opposing the oppression of the female sex as well as other forms of social injustice, since Christians believe that human beings are all equal before God. Cheng Guanyi, for instance, stated that Christians believe in love and equality, trying to spread the Gospel to everyone. In the Kingdom of God, which they earnestly pray may be realized on earth, there are no distinctions between classes or sexes.[72] The principle of equality was underscored by Li Guanfang, who grounded it in terms of the relationship between human beings and their God. "All human beings, no matter whether they are wise or foolish, rich or poor, can call upon God as Father. Human beings are the sons and daughters of God. In human relationships, there are distinctions: some are fathers, others are sons; some are masters, others are slaves. But in the eyes of God, all human beings are equal."[73]

Christianity thus provided religious sanctions for women in their struggle against hierarchical social relationships and sexual discrimination. It offered another symbolic universe from which to challenge the "sacred canopy" that legitimated women's inferior position in Chinese culture.[74] Women, such as Wang Huiwu, who fought for women's rights often saw Christianity as support for their struggle;

> We know that Christians also espouse equality between men and women, and support the abolition of classes. They strongly oppose inhumane practices, such as concubinage, the keeping of domestic maids, and prostitution, and do not contradict the feminist movement. In

> terms of belief, the feminist movement differs from gospel
> preaching, but in terms of concrete work in society, the
> feminist movement and Christianity both elevate women's
> position.[75]

The single most important contribution of Christianity, many
Christian men and women concurred, was the provision of female
education. For Jiang Hezhen, female education awakens the feminine
mind and enables women to participate in public affairs and social
welfare services.[76] Cheng Guanyi shared a similar view: "Education
is now transforming those women who were passive, bound, dependent, and lifeless into active, free, independent and lively constituents
of society."[77] According to Sun Wenxue, the provision of female
education was directly related to the emergence of the women's
movement in China:

> Christianity is a motivating force, which arouses women's
> self-consciousness. This is evident in the past history of
> our country. When Christianity was introduced into
> China, girls' schools were opened alongside the churches.
> Women, who for a long time had been accustomed to
> unequal social teachings, began to be aware of their own
> status, and to reevaluate their worth as human beings.
> Being emancipated from their families, women also
> demanded opportunities for economic independence and
> other women's rights. This was the origin of the women's
> movement in China.[78]

During the anti-Christian movement, the mission schools were
criticized for their use of English as a teaching medium, compulsory
chapel services and religious education, and as elitist training that
alienated the students from the masses. Zeng Baosun, who ran a girls'
school in Hunan, seemed to keep a more balanced view of the
matter: "Early girls' schools were founded by Christian missionaries,
on whom so much blame has been reaped in recent years that we
are apt to forget this great service they have rendered to the women
of China. Mission schools are certainly open to criticism in many
important respects, but their attitude towards women has been
consistently liberating."[79]

Besides awakening their minds, Christianity also acted as a moral
force empowering Christian women to condemn the evils of society.
Since they experienced the injustices of sexual discrimination,

Christian women were also aware of inequalities that existed in the treatment of the rich and the poor, the powerful and the powerless. Some writers encouraged their readers to follow the example of Jesus, who dared to stand up for justice and equality, identifying himself with the oppressed to challenge those in power.[80] The life of Jesus not only set a moral example but testified also that justice and truth would ultimately prevail.

Christian women realized that women as a group needed to raise their consciousness so that they could become agents of social change. Students in Ginling College lamented that the future of China would be without hope if half of her four-hundred million people remained illiterate and dependent on others.[81] Hu Binxia passionately asked: "If half of the nation is lazy and slothful like this, how can China fail to be poor? This is alright if women want to be the rubbish of society. However, if they do not want this and wish to develop perfect female character, they must be diligent and self-motivated, independent and helpful in the building of the nation."[82] Others encouraged women to cultivate their social consciousness and to acquire the analytic tools necessary to understand social issues, realizing that they were equally responsible for the future destiny of the nation.[83]

To broaden women's horizons, Christian women frequently cited examples of social reform and public service initiated by women in Europe and America. As we have mentioned already, the story of Frances Willard was widely publicized. Other prominent leaders discussed include Florence Nightingale and Jane Addams, the American pioneer who established social services in the poorest communities.[84] Reform movements initiated by women—such as the improvement of the prison system in England and temperance in the United States—were introduced,[85] as were benevolent actions such as the sheltering of homeless people, the care of orphans, and concern for child labor. The selective introduction of Western female leaders indicated the line of work the writers endorsed, for seldom did they cite those more radical feminist leaders such as Elizabeth Cady Stanton and Susan B. Anthony, who pushed for women's suffrage and other constitutional reforms.

Did women have a particular contribution to make because they were women? Although Christian women believed in the equality of the sexes, they also upheld the conviction that women had particular qualities and character traits that enabled them to contribute to society in unique ways. For instance, they thought women were innately more loving and compassionate, such that they were more able to extend their sympathy to those less fortunate than they. Zeng Baosun regarded women as more religious, too, and attributed this to women having to endure "more sorrow and suffering."[86] Shen Caizhen thought women were capable of leadership in social reform, because caring less for their self-interest, they were more able to love others with a much deeper compassion.[87] Cheng Guanyi also exhorted women to bring forth their innate loving character, so that they could serve as lights in the midst of darkness.[88]

This understanding of the gender distinction between men and women explains why these women opted for one particular social strategy for changing society over others. In 1912, Kang Cheng published the booklet *An Amazon in Cathay*, in which she contrasted the patriotic activities of two cousins.[89] One of the cousins, Hoying, who is a Christian, is gentle, cultured, and dresses in gowns "exquiste in their soft tints." During the revolution, she goes to serve selflessly as an assistant in a hospital for women and children. The other cousin, Pearl, is not a Christian. With patriotic fervor, she decides to join the "Dare-to-Die" military bands. Reminiscent of Hua Mulan, Pearl puts on men's attire, cutting her tresses when she enrolls in the all-female Amazon Corps.

As the story goes on, Pearl sorrowfully realizes that as a woman, she cannot possibly be a good soldier; for example, she dares not eat the flesh of a decapitated body. When others accuse her of lacking patriotism, she is in great distress, believing that she has betrayed her cause. After a suicide attempt, she is brought to the hospital where Hoying is working. Hoying tries to convince her to put her trust in God, and Pearl is finally converted to Christianity, dedicating herself to be a nurse caring for suffering women and children. In *An Amazon in Cathay*, Kang Cheng sought to contrast two ways of serving one's nation, as Jane Hunter eloquently says, "one based on glorious self-sacrifice, another on more subtle self-abnegation; one based on the assumption of male roles, the other on the expansion of womanly ones; one based on a transcendence of sex, the other on the submission to sex; one based on heroic, nearly theatrical action, the other on womanly feeling."[90]

Kang Cheng was not the only one who thought that the members of the Amazon Corps betrayed their own sex. Zhang Zhujun, as already mentioned, also opposed women joining military activities.

Zhang opted for serving the Red Cross during the revolution, while Kang, besides running a large hospital, provided protection and health care during the Northern Expedition. Among the women leaders, only Jiang Hezhen seemed to be less critical of the Amazons. Comparing the "Dare-to-Die" Corps to the American Minutemen of 1776, Jiang said, "Many girls have sacrificed their lives in the cause of democracy. . . . This certainly is no sign of either retrogression or of old-style inactivity among Chinese women."[91]

Christian women's denunciation of military activities may be attributed to two causes. First, martial virtues were opposed to the feminine qualities espoused both in Chinese culture and in evangelical Christianity. Second, Christian women were influenced by liberal thinking, which supports the idea that society can be changed through changing individuals. What China needed most, in Zeng Baosun's view, was not a political revolution but a spiritual regeneration. She pointed out the fact that the Chinese had tried various means—both political and educational—to solve their internal troubles and external pressures, but all had failed. They were looking for a "spiritual change," and "the true government of a nation can only be based on the principles of Christ's love."[92] Ding Shujing, perhaps best summarized women's view of social transformation during that period:

> The foundation of a national construction depends on people's personality; healthy personalities can build a healthy nation. If a person has a wholesome life, he or she will have a healthy personality, and this healthy personality is the most important foundation for national construction. If we build our nation on this foundation, it will be strong and firm. When this has been accomplished to a certain extent, then we can make a considerable contribution towards the world's culture.[93]

Women's Faith and Religious Quest

During the 1920's, in the midst of the anti-Christian movement, it was not easy to be a Christian and all the more so if one were a woman, as Christianity was regarded by some as out-dated and patriarchal. In the wake of the May Fourth movement, some radical writers criticized the Bible as androcentric, and the church as discriminatory against women. Unlike Christian men who simply had to demonstrate why Christianity was relevant to China, Christian women needed to defend their faith by showing that it was also beneficial to women.

Christian women in this period were not inclined to write about their religious experiences. A few conversion stories, however, have been preserved in the autobiographies and women's writings in religious journals of the 1920's; these help us to get in touch with the inner spiritual world of women. These stories, written mostly by graduates of mission schools, cannot be taken to represent the vast majority of female Christians. Recounted long after the conversion experience, these accounts were unavoidably colored by experiences of their adult lives. Still, they are a primary resource of understanding what Christianity meant to women in this period.

Some of the conversion stories are written by women who belonged to the well-to-do families of government officials. Cai Sujuan, a well-known evangelist, was born in 1890 as the seventh in a sequence of daughters to a vice-governor of Nanjing. Since her parents had wished for a son, she was given the nickname "Too Many," signifying her low status in the family. Adding to her misfortune, she was also born on an unlucky day, such that no mother-in-law would risk taking her as a future daughter-in-law. Her mother and many other family members were addicted to opium; her sisters, marrying into rich and upper-class families, often came back home crying, having been mistreated by their in-laws. Even in her youth, Cai was sensitive to hypocrisy in human relationships and wickedness in the world. Trying to seek refuge in the religious world, she followed a vegetarian diet and even applied to become a Buddhist nun. She encountered Christianity when she enrolled in a mission school in Nanjing, and subsequently she was converted during a gospel meeting.[94]

Huang Ying, a famous writer of the May Fourth period, was also born to an official's family. On the day when she was born, her grandmother died. She was considered to have brought bad luck to the family; her mother even refused to nurse her. Huang Ying was so neglected and deprived during her childhood that she cried much more often than her brothers. Once when the family was traveling on a ship, her crying infuriated her father to such an extent that he picked her up and almost threw her into the sea. Her family moved to Beijing after her father's death, and she was sent to the Methodist Mary Gamewell School as a boarder. Huang Ying did not like the school, complaining about coarse food and the older schoolmates who used to bully her. She was finally converted to Christianity because her heart felt so empty: "My mother did not love me, my brothers and sisters rejected me. My disease tortured me. . . . I cried bitterly. My empty heart accepted God at that time."[95]

Both Cai and Huang experienced overt oppression within their patriarchal families. Their conversions have been attributed to the emotional exhaustion because of the oppressive circumstances and the warm and friendly attitudes of their missionary teachers.[96] Although these external factors might be conducive to their conversion, we should not overlook their subjective response to Christianity. Cai remarked that Christianity helped her to see that the moral teachings of Confucianism were sheer moralism, and inside her she was full of evil. Christianity gave her a new found peace and power to act according to her faith, in spite of the oppositions of family members.[97] In retrospect, Huang confessed she was impressed by the noble character of Jesus and his spirit of love, hoping to follow his example at that time, though she later gave up her religious belief.[98] Christianity did provide them with consolation and encouragement during distress, but more importantly, it awakened them to a search for the meaning of life and to live in hope.

Unlike Cai and Huang, Zeng Baosun did not suffer familial oppression. She too came into contact with Christianity while studying at mission schools. The first school she attended, a Baptist school, had daily morning prayer and strict Sabbath observances. Zeng disliked the rituals but enjoyed the hymns. Later at Mary Vaughan High School, she was impressed by the kind and forgiving attitudes of her missionary teachers. While taking a walk around the West Lake at Hangzhou, she pondered the meaning of life, especially when her country was facing such enormous problems. She was amazed by the power that Christianity had to change human beings: "The Christian spirit is so wonderful, it can make ordinary people extraordinary. . . . But at that time I felt that China needed the spirit of Christian 'practice,' and I decided to become a Christian."[99]

Christian women leaders did not all come from rich and noble families. Fan Yurong's father was a water carrier; her mother, a hard-working seamstress. Her family was so dispossessed that she would not have been able to go to school if it had not been for the determination of her mother. Li Dequan, later the wife of General

Fung Yuxiang, was the daughter of an illiterate farmer in northern China, whose uncle and relatives were killed in the Boxer incident. Ding Shujing was born in a "drab town" on an utterly "drab plain" in Shandong. Her enrollment in a small mission school changed her life, but people were surprised that "she was allowed by her people to take such a seat."[100]

According to Ding Shujing, Christianity gave people wholeness of life. She lamented that people in the twentieth century were concerned primarily with material satisfaction, neglecting their spiritual well-being. Reminiscent of Zeng Baosun, she said Christianity enabled people to break out of their ordinary routines to seek life in its fullness, that is, the development of human potential and the attainment of the highest spiritual ideals.[101] For Yuan Peifen, the mother of two children, the Christian religion gave her the moral power to cultivate an ideal character, something she did not find in Confucianism or Buddhism. "The way of Jesus Christ is the eternal unchanging way, which we cannot cast aside for a minute. It liberates us from the bondage of sin and lust to attain sainthood."[102]

The conversion stories and religious testimonies of these and other women indicate that at that time educated women were attracted to Christianity not only for salvation from sin but also for the religious power to lead a meaningful life. Christianity opened their eyes to see reality in fresh ways, awakened them to their personal worth, and motivated them to make critical decisions that changed their lives. Cai decided to be an evangelist despite many admirable job offers, Huang quit school to be a writer, and Ding joined the staff of the Y.W.C.A.

In the 1920's, Christianity was under severe attack from students and left-wing intellectuals. The major criticisms were: (1) Christianity is unscientific, (2) it is a foreign religion, and (3) it has been used by Western imperialistic forces. The anti-Christian movement cast its shadow on the entire Christian community, prompting Christian leaders to write apologetics in defense of their religion. We do not have enough publications to reconstruct how Christian women in general responded to the situation, but there are indications that young female students in the schools were affected by the current debate at the time. Zhang Qunying says that ever since she was eleven, she had learned by heart religious hymns and biblical passages. At secondary school, however, when she was exposed to modern scientific knowledge, her faith was shaken. Influenced by the spirit of positivism, she started to question religion, which cannot be empirically proven, and to ask what objective basis can support religious claims to truth. She found it very difficult to accept the religious beliefs she had once embraced.[103]

Zhang's problem was not hers alone, for other female students faced a similar challenge. Wang Fanglian was born into a Christian family and had accompanied her family to church since childhood. At fourteen, she was baptized and joined the Church. When she attended Normal School, some of her schoolmates accused Christianity of being unscientific and superstitious, and she stopped going to morning prayers, Bible studies, and Sunday worship. Later when she continued her study at a Higher Normal school at Beijing, she started to attend a Bible-study class organized by the Y.W.C.A. At that time, Wu Leichuan and other Christians espoused a new religious outlook, emphasizing Christianity's similarities with Chinese culture and the social relevancy of the Gospel.[104] Wang was deeply attracted to this new religious quest, attacking her earlier evangelical faith—according to which the faithful go to heaven and the nonbelievers go to hell—as a system of belief designed to appease "foolish men and women."[105]

In response to the attack that Christianity was imperialistic and encouraged Christians to be less patriotic, some Christian women asked Christians to reflect upon the sincerity and relevancy of their faith.[106] Christians in China also developed an apologetics centered around the person of Jesus. Chinese theologians in the 1920's emphasized the humanity of Jesus, instead of his divinity. As Zhao Zichen (T. C. Chao) of the theological faculty of Yenching University wrote:

> It was not as God or the Son of God that Jesus attracted me: rather He commanded my attention and interest because He was a thoroughly human being. . . . Consequently, when Jesus declared Himself to be the Son of Man, whatever else that term may mean, I was glad, because here I could have ground for assurance that what He taught was true, for He was human.[107]

Jesus was portrayed as a real human being and a moral exemplar. His uniqueness was seen to rest not so much on his divinity, and thus beyond all human beings, as on his moral and spiritual perfection. His death was thought to be not so much a sacrifice to expiate sin as a demonstration of his radical obedience and his absolutely altruistic love. Human beings were exhorted to follow the footsteps of Jesus in order to discover the "divine element" within each of us. According to Xu Baoqian, a Y.M.C.A. secretary: "If God means a being who is entirely different from me, or, in other words, if there is no divine element in me, then Jesus is not God to me."[108]

Unlike their male counterparts, Christian women did not write theological treatises, but their religious writings indicate that they shared a similar humanistic understanding of Jesus, for example, Ding Shujing regarded Jesus as a man who lived to the fullest:

> The life of Jesus is an exemplar, unique both in the past and in the present. He has perfect knowledge of God and is in complete harmony with God. He has genuine love for humankind. With steadfast and relentless power, he fulfills the task of saving human beings and the world. Therefore, he has lived a glorious and radiant life, accomplishing fullness of life.[109]

Ding was joined by Zeng Baosun, who referred to Jesus as the perfect human being. "As a perfect human being, Jesus sacrificed himself on behalf of human beings, thus elevating human personality nearer to God. Through his incarnation—the Son of God became the Son of Man—He showed us how to attain God's favor and forgiveness."[110]

Christian women were particularly moved by one salient aspect of Jesus' life, that is, his revolutionary attitude towards women. According to Cheng Guanyi, "Jesus always elevated the worth of women and women's position." He preached the Kingdom of God to the Samaritan women at the well, and he told the parable of the "lost pearl" to a Canaanite women. When he was alive, his food and material needs were supplied by women; after his death, he appeared first to women.[111] Ding Shujing stated that Jewish customs were extremely patriarchal, but Jesus dared to challenge the prejudice and injustice of tradition. He expressed filial piety toward his mother and respect for his women friends. Trying to abolish the hierarchical distinction between men and women, he restored women to their rightful position.[112] Zeng Baosun came very close to writing a new credal formula by saying: "Chinese women can only find full life in the message of Christ, who was born of a woman, revealed His messiahship to a woman, and showed His glorified body after His resurrection to a woman.''[113]

Available accounts of women's religious experience indicate that women have adapted Christian faith to their own situations. Contrary to a general assumption that women tend to be sentimental in their religion, these female authors demonstrate a capacity to reason their faith. Although most female believers still upheld an individualistic faith propagated by evangelical Christianity, a small minority of Christian women had begun to search for a liberating faith that both recognized their dignity as women and addressed the situation of China at that time. In particular, they found a humanistic understanding of Christology as uplifting for women, enabling them to live a meaningful life.

Women and the Church

At the Second National Convention of the Y.W.C.A. in 1927, Ding Shujing presented a memorable speech, entitled ''The Position of Women in the Church.'' The Church, she said, was a holy fellowship called together by the love of Christ. Everyone who believed in Christ had new life, which needed to grow in the spiritual communion of believers. Christians gathered together because they were moved by the love of God and wished to follow Jesus' commandment to love one another. The power that bound them was the power of love. This fellowship of love could serve two functions. Inwardly, it enabled Christians to come together for mutual learning and support, so that they could help each other to develop their faith, character, temperament, and interests. Outwardly, it united Christians, strengthening them to work for the public good, looking forward to the day when the whole society could be Christianized. This fellowship, according to Ding, was the church of Christ, or *Ecclesia*, which had five characteristics: (1) it consisted of a spiritual and holy union of Christians, (2) and this union was based on love, (3) and the cultivation of fellowship, (4) serving the needs of society, and (5) maintaining a force to Christianize society.[114]

Based on this theological understanding of the Church, Ding and other female leaders demanded that women be treated as full participants in the body of Christ. Because the Christian Church was a fellowship based on love, it had to recognize the worth of each individual member. Furthermore, Jesus respected women, preaching to them and healing them, and women participated in his ministry through supporting his needs. What Jesus did was indeed contrary to the customs of his time, as Li Guanfang pointed out: "Christ, the Supreme leader of all times did not blindly follow other leaders of His day. He struck out for Himself. He dared to preach new doctrines, to do things differently. . ."[115] Discrimination against women, for these Christians, contradicted the principles of Christianity.

Apart from theological and biblical reasons, Christian women argued that the Chinese church needed the participation of women at a time when it was under mounting pressure from the outside. In dealing with the anti-Christian attack, one of the immediate tasks of Chinese Christians was to build a native Chinese church. Hu Binxia noted: "It is true that unless the Church is made indigenous, Christianity will remain a foreign religion."[116] Since this required the effort of both women and men, Cheng Guanyi appealed to her Christian sisters: "We must fulfill our responsibilities as a part of Christ and with Christ as the Head, let us build the Church in China."[117]

Christian women understood that Chinese Christians had to bear the responsibility to carry on the work the missionaries had begun. Although they did not think the missionary days were over, they were aware that China might require a new type of missionary, missionaries who:

> needed to be filled with buoyant courage to speak out plainly in matters of international justice; and in approaching international questions arising between other countries and China, their judgement should be based on a high regard for personal human values. . . .[118]

Ding Shujing thought that these attitudes would demonstrate to the non-Christians that "Christian work in China is not imperialistic and capitalistic, but works for the coming of the Kingdom of God, which is goodwill and brotherhood among all men."[119]

If the Chinese church required a greater number of competent leaders, the urgency of developing female leadership had to be recognized. Many Christian women were dismayed that the degree of their participation in the Christian community was far from being satisfactory and that many people still held onto a traditional, stereotypical view of the sexes. Sun Wensue, for instance, observed there were Christians who insisted that male and female evangelists should receive different wages. Teachers in female mission schools continued to uphold moral standards that were two-hundred years old. At the time when the feminist movement was at its peak in China, Sun rightly pointed out that such phenomena would easily give non-Christians an excuse to criticize Christianity. For Sun and other Christian women, it was regrettable that Christianity, having made such a contribution to elevating the position of Chinese women, was to be attacked by modern Chinese women as patriarchal and out-dated.[120]

Christian women regarded the discrimination against women as a barrier to the development of God's ministry. Women have their special talents and gifts that men lack, just as men have qualities that women do not possess. Ding Shujing asserted: "If the position of men and women is not equal in the church, the original mission of the church will not be fulfilled, and the development of church ministry will also be hampered."[121] Cheng Guanyi shared her view:

> Have we not found how Christ, the Leader of the Church handed His most precious doctrine to women, how He gave the best opportunity to women so that they could give their contribution to the Kingdom of God? Does not the present Chinese Church suffer deeply from the pain of wrong conditions? Do we realize that the unprogressive state in the Church is due to the fact that the women in the Church have not the opportunity of enjoying their privileges to the full?[122]

Christian women made concrete suggestions to rectify the situation. First, at the National Christian Conference of 1922, Cheng Guangyi called attention to the question of the ordination of women. Since China needed to build her own church, she questioned whether the Western church tradition should be strictly followed:

> People in some places think that the ordination of women is out of the question and women pastors are simply impossibilities. I do not intend to advocate that the Church ought to have women pastors, but I would simply like to ask the reason why women cannot have such rights. If the Western Church because of historical development and other reasons has adopted such an attitude, has the Chinese Church the same reason for doing so? If the ancient Church with sufficient reasons, considered that women could not have such rights are those reasons sufficient enough to be applied to the present Church?[123]

Cheng's opinions were shared by some open-minded men in the Christian community, who wrote in support of women's ordination. Since women now enjoyed greater equality and freedom in Chinese society, they argued, the church should not stick to the earlier tradition, denying them the right to be ordained in the Christian ministry. These men challenged the prejudice that women were inferior to men based on a belief that Eve was the one who sinned first. Reminding the audiences that the blood of Jesus was shed for all, they affirmed that men and women both were reconciled to God. Furthermore, if Christains really believed that men and women were equal, there was no reason why women could not be ordained.[124]

Second, Christian women asked for greater representation of women in the making of decisions because of the small number of women serving on church boards and executive committees or appointed as delegates to church synods and national conferences. It was not enough that several women were offered "token" representation on certain committees or that a certain number of seats were reserved for women. If women were really qualified for such tasks, there should be no artificial rules to limit their participation. Instead, they called the church to recognize women as integral partners in the church and their talents as gifts of the Christian fellowship.[125]

Third, they emphasized that leadership training for women should be strengthened and implemented on different levels. In the Church, the awareness of both men and women on women's issues needed to be raised through preaching and literature. Special lectures for women could be organized to broaden their horizons, especially on current world affairs and new ideas. Women with specific talents could be selected to receive advanced training so that they could better serve the Church. In the Christian colleges and seminaries, equal opportunity should be offered men and women, and the Church as a whole should draw the attention of the public to the importance of higher education for women in general.[126]

Christian women envisioned the Church as the visible sign of a new community in which the relation of the sexes was based on equality and mutuality. Ding Shujing described the new relationship between men and women as one based on equality, interdependency, complementarity, and cooperation. The Church should be the pioneer of society, she claimed, and by treating women on an equal basis, the Church would contribute toward social progress. Fan Yurong openly shared Ding's bold dream in her short address to the

National Christian Conference: "Therefore let us strive for the day when men and women stand on the same level to reform the home, to improve society, and to establish the Church of God in the world, the best they know how."[127]

In this chapter, we have seen the development of the consciousness of Christian women, which involved questioning traditional roles and images, recognizing their own issues and predicament, and awareness of themselves as agents of social change. This complex process took place in a rapidly changing social matrix: the mushrooming of women's journals, the accessibility of female education, the early industrialization of coastal cities, and women's participation in the 1911 Revolution and the May Fourth movement. But as Christian women, they were influenced also by their religious faith, which they had begun to reflect upon from their particular perspective as Chinese women.

Apart from other criticisms, the anti-Christian movement specifically attacked Christianity for discriminating against women. This prompted female Christian leaders to defend their Christian identity. The writings of Christian women express their reexamination of the relation between women and Christianity from both historical and theological perspectives. They argued that the Protestant Christain mission had, indeed, initiated the education of women and various other social reforms aiming at improving women's position in China. Christian women themselves served as leaven in their society through their involvements in the anti-footbinding movement, the temperance movement, the publishing of women's journals, and the campaign against concubinage. This historical consciousness allowed them both to celebrate their past and to critique the present. They voiced their opinions on the ongoing discrimination against women in the Christian church, especially in respect to the ordination of women and female leadership, challenging the church to fulfill her original mission to be the sign of a new community.

Theologically, they responded positively to the person of Jesus, who respected women and recognized their worth. As we can recall from earlier chapters, male missionaries such as Charles Hartwell mentioned Jesus' relationship with women in their religious tracts and pamphlets, and women missionaries reiterated the message in the late nineteenth century to justify social reforms for women. In the 1920's, Christian women developed further the humanistic understanding of Jesus, both as a foundation for their own confession of faith and as a religious sanction for the feminist movement.

In their religious testimonies, Christian women emphasized two dimensions to their concept of God. God was a loving and compassionate God, who took care of human beings and helped those in need. Christian women realized that to confess "God is love" in a world in which injustice and violence seemed to prevail was an act of faith.[128] God was described as the creator of the universe, who sustained the world and gave it meaning and purposefulness. Some Christian women referred to the creator as the father of all human beings. However, the "father image" did not derive from the Chinese human family, in which the father dominated, but served to challenge all patriarchal and hierarchical relations. God as the ultimate father relativized all claims of authority on earth, because all were equally sons and daughters of God. In this way, the image of God the Father was not understood to be a legitimation of the patriarchal structure of the Chinese household.

Christianity provided women with symbolic resources for affirming their identities and enabling them to step outside familiar domains to act as agents for social change. Christian women saw the liberation of women in China as a critical component in the struggle for national survival and reconstruction. Assuming a liberal stand, they affirmed that by transforming the individual person, Christianity could be a positive force in the salvation of China. The writings of Christian women demonstrated a strong recognition of their identity as Chinese women, and their sincere and deepened patriotism. In the turbulent years of the early twentieth century, they had tried to live out their multiple identities as Chinese, Christian, and women.

Notes

1. Yuan Yuying, "Zhongguo nüjie baozhi zhi xianzhuang" (The present condition of Chinese women's newspapers), *Nianjian* 5 (1918): 167; and Hu Binxia, "Magazines for Chinese Women," by Mrs. T. C. Chu, *Year Book* 8 (1917): 454-458.

2. The Library of the National Committee of the Chinese Christian Three-Self Patriotic Movement at Shanghai holds a nearly complete set, missing only a few issues.

3. Xu Zhihe, "Fakan ci" (Remarks on the beginning of publication), *NDB* 1/1 (April 1912): 3. A *duo* was a big bell in ancient China that was struck to warn people when a new law was going to be promulgated.

4. Yuan Yuying, "Zhongguo nüjie baozhi," 168.

5. Due to these changes, some of the issues have volumes and numbers, whereas others just list the month and the year. I have tried to give all available data in the footnotes. It is unfortunate that a complete set cannot be located either in China or in the libraries and archives I have consulted in the United States. Some earlier issues can be found in the Shanghai Y.W.C.A. headquarters, the Shanghai Library, and the Library of the National Committee of Chinese Christian Three-Self Patriotic Movement. The Harvard-Yenching Library holds an incomplete set of issues from 1928 to 1933.

6. Hilda L. Smith, "Women's History and Social History: An Untimely Alliance," *Organization of American Historians Newsletter* 12/4 (November 1984): 6.

7. Ethel Klein, *Gender Politics*, 5.

8. Ibid.

9. Charlotte L. Beahan, "The Women's Movement and Nationalism in Late Ch'ing China." Ph.D diss., Columbia University, 1976.

10. Jessie Gregory Lutz, *China and the Christian Colleges*, 132-138.

11. See Roxane Heater Witke, "Transformation of Attitudes towards Women during the May Fourth Era of Modern China," Ph.D. diss., University of California, Berkeley, 1970.

12. Hu Binxia, "The Emancipation of Chinese Women," by Mrs. T. C. Chu, *CR* 50 (1919): 655.

13. Cheng Wanzhen, "The Woman's Movement in China," by Zung Wei Tsung, *The Y.W.C.A. Magazine* (June 1923): 1.

14. Yuan Yuying, "Funü yu zhanshi zhi guanxi" (The relationship between women and war), *NDB* 2/3 (June 1913): 5-6.

15. Cao Fangyun, "Yifu lüeshuo" (A brief talk on clothes), *NDB* 2/4 (July 1913): 13.

16. Xu Guifen, "Nüzi aiguo lun" (On women's patriotism), *NDB* 1/6 (September 1912): 29; Cao Fangyun, "Yifu lüeshou," 12.

17. Tan Huiran, "Duiyu nüquan yundong zhi wojian" (My views on the feminist movement), by Mrs. Ou Bin, *NDB* 11/11 (February 1923): 2.

18. Qiu Yinlan, "Jiating jiaoyu shou zai xianmu" (A virtuous mother is most important in family education), *NDB* 2/4 (July 1913): 45

19. Xu Guifen, "Nüzi aiguo lun," 29.

20. Hu Binxia, "The Emancipation of Chinese Women," 658.

21. Jiang Hezhen, "The Modern Chinese Woman: Her Work and Problems," by Anna Kong Mei, *International Review of Missions* 13 (1924): 568.

22. Guo Fangyun, "Gaizao shehui de funü lingxiu" (Women leaders who transform society), *Nüqingnian bao* (May 1923): 1.

23. Shen Caizhen, "Gaizao shehui de funü lingxiu" (Women leaders who transform society), *Nüqingnian bao* (April 1923): 2.

24. Wang Huiwu, "Nüquan yundong yu nü Jidutu" (The feminist movement and female Christians), *Nüqingnian bao* (October 1922): 8.

25. Cheng Wanzhen, "The Woman's Movement in China," 2-3; Li Ang, "Zhongguo de funü wenti" (Chinese women's problems), *NDB* 13/7 (October 1924): 1-7.

26. Zeng Baosun, "The Chinese Woman Past and Present," by P. S. Tseng, in *Symposium on Chinese Culture*, ed., Sophia H. Chen (Shanghai: China Institute of Pacific Relations, 1931), 281-292.

27. Ibid., 282.

28. Ibid., 283.

29. Ibid.

30. A Chinese anthropologist also noted that requirements of female chastity tightened in the Song Dynasty; see Chiao Chien, "Female Chastity in Chinese Culture," *Minzu xue yanjiu jikan* (Journal of ethnographic studies), 31 (1971): 205-211.

31. Zeng Baosun, "The Chinese Woman Past and Present," 286.

32. Ibid., 288.

33. Liu Jingying, "Lun jiu jiating gailiang zhi biyao" (On the necessity to reform the traditional family), *NDB* 11/1 (April 1922): 11; Fang Suxin, "Nüzi de zhuquan" (Women's rights), *NDB* 15/5 (August 1925): 3.

34. For example, Zhu Yansheng, "Liangceng lijiao xia Zhongguo nü xintu de hunyin wenti" (Chinese Christian women's marriage issues in a society with double moral standard), *Shengming* 5/3 (December 1924): 74-77; and Xu Baoqian, "Liangxing daode biaozhun zhi bianqian ji Jidu jiaoyi" (Changes in the moral standard between the sexes and Christian doctrine), *Zhenli yu shengming* (Truth and life) 2/16 (1927): 500-503.

35. Ginling College Girls, "Students and Marriage Customs in China," *CR* 57 (1926): 496.

36. Chen Ruilan, "Lun nüzi ziyou jiehun zhi buke bushen" (On the topic of women needing to take greater care concerning free marriage), *NDB* 4/2 (May 1915): 1-6.

37. For example, *The Church Missionary Gleaner* 16 (1866): 2; and *Missionary Herald* 72 (1876): 220 and 78 (1882): 23-26. See also missionary reports: Elsie M. Garretson and Irene L. Dorublaser, "Foochow Girls' College: Report for 1911," ABC 16.3.6 (3); and Luella Miner, "Annual Report of Bridgman Academy," ABC 16.3.12 (3), no. 113.

38. See the articles by Charles Hartwell and D. G. Sheffield, "Questionable Practices Connected with Marriage and Funeral Ceremonies,"

in *Records 1877*, 387-392, 393-396.

39. "A Visit with Deng Yuzhi (Cora Deng)" *China Update* (August 1983): 11-12. My personal interview at Shanghai, November, 1987.

40. For example, Yao Fubao, "Wenming jiehun" (Civilized marriage), *NDB* 4/9 (December 1915): 67-68.

41. Bian Yuying, "Lun quqie yu weiqie zhi louxi" (On the bad habits of taking a concubine or becoming a concubine), *NDB* 3/7 (October 1914): 2-8.

42. Ginling College Girls, "Students and Marriage Customs," 495.

43. National Committee of the Y.W.C.A. in China, *Diyici quanguo dahui jilu*, 163.

44. Jiang Hezhen, "Making the Home Christian," by Mrs. H. C. Mei, *CR* 53 (1922): 473.

45. Ding Shujing, "Feibi yundong" (The movement to abolish domestic maids), *Nüqingnian* 7/2 (March 1928): 54.

46. Long Deyuan, "Zhongguo jiating de gaijin" (Reforming the Chinese family), *Nüqingnian* 7/2 (1928): 27; Liu Jingying, "Lun jiu jiating gailiang," 10.

47. Liu Jingying, "Lun jiu jiating gailiang," 11.

48. Jiang Hezhen "Making the Home Christian," 472-473.

49. Zhu Yansheng, "Liangceng lijiao," 75.

50. Ginling College Girls, "Students and Marriage Customs," 494.

51. Fang Suxin, "Nüzi de zhuquan," 2.

52. Cheng Guanyi, "Zhonghua Jidujiao nüzi gaodeng jiaoyu jinzhuang" (The current situation of Chinese Christian higher education for women), *Nianjian* 6 (1921): 95.

53. Xu Maoli, "Jinri nü xuetang yi zengshe shiye ke lun" (Recommending that girls' schools offer practical subjects) *NDB* 1/11 (February 1913): 44-45.

54. Zhan Yanlai, "Zhongguo funü yu zhengqu dao nannü pingdeng de genben wenti" (Basic issues of Chinese women's struggle for sexual equality), *NDB* 14/7 (October 1925): 12.

55. Cheng Wanzhen, "Nüzi zhiye wenti" (Issues on women's jobs), *Nüqingnian bao* 5/1 (March 1921): 1; and Zhao Minshu, "Nüxing yu zhiye" (Women and jobs) *Nüqingnian* 8/7 (July, 1929): 11.

56. Hu Shi, "Meiguo de furen" (American women) in vol. 1 of *Hu Shi Wencun* (Collected essays of Hu Shi) (Taibei: Yuandong tushu gongsi, 1953), 648-664. The article was originally published in 1918. Lu Xun's well-known address in December, 1923 also talked about the economic independence of women; see "Nuola zouhou zenyang" (What happens to Nora after she leaves?) in *Fen* (Graves) collected in vol. 1 of *Lu Xun quanji* (Complete works of Lu Xun) (Beijing: People's Press, 1973), 143-151.

57. Guo Fangyun quoted a lengthy paragraph from Hu Shi's article, see "Gaizao shehui," 2-3. See also Zhan Yanlai, "Zhongguo funü yu zhengqu dao nannü pingdeng," 12-13.

58. Li Zhezhen, "Yige shou jiaoyu de nüzi ying ruhe gailiang tade guo" (How can an educated woman reform her nation?), *NDB* 12/3 (November 1923): 7.

59. Jane Hunter notes that Christian women's decisions to remain single may be due to their sense of obligation to the nation, and the example of single women missionaries. See Hunter, *The Gospel of Gentility*, 249-250.

60. Hu Binxia, "Nüzi yu guoyun" (Women and the destiny of the nation), *NDB* 11/2 (May 1922): 5.

61. Shen Caizhen, "Gaizao shehui," 2.

62. Hu Binxia, "The Emancipation of Chinese Women," 656-657.

63. Zhu Shouheng, "Gaizao shehui de funü lingxiu" (Women leaders who transform society), *Nüqingnian bao* (February 1923): 3.

64. Cheng Wanzhen, "The Chinese Church and the New Industrial System," by Zung Wei Tsung, *CR* 53 (1922): 190.

65. See Cheng Wanzhen, "The Woman's Movement in China," 2.

66. Wang Liming, "The Chinese Woman's Movement and Magazines," by Mrs. Herman C. E. Liu, *CR* 69 (1934): 85.

67. Cheng Wanzhen, "The Woman's Movement in China," 2.

68. Feibi, "Nüzi canzheng yundong de shangque" (Discussion on women's political movement) *Ginling College Magazine* 1/3 (April 1925): 2-4.

69. Shi Meiyu, "What Chinese Women Have Done," 239-245.

70. Kang Cheng, "The Place of Chinese Christian Women in the Development of China," by Ida Kahn, *CR* (1919): 659.

71. Ibid., 660-661.

72. Cheng Guanyi, "Zhonghua Jidujiao nüzi gaodeng jiaoyu jinzhuang," 95.

73. Li Guanfang, "Zhongguo shehui ruhe keyi pingdeng" (How can equality be achieved in Chinese society?), *NDB* 9/6 (September 1920): 6.

74. "Sacred canopy" refers to religious legitimation of the established order of society; see Peter Berger, *The Sacred Canopy: Elements of a Sociological Theory of Religion* (Garden City, N.Y.: Doubleday and Co., 1969).

75. Wang Huiwu, "Nüquan yundong," 8.

76. Jiang Hezhen, "The Modern Chinese Woman," 570-571.

77. Cheng Guanyi, "Women and the Church," by Ruth Cheng, *CR* 53 (1922): 538.

78. Sun Wenxue, "Jidujiao duiyu funü yundong de gongxian" (The contribution of Christianity to the women's movement), *Nüqingnian* 7/3 (April 1928): 23.

79. Zeng Baosun, "The Chinese Woman Past and Present," 286.

80. Li Guanfang, "Zhongguo shehui ruhe keyi pingdeng," 7.

81. Wu Ming-ying, "Women and Education," *Ginling College Magazine* 1/1 (June 1924): 23.

82. Hu Binxia, "Nüzi yu guoyun," 3.

83. Shen Caizhen, "Gaizao shehui," 3; and Kong Xianglin, "Zhongguo nü xuesheng yingchi zhi taidu" (The attitudes Chinese female students should have), *NDB* 14/4 (July 1925): 7.

84. Shanghai Y.W.C.A., "Nüzi duiyu shehui zhi yiwu" (Women's duty toward society), *NDB* 3/3 (June 1914): 2.

85. Cheng Guanyi, "Funü duiyu ziyou de gongxian" (Women's contribution to freedom), *NDB* 10/11 (February 1922): 5; and Chen Yuling, "Wanguo funü jiezhi hui," 85-86.

86. Zeng Baosun, "China's Women and Their Position in the Church," by P. S. Tseng, *Church Missionary Review* 68 (1917): 375.

87. Shen Caizhen, "Gaizao shehui," 3.

88. Cheng Guanyi, "Funü duiyu ziyou de gongxian," 6.

89. Kang Cheng, *An Amazon in Cathay*, by Ida Kahn (Boston: Woman's Foreign Missionary Society, 1912).

90. Jane Hunter, *The Gospel of Gentility*, 259.

91. Jiang Hezhen, "The Modern Chinese Woman," 568.

92. Zeng Baosun, "China's Women and Their Position in the Church," 376.

93. Ding Shujing, "Fengman de shengming" (Fullness of life), *Nüqingnian* 7/4 (May 1928), 5.

94. Cai Sujuan, *Anshi zhi hou* (Hong Kong: The Bellman House, 1982), Chinese translation of Christiana Tsai, *Queen of the Dark Chamber*, as told to Ellen L. Drummond (Chicago: Moody Press, 1953).

95. Huang Ying, "Lu Yin zizhuan," 561.

96. Jane Hunter, *The Gospel of Gentility*, 258.

97. Cai Sujuan, *Anshi zhi hou*, 98-105.

98. Huang Ying, "Lu Yin zizhuan," 603.

99. Zeng Baosun, *Zeng Baosun huiyilu*, 35.

100. *Women Leaders of Present Day China: Chinese Christians Worth Knowing* (Boston: Women's Board of Missions, n.d.), 3, 6, 8.

101. Ding Shujing, "Fengman de shengming," 3-7.

102. Yuan Peifen, "Wo weihe wei Jidutu" (Why am I a Christian?), *Nianjian* 6 (1921): 240.

103. Zhang Qunying, "Wo de zongjiao xinyang de kunnan" (The difficulty of my religious faith), *Shengming* 3/7-8 (April 1923): 1-2. (The pagination in this volume does not follow numerical order. Each article starts with page one. Thus the pagination of this article is the same as that in footnote 105).

104. Wu Liming, *Jidujiao yu shehui bianqian* (Christianity and Social Change in China) (Hong Kong: Chinese Christian Literature Council, 1981), 225-230.
105. Wang Fanglian, "Wo geren de zongjiao jingyan" (My own religious experience), *Shengming* 3/7-8 (April 1923): 1-2.
106. Bai Yurong, "Zai fan zongjiao nonghou de kongqi li suosheng de chuti" (Alertness in the midst of strong anti-religious sentiment), *Zhenli yu shengming* 4/5 (1929): 33-35.
107. Zhao Zichen, "Jesus and the Reality of God," quoted in *Chinese Theology in Construction* by Wing-hung Lam, 37.
108. Xu Baoqian, "The Uniqueness of Christ from a Chinese Standpoint," quoted in *Chinese Theology in Construction* by Wing-hung Lam, 38.
109. Ding Shujing, "Fengman de shengming," 7.
110. Zeng Baosun, "Wo de Jidujiao xinyang" (My Christian faith), in *Jidujiao yu xin Zhongguo* (Christianity and a new China), ed., Wu Yaozong (Shanghai: Qingnian xiehui shuju, 1940), 241. The emphasis of Jesus as a perfect human being was shared even by some non-Christians. A notable example was Chen Duxiu, later the founder of the Chinese Communist Party; see his "Jidujiao yu Zhongguo ren" (Christianity and Chinese people), *Xin qingnian* 7/3 (1 February 1920): 15-23.
111. Cheng Guanyi, "Funü dui yu ziyou de gongxian," 5.
112. Ding Shujing, "Funü zai jiaohui zhong de diwei" (The position of women in the church) *Nüqingnian* 7/2 (March, 1928): 22.
113. Zeng Baosun, "Christianity and Women as Seen at the Jerusalem Meeting," 443.
114. Ding Shujing, "Funü zai jiaohui," 21-22.
115. See *NCC 1922*, 599.
116. Hu Binxia, "My Impression of the National Christian Conference," by Mrs. T. C. Chu, *CR* 53 (1922): 410.
117. Cheng Guanyi, "Women and the Church," 541.
118. Ding Shujing, "Chinese Women Leader's Conception of the Missionary," by Ting Shu Ching, *CR* 57 (1926): 122.
119. Ibid.
120. Sun Wenxue, "Jidujiao dui yu funü yundong," 23-24.
121. Ding Shujing, "Funü zai jiaohui," 23.
122. Cheng Guanyi, "Women and the Church," 539.
123. Ibid., 540.
124. "Jiaohui funü yingfou fengzhi zhi shangque" (Discussion on the ordination of women in the church), *NDB* 14/8 (November 1925): 50-52; Chen Xiedong, "Lun jiaohui ying zhongshi nüquan" (On the church should respect women's rights), *Zhenli zhoukan* 3/25 (20 September 1925): 2.
125. Ding Shujing, "Funü zai jiaohui," 23-24.

126. Ibid., 24-25.
127. Fan Yurong, "Women Leaders," by Fan Yu Jung, in *NCC 1922*, 598.
128. Zeng Baosun, "Wo de Jidujiao xinyang," 240.

Conclusion

In the latter half of the nineteenth century, a small number of Chinese women, especially those marginalized in society, overcame many social and cultural barriers in order to follow a foreign religion. Christianity introduced new symbolic resources to these female converts, showing an alternative way of looking at the world and at themselves was possible. I have discussed in chapter two how in the process of adaptation to the Chinese context Christian symbolism was feminized in order to increase its appeal to both Chinese men and women. Female converts found religious values relevant to their own needs in the message of a God who was both loving and compassionate, a Jesus who befriended women, and a Mary who was a model of ideal motherhood. Although we do not have many writings of Chinese Christian women from the nineteenth century, there is clear evidence that in repudiating their former religious practices and refusing to follow traditional family rituals in order to join the Christian church they accepted the Christian teachings with seriousness and commitment.

Similarly to the Chinese popular religious sects, the Christian congregations offered women channels to form bonds with their peers and to provide group support in times of personal and family crises. Girls in impoverished families, who were otherwise denied educational opportunities, could enrol in mission schools, which often provided food and board in addition to free tuition. Older women, especially widows, found that they could learn Chinese characters and songs in church and a few were even employed as Bible women. Situated at the boundary of society in terms of both social class and religious orientation, women in the church were relatively free from the old cultural order. They were the ones who initiated social reforms such as anti-footbinding and anti-concubinage in the local communities.

Missionaries in the nineteenth century brought the cultural construction of gender from their home countries. They subscribed to the values of small nuclear family, domesticity of womanhood, and female education for nurturing the young. They also approved the public roles of women in organizing religious activities and voluntary services for the poor and the needy. Chinese reformers, too, saw that women's domestic roles and maternal duties had a social effect on strengthening the nation. Assuming that educated mothers could bring up better children, they argued that greater opportunities be given to women, especially in terms of education.

Since the 1890's, Christian women experienced a growing participation in church and society, based on the creation of a separate women's sphere and a recognition of women's roles in reproducing and nurturing healthier and stronger offspring. Women's groups in the churches and mission schools provided the training necessary for church women to move into the public arena. In chapter four, we saw that in the name of "social housekeeping," Christian women participated in health campaigns, the W.C.T.U., and the Y.W.C.A. in order to improve social hygiene and child welfare, to care for female students and workers in the cities, as well as to protect the home from the abuses of alcoholism and opium smoking.

Women's rising consciousness in this period was demonstrated by the publication of women's journals and newspapers, notably in Shanghai and Beijing. Rejecting the stereotypical roles of women, this wider feminist movement based its auguments on a belief in the equality of the sexes rather than on women's femininity. Sexual equality, for the radical feminists, was rooted in the natural rights of all human beings. They called the feminist movement *nüquan yundong*, or the "women's rights movement." In addition to propagating new ideas, some iconoclastic feminists went one step farther and actually put these ideas into practice. The revolutionary martyr Qiu Jin cut her hair, assumed a masculine name, and organized military corps directed against the Manchu government. Although Qiu Jin may have imitated Hua Mulan, the legendary heroine who wore male dress and fought in the army, she was also "demanding the right as a woman to play male roles," as historian Mary Backus Rankin has observed.[1]

Furthermore, during the anti-Christian movement, some people with a heightened feminist consciousness criticized Christianity for being conservative and patriarchal. Timothy Richard and Young J. Allen, in the late nineteenth century, propagated the idea that in the West Christianity contributed to the emancipation of women. But twentieth-century Chinese intellectuals, with a more sophisticated knowledge of the West, were able to discern that Christianity was only one of many institutions contributing to the phenomenon, and its influence was, in fact, declining due to the process of secularization. Moreover, socialist literature introduced a more radical strategy for women's liberation, capturing the imagination of Xiang Jingyu and others like her who were impatient with the reformist approach associated with Christianity.

The growing feminist consciousness among women in China and the demand for sexual equality challenged Christian women in a number of ways. First of all, it provided a critical context for them to learn that the traditional roles of women might not be adequate for modern times and that other social roles were possible. Accepting this wider view, Christian women began to explore new images for modern women and to discuss a range of topics, such as female education, women and work, and women's political participation. Borrowing the rhetoric and insights of the feminist movement, Christian women also broadened their feminist agenda to strive for equal participation of women in areas of law, economics, education, politics, and so on. But on the other hand, influenced by the ideas of womanhood learned in church and mission schools, Christian women tended to pay more attention to reform activities related to the home and child care. They were also more willing to support a liberal approach of gradual reform than drastic measures such as revolutionary and military activities, which were seen as beyond the bounds of accepted feminine behavior.

The feminist movement in China can be compared to feminism as it developed in the United States in several ways. In both cases, a tension existed arising from conflicting visions, that is, whether to base feminist activities on an ideology that defined women's separate sphere and distinct feminine qualities or on a conviction of the equality of the sexes.[2] The former justified women's participation in moral and temperance reforms, while the latter provided the foundation for more radical political and economic changes. Again, in both situations, the Christian church has played a complex role in the women's movement. The church provided the training ground for American women to organize their own mission and reform societies, but as Elizabeth Cady Stanton has pointed out, the Bible and Christian teachings comprise also certain patriarchal components that can be used to condemn women to a secondary status.[3] In China, the influence of Christianity on the women's movement was even more ambiguous given the small number of female Christians and the majority of feminists as non-Christians. Christianity certainly provided religious resources to counteract dominant patriarchal cultural order. But on the other hand, the gender construction of the Christian community and missionary circles also limited the range of options for social change Christian women could adopt.

The feminist movement in China differed from that in the West in one significant aspect. As Kumari Jayawardena has pointed out, feminist movements in Third World countries were heavily colored by nationalism, and China was no exception.[4] Women suffering multiple oppressions had the double burden of striving to liberate themselves and their entire people. Christian women in China did not see the two aspects as contradictory, because they assumed that the emancipation of one-half of the population would inevitably lead to the strengthening of the nation. Their Marxist contemporaries, nevertheless, did not see it in the same way and criticized them as too Westernized and bourgeois, concerned only with "women's rights." Subsequent Marxist statements insisted that the liberation of women in China must be an integral part of the overall liberation of the people. But it must be pointed out that though the Marxist revolution promised the emancipation of women, most current studies indicated that Chinese women have yet to be liberated in many areas. Margery Wolf aptly titles her most recent book on Chinese women *Revolution Postponed.*[5] It seems to me that many of the issues raised in the 1920's by both Christian and secular feminists are still valid for those of us who are concerned about feminism in China today.

This study focuses also on the interesting fact of the role of women missionaries in the development of feminist consciousness of women in China. Chinese Christian women, in this cultural contact, benefited from the role modelling of the female missionaries as well as the introduction of women's organizations from the West. However, my observation is that it was the wider women's movement that heightened and shaped the development of the feminist consciousness of Christian women. The demand for sexual equality in the church began as women were offered more educational and economic opportunities, and the discrimination against women in ritualistic and pastoral leadership was more keenly felt when women demonstrated for equal rights with men.

In the 1920's, during the heyday of the anti-Christian movement, female Christians were prompted to reflect more specifically about women and Christianity. Looking back at the history of Christianity in China, they generally felt that Christian mission had contributed to the uplift of women, citing the provision of female education as the most outstanding example. In addition, they evaluated positively the involvement of Christian women in the anti-footbinding movement and other reform activities.

On the other hand, they realized that the patriarchal structure of the church should be transformed and the androcentric elements in Christian doctrines critiqued. The writings of Christian women challenged those Christian teachings that circumscribed the power and role of women in the church and society. With her characteristic boldness, Zhang Zhujun denounced Paul's teaching that women should not preach in church. Cheng Guanyi promoted the ordination of women, and she questioned the legitimacy of applying biblical teachings unconditionally within another cultural context. Some Christian women leaders even attempted to reformulate certain crucial Christian doctrines, although they could not fully develop these ideas due to their lack of theological training. Zeng Baosun, for example, suggested a statement of faith centered around the humanity of Jesus and his relationship with women. Ding Shujing presented a more egalitarian and inclusive understanding of the doctrine of the church as a basis for greater participation of women.

The adaptation of Christianity to new cultural contexts has been full of tension and conflict, as well as accommodation and adjustment, ever since the very beginning when the primitive Church encountered the Hellenistic world.[6] Similar phenomena can be observed in the historical encounter between Christianity and the Chinese tradition since the nineteenth century. The Christian church both adapted to and challenged the dominant cultural pattern at the time. Chinese theologians, and feminist theologians in particular, have to be alert to how the androcentric bias of Christianity has been reinforced by the cultural and religious legitimations of Chinese patriarchal traditions. On the other hand, they also have to reclaim the liberating elements in both the history of the church and in their own traditions.[7]

This study has led me to believe that feminist theology in a Third World context must take into consideration women's historical experience of Christianity. In the Chinese case, Christian women have found in Christianity symbolic resources that give meaning to their lives and that empower women to struggle for dignity. Together with other Asian Christian women, they have witnessed to the potential of Christianity to liberate women from the underside of history.[8] Christians in the Third World, women in particular, must continue to learn from the past, drawing upon their heritage for insights into their present-day struggle. Such a historical consciousness has been indispensable in the development of theologies of oppressed peoples, including Africans, Asians, Afro-Americans, and Latin Americans, and women as a whole.

Third World feminist theology, rooted in its particular history and sociopolitical contexts, will be different from that developed by Western feminists. In the Chinese situation, for example, some of the major themes of feminist theology will include discussions on a wholistic interpretation of the divine based on Chinese philosophical and religious insights, the salvific role of Jesus in relation to the pluralistic religious tradition of China where female figures have been mediums of both enlightenment and salvation, the promise of Christianity as a force for emancipation of women in comparison with other faiths and ideologies, such as Daoism and Marxism, the relation of women's emancipation to the overall liberation of the Chinese people, and the role of the Church as a transforming agent in the Chinese society.

Third World feminist theology can offer a cross-cultural critique of Western feminist theology that is particularly relevant, because the religious histories of Western women and Third World women intersected, albeit ambiguously, during the missionary movement. Third World feminists consistently challenge Western feminist theologians to construct a kind of theology that does not work simply toward the self-aggrandizement of white women but takes into consideration the plight of women in the Third World. Conscious of the fact that Christian symbolism functions variously in different contexts, they challenge others to broaden their investigations to include the historical experience of women in different settings and religious traditions. Although the old missionary days are gone, new opportunities of cross-cultural encounter between women in which all parties can benefit from mutual learning need to be fostered. We live in a world in which human problems are increasingly intertwined, and only through genuine dialogue can we discover a religious vision that will open the way toward the salvation of ourselves and our planet.

Notes

1. Mary Backus Rankin, "The Emergence of Women at the End of the Ch'ing: The Case of Ch'iu Chin," in *Women in Chinese Society*, ed., Margery Wolf and Roxane Witke, 52.

2. For the American case, see Nancy F. Cott, *The Bonds of Womanhood*, 197-201.

3. Elisabeth Griffith, *In Her Own Right: The Life of Elizabeth Cady Stanton* (Oxford: Oxford University Press, 1984), 210-213.

4. Kumari Jayawardena, *Feminism and Nationalism in the Third World* (London: Zed Press, 1986).

5. Margery Wolf, *Revolution Postponed: Women in Contemporary China* (Stanford: Stanford University Press, 1986).

6. See Rudolf Bultmann, *Primitive Christianity in Its Contemporary Setting*, trans., R. H. Fuller (London: Thames and Hudson, 1956).

7. See Kwok Pui-lan, "Claiming a Boundary Existence: A Parable from Hong Kong," *Journal of Feminist Studies in Religion* 3/2 (Fall 1987): 123.

8. For the Japanese case, see Yasuko Morihara Grosjean, "Japan: The 'Silent Victim' Speak," *Journal of Feminist Studies in Religion* 3/2 (Fall 1987): 107-113; for the Korean case, see Sung-Hee Lee, "Women's Liberation Theology as the Foundation for Asian Theology," *East Asia Journal of Theology* 4/2 (1986): 2-13.

Bibliography

Allen, Young J. "Jidujiao youyi yu Zhongguo shuo" 基督教有益於中國說 (Christianity is beneficial to China). *WGGB* n.s. 7/83 (December 1895): 6b-8.

——. *Quandi wu dazhou nüsu tongkao* 全地五大洲女俗通考 (Women of all lands). 21 juan. Shanghai: Christian Literature Society for China, 1903.

——. "Wanguo gongbao gaobai" 萬國公報告白 (*Wanguo gongbao* advertisement). *WGGB* 7 (7 August 1875): 670b.

——. "Xianyu dui xia" 險語對下 (Words of warning), part one. *WGGB* n.s. 8/86 (March 1896): 8-12.

Allen, Young J., et al. *Yesu shengjiao ruhua* 耶穌聖敎入華 (Memorial on the aims of Protestant mission in China). N.p., 1895.

American Board of Commissioners for Foreign Missions Archives. Houghton Library, Harvard University, Cambridge, Massachusetts.

Andrews, Mary Elizabeth. *Shengjing yaoyan* 聖經要言 (Important words of Scripture). Beijing: Huabei shuhui, 1890.

A. R. M. "Girls' Schools: Use Versus Ornament." *WWFE* 21/1 (May 1901): 20-22.

Ashmore, William. "Why We Should Study the Old Testament." *CR* 23 (1892): 249-255.

Bai Yurong 白玉榮. "Zai fan zongjiao nonghou de kongqi li suosheng de chuti" 在反宗敎濃厚的空氣裏所生的忧惕 (Alertness in the midst of strong anti-religious sentiment). *Zhenli yu shengming* 4/5 (1929): 33-35.

Baldwin, Caleb C. *Shengxue wenda* 聖學問答 (A catechism on sacred learning). 8 juan. Fuzhou colloquial. Fuzhou, 1864.

Balme, Harold. *China and Modern Medicine: A Study in Medical Missionary Development.* London: United Council for Missionary Education, 1921.

——. "Medical Missionaries in Conference." *CR* 46 (1915): 184.

Baozhuo zi 抱拙子. "Quanjie chanzu" 勸戒纏足 (Exhortation against footbinding). *WGGB* 15 (14 October 1882): 83b-85.

Barnes, Irene H. *Behind the Great Wall: The Story of the Ç.E.Z.M.S. Work and Workers in China*. London: Marshall Brothers, 1896.

Barnett, Suzanne Wilson, and John King Fairbank, eds. *Christianity in China: Early Protestant Missionary Writings*. Cambridge, Mass.: Committee on America-East Asian Relations of the Department of History, Harvard University, 1985.

Barrett, Michèle. *Women's Oppression Today: Problems in Marxist Feminist Analysis*. London: NLB, 1980?

Bays, Daniel H. "Christianity and the Chinese Sectarian Tradition." *Ch'ing-shih wen-ti* 4/7 (1982): 35-55.

Beahan, Charlotte L. "Feminism and Nationalism in the Chinese Women's Press, 1902-1922." *Modern China* 1 (1975): 379-416.

——. "The Woman's Movement and Nationalism in Late Ch'ing China." Ph.D. diss., Columbia University, 1976.

Beattie, Andrew. "Partitions." *CR* 34 (1903): 95.

Beaver, R. Pierce. *All Love Excelling: American Protestant Women in World Mission*. Grand Rapids, Mich.: Wm. B. Eerdmans, 1968.

Bennett, Adrian A. *Missionary Journalist in China: Young J. Allen and His Magazines, 1860-1883*. Athens, Georgia: University of Georgia Press, 1983.

——. comp. *Research Guide to the chiao-hui hsin-pao (The church news), 1868-1874*. San Francisco: Chinese Material Center, 1975.

——. comp., *Research Guide to the Wan-kuo kung-pao (The globe magazine), 1874-1883*. San Francisco: Chinese Material Center, 1976.

Bentley, W. P. *Illustrious Chinese Christians*. Cincinnati: Standard Publishing Co., 1906.

Berger, Peter. *The Sacred Canopy: Elements of a Sociological Theory of Religion*. Garden City, N.Y.: Doubleday and Co., 1969.

Bian Yuying 卞豫英. "Lun quqie yu weiqie zhi louxi" 論娶妾與爲妾之陋習 (On the bad habits of taking a concubine or being a concubine). *NDB* 3/7 (October 1914): 2-8.

Blodget, Henry. *Sanzi jing* 三字經 (Trimetrical classic). N.p., 1875.

——. *Zhenli wenda* 眞理問答 (A catechism on truth). Beijing, 1873.

Blodget, Henry, and Caleb C. Baldwin. *Sketches of the Missions of the American Board in China*. Boston: American Board of Commissioners for Foreign Missions, 1896.

Boggs, M. Pearl. "The Nanking Woman's Christian Temperance Union."

WWFE 32/2 (June 1911): 82-84.

Bonafield, Julia. "Some Observations on Foot-Binding." *WWFE* 13/2 (May 1893): 121-123.

Boone, William J. "An Essay on the Proper Rendering of the Words *Elohim* and *Theos* into the Chinese Language." *Chinese Repository* 17 (1848): 17-53, 57-89.

——. "Defense of an Essay on the Proper Rendering of the Words *Elohim* and *Theos* into the Chinese Language." *Chinese Repository* 19 (1850): 345-385, 409-444, 465-478, 569-618, 625-650.

Bowker, (Mrs.) Albert, and Mrs. J. A. Copp. "To Christian Women, in Behalf of Their Sex in Heathen Lands." *The Missionary Herald* 64 (1968): 139.

Broomhall, Marshall. *The Jubilee Story of the China Inland Mission.* London: Morgan and Scott, 1915.

——. *Robert Morrison: A Master Builder.* New York: George H. Doran Co., 1924?

Bultmann, Rudolf. *Primitive Christianity in Its Contemporary Setting.* Translated by R. H. Fuller. London: Thames and Hudson, 1956.

Burt, E. W. *After Sixty Years: The Story of the Church Founded by the Baptist Missionary Society in North China.* London: Carey Press, 1937.

Burton, Margaret. *Comrades in Service.* New York: Board of Foreign Missions of the Presbyterian Church in the U.S.A., 1915.

——. *The Education of Women in China.* New York: Fleming H. Revell Co., 1911.

——. *Notable Women of China.* New York: Fleming H. Revell Co., 1912.

Bynum, Caroline Walker, Steven Harrell, and Paula Richman, eds. *Gender and Religion: On the Complexity of Symbols.* Boston: Beacon Press, 1986.

C. "In What form Shall We Give the Bible to the Chinese." *CR* 21 (1890): 453-457.

Cai, Sujuan (Christiana Tsai) 蔡蘇娟. *Anshi zhi hou* 暗室之后 (Queen of the dark chamber). Hong Kong: The Bellman House, 1982. (Chinese translation of her *Queen of the Dark Chamber* as told to Ellen L. Drummond, Chicago: Moody Press, 1953.)

Cao Fangyun 曹芳雲. "Yifu lüeshuo" 衣服略說 (A brief talk on clothes). *NDB* 2/4 (July 1913): 12-14.

Cao Jingrong (Cao Ziyu) 曹景榮 (曹子漁). "Chanzu lun" (On footbinding). *JHXB* 2 (21 May 1870): 182-183.

——."Le chengrenmei lun" 樂成人美論 (The pleasure of helping others attack footbinding). *WGGB* 7 (24 April 1875): 456b-457b; 7 (1 May 1875): 474-474b; 7 (15 May 1875): 500-500b.

Carlson, Ellsworth C. *The Foochow Missionaries, 1847-1880*. Cambridge, Mass.: East Asian Research Center, Harvard University, 1974.

Chau, Virginia Chui-tin. "The Anti-Footbinding Movement in China (1850-1912)." M.A. Thesis, Columbia University, 1965.

Chen Duxiu 陳獨秀. "Jidujiao yu Zhongguo ren" 基督教與中國人 (Christianity and Chinese people). *Xin qingnian* 7/3 (1 February 1920): 15-23.

Chen Hongmou 陳宏謀. *Jiaonü yigui zhaichao* 教女遺規摘鈔 (Selections from instructions to girls). Chongwen shuju, 1868.

Chen Ruilan 陳瑞蘭. "Lun nüzi ziyou jiehun zhi buke bushen" 論女子自由結婚之不可不慎 (On the topic of women needing to take greater care concerning free marriage). *NDB* 4/2 (May 1915): 1-6.

Chen, Sophia H. (Chen Hengzhe) 陳衡哲. "A Non-Christian Estimate of Missionary Activities." *CR* 65 (1934): 110-119.

Chen Xiedong 陳協東. "Lun jiaohui ying zhongshi nüquan" 論教會應重視女權 (On the church should respect women's rights). *Zhenli zhoukan* 3/25 (20 September 1925): 2.

Chen Yuling 陳玉玲. "Wanguo funü jiezhi hui" 萬國婦女節制會 (Woman's Christian Temperance Union). *Nianjian* 3 (1916): section wei, 85-87.

Cheng Guanyi (Ruth Cheng) 誠冠怡. "Funü duiyu ziyou de gongxian" 婦女對於自由的貢獻 (Women's contribution to freedom). *NDB* 10/11 (February 1922): 4-6.

——."Women and the Church." *CR* 53 (1922): 538-541.

——."Zhonghua Jidujiao nüzi gaodeng jiaoyu jinzhuang" 中華基督教女子高等教育近狀 (The current situation of Chinese Christian higher education for women). *Nianjian* 6 (1921): 94-96.

Cheng Wanzhen (Zung Wei Tsung) 程婉珍. "The Chinese Church and the New Industrial System." *CR* 53 (1922): 186-190.

——."Nüzi zhiye wenti" 女子職業問題 (Issues on women's jobs). *Nüqingnian bao* 5/1 (March 1921): 1-3.

——."The Woman's Movement in China." *The Y.W.C.A. Magazine* (June 1923): 1-3.

Chiao Chien 喬健. "Female Chastity in Chinese Culture." *Minzu xue yanjiu jikan* 31 (1971): 205-211.

China Centenary Missionary Conference Records: Report of the Great Conference Held at Shanghai, April 25 to May 8, 1907. New York:

American Tract Society, n.d.

The China Christian Year Book. Successor to the *China Mission Year Book*. Shanghai, 1926-1938.

China Educational Commission. *Christian Education in China: A Study Made by an Educational Commission Representing the Mission Boards and Societies Conducting Work in China*. New York: The Foreign Missions Conference of North America, 1922.

China Medical Commission of the Rockefeller Foundation. *Medicine in China*. New York: Rockefeller Foundation, 1914.

The China Mission Year Book. Shanghai, 1910-1925.

The Chinese Church as Revealed in the National Christian Conference Held in Shanghai, May 2 to May 11, 1922. Shanghai: Oriental Press, n.d.

The Chinese Recorder and Missionary Journal. Fuzhou, 1868-1872; Shanghai, 1874 et seq.

Chiping sou 持平叟. "Yesujiao yu Tianzhujiao yitong bian" 耶穌教與天主教異同辯 (Differences and similarities in Protestantism and Roman Catholicism). *JHXB* 2 (29 January 1870): 109-110.

Chittenden, C. E. "Mrs. Diong Cing-hoing, Bible Woman." *Life and Light* 32 (1902): 208-212.

"Chivalry to Women as Christian Sentiment." *CR* 22 (1891): 266.

Clark, Alice, "Training of Men and Women Nurses in China." *Year Book* 7 (1916): 326-329.

Cohen, Paul A. *China and Christianity: The Missionary Movement and the Growth of Chinese Anti-Foreignism, 1860-1870*. Cambridge, Mass.: Harvard University Press, 1963.

——. "Christian Missions and Their Impact to 1900." In *The Cambridge History of China*. Vol. 10, *Late Ch'ing, 1800-1911*, edited by John King Fairbank. Cambridge: Cambridge University Press, 1978.

"Contemporaneous Chinese Leaders: Mrs. H. C. Mei." *CR* 58 (1927): 576-577.

Cott, Nancy F. *The Bonds of Womanhood: "Women's Spheres" in New England, 1780-1835*. New haven: Yale University Press, 1977.

Crawford, A. R. "Shall Men and Women Be Separated in Our Public Chinese Services?" *CR* 34 (1903): 378-382.

Croll, Elisabeth. *Feminism and Socialism in China*. London: Routledge and Kegan Paul, 1978.

Daly, Mary. *Beyond God the Father: Toward a Philosophy of Women's*

Liberation. Boston: Beacon Press, 1973.

——. *The Church and the Second Sex*. Boston: Beacon Press, 1968.

Davies, M. Faith. "Anti-Foot-Binding in Foochow City." *WWFE* 27/3 (September 1906): 116-119.

DeGroot, J. J. M. *Sectarianism and Religious Persecution in China*. 2 vols. Amsterdam: Johannes Muller, 1903.

"Dezheng kechuan" 德政可傳 (Guangdong officials assist a woman in Buddhist rites). *WGGB* 14 (17 December 1881): 171-171b.

Ding Ai-nyok (Mrs.). "Results of Unbinding My feet." *WWFE* 17/2 (November 1896): 119-121.

Ding Shujing (Ting Shu Ching) 丁淑靜. "Beijing Jidujiao nü qingnianhui" 北京基督敎女青年會 (Beijing Y.W.C.A.). *Nianjian* 5 (1918): 201-204.

——. "Chinese Women Leader's Conception of the Missionary." *CR* 57 (1926): 122.

——. "Feibi yundong" 廢婢運動 (The movement to abolish domestic maids). *Nüqingnian* 7/2 (March 1928): 54-55.

——. "Fengman de shengming" 豐滿的生命 (Fullness of life). *Nüqingnian* 7/4 (May 1928): 3-7.

——. "Funü zai jiaohui zhong de diwei" 婦女在敎會中的地位 (The position of women in the church). *Nüqingnian* 7/2 (March 1928): 21-25.

——. "Jinri Zhongguo Jidujiao nü qingnianhui de shiming" 今日中國基督敎 女青年會的使命 (Mission of the Chinese Y.W.C.A. today). *Nüqingnian* 7/7 (November 1928): 3-10.

——. "What Chinese Women Are Doing?" *Year Book* 16 (1929): 107-111.

Dodd, Samuel. "The Relation of Christianity to Polygamy." *CR* 2 (1869): 31-35.

Donavan, Mary Sudman. "Zealous Evangelists: The Woman's Auxiliary to the Board of Missions." *Historical Magazine of the Protestant Episcopal Church* 51 (1982): 371-383.

Doolittle, Justus, comp. *Quanshan liangyan* 勸善良言 (Good words exhorting one to virtue). Fuzhou colloquial. N.p., 1856.

Doty, E. *Yesu zhengjiao wenda* 耶穌正敎問答 (A catechism on the Christian true religion). Xiamen, 1854.

Douglas, Carstairs. "*Spirit* and *God*: How Should They Be Translated?" *CR* 7 (1876): 68-74.

Drucker, Alison R. "The Influence of Western Women in the Anti-Footbinding Movement, 1840-1911." In *Women in China: Current*

Directions in Historical Scholarship, edited by Richard W. Guisso and Stanley Johannesen. New York: Philo Press, 1981.

——. "The Role of the Y.W.C.A. in the Development of the Chinese Women's Movement, 1890-1927." *Social Service Review* 53 (1979): 421-440.

Dudgeon, J. "The Small Feet of Chinese women." *CR* 2 (1869): 93-96, 130-133.

Edkins, Joseph. "Buddhist Phraseology in Relation to Christian Teaching." *CR* 9 (1878): 283-295.

Esherick, Joseph W. *The Origins of the Boxer Uprising*. Berkeley and Los Angeles: University of California Press, 1987.

Faber Ernst. *Zixi cudong* 自西徂東 (From the West to the East). 5 juan. N.p., 1884.

Fan Yurong 范玉榮. "Women Leaders." In *NCC 1922*, 597-598.

Fang Suxin 房素馨. "Nüzi de zhuquan" 女子的主權 (Women's rights). *NDB* 15/5 (August 1925): 1-3.

Feibi 飛碧. "Nüzi canzheng yundong de shangque" 女子參政運動的商榷 Discussion on women's political movement). *Ginling College Magazine* 1/3 (April 1925): 1-6.

Fisher, Elizabeth M. "The Enlightenment of Our Native Christian Women. How Can It Be Accomplished?" *CR* 21 (1890): 390-396.

Forsythe, Sidney A. *An American Missionary Community in China, 1895-1905*. Cambridge, Mass.: Harvard University Press, 1971.

Foster (Mrs.). "The Nü Hiao King." *Woman's Work in China* 7/1 (November 1883): 69-70.

Foster, L. S. *Fifty Years in China: An Eventful Memoir of Tarleton Parry Crawford, D. D.* Nashville: Bayless-Pullen Co., 1909.

Fulton, Mary. "Letter from Canton." *WWFE* 21/2 (November 1900): 115-116.

Furth, Charlotte. "Concepts of Pregnancy, Childbirth, and Infancy in Ch'ing Dynasty China." *Journal of Asian Studies* 46/1 (1987): 7-35.

Gamewell, Mary Porter. "The Christian and the Chinese Idea of Woman and How the Former Can Be Propagated in Our Girls' Schools." *WWFE* 20/2 (November 1899): 132-141.

Garrett, Shirley S. *Social Reformers in Urban China: The Chinese Y.M.C.A., 1895-1926*. Cambridge, Mass.: Harvard University Press, 1970.

Gernet, Jacques, *China and the Christian Impact: A Conflict of Cultures*. Translated by Janet Lloyd. Cambridge: Cambridge University Press, 1985.

Gibson, John C. "Christian Terminology in Chinese." *CR* 23 (1892): 255-259; 24 (1893): 51-54.

Gibson, Otis. *Chuxue wenda* 初學問答 (Easy questions for beginners). English and Chinese. Fuzhou, 1892.

Ginling College Girls. "Students and Marriage Customs in China." *CR* 57 (1926): 493-497.

Goodrich, Chauncey. *Sanzi jing zhujie* 三字經註解 (Trimetrical classic with commentary). N.p., 1865.

———. "Tracts and Terms." *CR* 35 (1904): 385-396.

Goodrich, Grace. "Beer: Study Number Three." *WWFE* 35/1 (March 1914): 42-46.

———. "Cigarettes: Study Number One." *WWFE* 34/2 (June 1913): 88-91.

Goodrich, Sara. "The Anti-Alcohol Campaign." *WWFE* 35/4 (December 1914): 189-194.

———. "Shall We Not Inaugurate a United and Earnest Anti-Cigarette Campaign." *WWFE* 34/1 (March 1913): 39-42.

———. "Woman's Christian Temperance Union." *Year Book* 2 (1911): 452-455.

———. "Woman's Christian Temperance Union of China." *Year Book* 7 (1916): 488-492.

Graham, A. C. *Two Chinese Philosophers: Ch'êng Ming-tao and Ch'êng Yi-ch'uan*. London: Percy Lund, Humphries, and Co., 1958.

Graves, R. H. "Fifty Years Service in South China." *CR* 38 (1907): 81-91.

Gray, Arthur R., and Authur M. Sherman. *The Story of the Church in China*. New York: The Domestic and Foreign Missionary Society of the Protestant Episcopal Church in the U.S.A., 1913.

Griffith, Elisabeth. *In Her Own Right: The Life of Elizabeth Cady Stanton*. Oxford: Oxford University Press, 1984.

Grosjean, Yasuko Morihara. "Japan: The 'Silent Victims' Speak." *Journal of Feminist Studies in Religion* 3/2 (Fall 1987): 107-113.

Gu Ziren 顧子仁. "Yijiuersi nian zhi guoji jinyan huiyi ji woguo zhi judu wenti" 一九二四年之國際禁煙會議及我國之拒毒問題 (The 1924 international anti-opium conference and problems of opium suppression in China). *Nianjian* 8 (1925): 225-231.

Guo Fangyun 郭芳雲. "Gaizao shehui de funü lingxiu" 改造社會的婦女領袖 (Women leaders who transform society). *Nüqingnian bao* (May 1923): 1:4.

Gützlaff, Charles. *Jiushizhu Yesu Jidu xinglun zhi yaolüe zhuan* 救世主耶穌基督行論之要略傳 (A concise story of the life of Jesus Christ the savior). 9 juan. N.p. 1834.

——. *Songyan zanyu* 頌言讚語 (Eulogy and praise). Singapore: Jianxia shuyuan, 1838.

Hansen, Chad. *Language and Logic in Ancient China.* Ann Arbor: University of Michigan Press, 1983.

Hartwell, Charles. *Jiaohui xinlu* 教會信錄 (Church creed). Fuzhou: Taiping jie fuyin tang, 1870.

——. *Quan xiangren shize* 勸鄉人十則 (Ten sermons). Fuzhou: Taiping jie fuyin tang, 1874.

——. *Shangdi zonglun* 上帝總論 (On the doctrine of God). Fuzhou, 1878.

——. *Shangjiao sanzi jing* 聖敎三字經 (Sacred trimetrical classic). Fuzhou: Taiping jie fuyin tang, 1870.

——. *Wuzijing zhujie* 五字經註解 (Five character classic with commentary). Fuzhou: Taiping jie fuyin tang, 1871.

——. *Xiaoxue sizi jing* 小學四字經 (Primary four-character classic). Fuzhou: Meihua shuju, 1874.

——. *Zhengdao qimeng* 正道啓蒙 (Enlightenment on truth). Fuzhou colloquial. Fuzhou: Taiping jie fuyin tang, 1871.

——. ed. *Guang xiao ji* 廣孝集 (On filial piety). Fuzhou: Nantai jiuzhu tang, 1882.

Haven, Ada. *Fuyin cuoyao* 福音撮要 (Selections from the gospels). N.p., 188?

He Yuquan 何玉泉. "Tiandao hecan" 天道合參 (A comparison of the Dao in Confucianism and Christianity). *WGGB* 10 (29 September 1877): 86b-88b; 10 (8 December 1877): 225b-228b.

Hershatter, Gail. *The Workers of Tianjin, 1900-1949.* Stanford: Stanford University Press, 1986.

Hill, Patricia R. *The World Their Household: The American Woman's Foreign Mission Movement and Cultural Transformation, 1870-1920.* Ann Arbor: University of Michigan Press, 1985.

Hoch-Smith, Judith, and Anita Spring, eds. *Women in Ritual and Symbolic Roles.* New York: Plenum Press, 1978.

Holcomb, Chester. *Yesu yanxing lu* 耶穌言行錄 (The life of Jesus). Beijing: Meihua shuguan, 1872.

Hong Xiuquan 洪秀全. "The Taiping Heavenly Chronicle." In Vol. 2 of

The Taiping Rebellion: History and Documents, edited by Franz Michael. Seattle: University of Washington Press, 1971.

Honig, Emily. *Sisters and Strangers: Women in the Shanghai Cotton Mills, 1919-1949*. Stanford: Stanford University Press, 1986.

Houston, M. H. "Woman Speaking in the Church." *CR* 28 (1897): 56-66.

Howard, Edith J. "Is China Ready for Women Nurses in Men's Hospital?" *The China Medical Journal* 33/2 (March 1919): 174-177.

Howe, Gertrude. "Danforth Memorial Hospital." *WWFE* 23/2 (June 1902): 57-59.

Hu Binxia (Mrs. T. C. Chu) 胡彬夏 (朱庭祺夫人). "The Emancipation of Chinese Women." *CR* 50 (1919): 655-658.

——. "Magazines for Chinese Women." *Year Book* 8 (1917): 454-458.

——. "My Impression of the National Christian Conference." *CR* 53 (1922): 409-411.

——. "Nüzi yu guoyun" 女子與國運 (Women and the destiny of the nation). *NDB* 11/2 (May 1922): 1-6.

——. *Zhongguo nü qingnianhui xiaoshi* 中國女青年會小史 (A short history of the Chinese Y.W.C.A.). N.p., 1923.

——. "Zhu Gongaihui zhi qiantu" 祝共愛會之前途 (Celebrating the future of the Common love society). In vol. 2 of *Jindai Zhongguo nüquan yundong shiliao, 1842-1911* 中國女權運動史料, 1842-1911 (Documents of the feminist movement in modern China, 1842-1911), edited by Li Youning and Zhang Yufa, 916-917. Taibei: Zhuanji wenxue she, 1975.

Hu Shi 胡適. "Meiguo de furen" 美國的婦人 (American Women). In vol. 1 of *Hu Shi wencun* 胡適文存 (Collected essays of Hu Shi). Taibei: Yuandong tushu gongsi, 1953.

Huang Pinsan 黃品三. "Da Lu Congzhou" 答路從周 (Reply to Lu Congzhou). *JHXB* 2 (25 September 1869): 20-20b.

——. "Shenghao lun" 聖號論 (On holy titles). *WGGB* 9 (21 July 1877): 674b-675.

——. "Xinnü Yao shi ji" 信女姚氏記 (On a Christian woman, Mrs. Yao). *WGGB* 11 (7 December 1878): 230-230b.

Huang Ying 黃英 (Lu Yin 廬隱). "Lu Yin zizhuan" 廬隱自傳 (Autobiography of Lu Yin). In vol. 1 of *Lu Yin xuanji* 廬隱選集 (Selected works of Lu Yin), edited by Qian Hong 錢虹. Fuzhou: Fujian People's Press, 1985.

Hunter, Jane. *The Gospel of Gentility: American Women Missionaries in*

Turn-of-the-Century China. New Haven: Yale University Press, 1984.

Hutchison, William R. *Errand to the World: American Protestant Thought and Foreign Missions.* Chicago: University of Chicago Press, 1987.

"The Hwangmei and North Kiangsi Districts Conference." *The China Christian Advocate* 12/5 (June 1925): 19-20.

Hyatt, Jr., Irwin T. *Our Ordered Lives Confess: Three Nineteenth-Century American Missionaries in East Shantung.* Cambridge, Mass.: Harvard University Press, 1976.

"In Remembrance: Miss Fan Yu-jung." *CR* 58 (1927): 55-56.

Institute of Modern History, Academia Sinica, ed. Vol. 1 of *Jiaowu jiaoan dang* 教務教案檔 (Archives on missionary affairs and cases). Taibei: Institute of Modern History, Academia Sinica, n.d.

Jaggar, Alison M. *Feminist Politics and Human Nature.* Totowa, N. J.: Rowman and Allanheld, 1983.

Jayawardena, Kumari. *Feminism and Nationalism in the Third World.* London: Zed Press, 1986.

Jia Fu 賈復. "Chanzu lun" 纏足論 (On footbinding). *WGGB* n.s. 8/1 (August 1896): 4b-5b.

Jiang Hezhen (Anna Kong Mei) 江和貞 (梅華銓夫人). "Making the Home Christian." *CR* 53 (1922): 472-476.

——. "The Modern Chinese Woman: Her Work and Problems." *International Review of Missions* 13 (1924): 565-572.

"Jiaohui funü yingfou fengzhi zhi shangque" 教會婦女應否封職之商榷 (Discussion on the ordination of women in the church). *NDB* 14/8 (November 1925): 50-52.

Jiaohui xinbao 教會新報 (The church news). Shanghai, 1868-1874.

John, Griffith. "The Chinese Circular on Mission." *CR* 4 (1871): 149-151.

Johnson, Kay Ann. *Women, the Family and Peasant Revolution in China.* Chicago: University of Chicago Press, 1983.

Judd, C. H. "Woman's Place in the Church as Taught in Holy Scripture." *CR* 27 (1896): 261-266.

Kang Cheng (Ida Kahn) 康成. *An Amazon in Cathay.* Boston: Woman's Foreign Missionary Society, 1912.

——. "The Doctor's Opportunity in Visiting Homes." *WWFE* 35/4 (December 1914): 170-174.

——. "The Place of Chinese Christian Women in the Development of China." *CR* 50 (1919): 659-662.

Kang Youwei 康有爲. "Qingchi gesheng gai shuyuan yinci wei xuetang zhe" 請飭各省改書院淫祠爲學堂摺 (Memorial on transforming Chinese academies and temples into modern schools). In vol. 2 of *Wuxu bianfa* 戊戌變法 (Reform of 1898), edited by Jian Bozan 翦伯贊 et al. Shanghai: Shenzhou guoguang she, 1953.

——. "Qingjin funü guozu zhe" 請禁婦女裹足摺 (Memorial on forbidding women to bind their feet). In vol. 2 of *Wuxu bianfa*, 戊戌變法 edited by Jian Bozan 翦伯贊 et al.

Kelly, Mary, "A Consecrated, Capable Chinese Woman." *WWFE* 22/2 (November 1901): 85-88.

Kerr, J. G. "Small Feet." *CR* 2 (1869): 169-170; 3 (1870): 22-23.

Klein, Ethel. *Gender Politics: From Consciousness to Mass Politics.* Cambridge, Mass.: Harvard University Press, 1984.

Kong Xianglin 孔祥麟. "Zhongguo nü xuesheng yingchi zhi taidu" 中國女學生應持之態度 (The attitudes Chinese female students should have). *NDB* 14/4 (July 1925): 4-8.

Kuang Rixiu 鄺日修. "Shenghao lunheng" 聖號論衡 (On holy titles). *WGGB* 10 (25 May 1878): 549-550.

Kulp, II, Daniel H. *Country Life in South China: The Sociology of Familism.* New York: Columbia University Press, 1925.

Kwok Pui-lan 郭佩蘭. "Claiming a Boundary Existence: A Parable from Hong Kong." *Journal of Feminist Studies in Religion* 3/2 (Fall 1987): 121-124.

Lacy, Walter N. *A Hundred Years of China Methodism.* New York: Abingdon-Cokesbury Press, 1948.

Lam Wing-hung 林榮洪. *Chinese Theology in Construction.* Pasadena, Calif.: William Carey Library, 1983.

Latourette, Kenneth S. *A History of Christian Missions in China.* New York: Macmillan Co., 1929.

Lee, Sung Hee. "Women's Liberation Theology as the Foundation for Asian Theology." *East Asia Journal of Theology* 4/2 (1986): 2-13.

Legge, James. *An Argument for Shang Te as the Proper Rendering of the Words Elohim and Theos in the Chinese Language: With Strictures on the Essay of Bishop Boone in Favour of the Term Shin, etc. etc.* Hong Kong: Hong Kong Register Office, 1850.

——. *Confucianism in Relation to Christianity: A Paper Read before the Missionary Conference in Shanghai, on May 11th, 1877.* Shanghai: Kelly and Walsh, 1877.

——. *Letters on the Rendering of the Name God in the Chinese Language.* Hong Kong: Hong Kong Register Office, 1850.

——. *The Notions of the Chinese Concerning God and Spirits: With an Examination of the Defense of an Essay on the Proper Rendering of the Words Elohim and Theos into the Chinese Language by William J. Boone, D.D.* Hong Kong: Hong Kong Register Office, 1852.

Leith, Suzette. "Chinese Women in the Early Communist Movement." In *Women in China: Studies in Social Change and Feminism*, edited by Marilyn Young. Ann Arbor: Center for Chinese Studies, University of Michigan, 1973.

"A Letter from Mrs. Zaw, a Native Christian Woman, to Mrs. Lambuth." *Woman's Work in China* 8/1 (November 1884): 64-65.

Lewis, Ida Belle. *The Education of Girls in China.* New York: Teachers College, Columbia University, 1919.

Li Ang 李昂. "Zhongguo de funü wenti" 中國的婦女問題 (Chinese women's problems). *NDB* 13/7 (October 1924): 1-7.

Li Guanfang 李冠芳. "Zhongguo shehui ruhe keyi pingdeng" 中國社會如何可以平等 (How can equality be achieved in Chinese society?). *NDB* 9/6 (September 1920): 4-8.

Li Zhezhen 李哲眞. "Yige shou jiaoyu de nüzi ying ruhe gailiang tade guo" 一個受教育的女子應如何改良他的國 (How can an educated woman reform her nation?). *NDB* 12/3 (November 1923): 1-9.

Liang Fa 梁發. *Qiufu mianhuo yaolun* 求福免禍要論 (Important discourse on seeking happiness and avoiding misfortune). Singapore: Jianxia shuyuan, 183?

——. *Quanshi liangyan* 勸世良言 (Good Words to admonish the age). In *Liang Fa zhuan* 梁發傳 (Life of Liang Fa), by Mai Zhanen 麥湛恩. Hong Kong: The Council on Christian Literature, 1959, Appendix.

——. *Zhendao wenda qianjie* 眞道問答淺解 (A catechism on the true way). Malacca, 1829.

Liang Fen-siu. "The Y.W.C.A. in Ginling College." *Ginling College Magazine* 1/1 (June 1924): 27-28.

Liang Qichao 梁啓超. "Changshe nü xuetang qi" 倡設女學堂啓 (On establishing girls' schools). In *Yinbingshi heji* 飲冰室合集 (Collected essays of Yinbingshi), collected in vol. 2 of *Liang Rengong wenji* 梁任公文集 (Collected works of Liang Qichao), by Liang Qichao. Shanghai: Zhonghua shuju, 1936.

——. "Ji Jiangxi Kang nüshi" 記江西康女士 (On Miss Kang of Jiangxi). In vol. 2 of *Liang Rengong wenji* 梁任公文集, by Liang Qichao.

——. "Shiban Buchanzu hui jianming zhangcheng" 試辦不纏足會簡明章程 (Concise rules for founding an anti-footbinding society). In vol. 2 of *Liang Rengong wenji* 梁任公文集, by Liang Qichao.

"List of Delegates to the Conference." *CR* 44 (1913): 237-239.

Little, Alicia. *In the Land of the Blue Gown.* London: T. Fisher Unwin, 1902.

Little, Sophia Martin. *Xunnü sanzi jing* 訓女三字經 (Trimetrical classic to instruct girls). N.p., 1832.

Liu (Miss). "How to Make the Girls Responsible for Social Service?" *WWFE* 38/3 (September 1917): 95-100.

Liu Jingying 劉京英. "Lun jiu jiating gailiang zhi biyao" 論舊家庭改良 之必要 (On the necessity to reform the traditional family). *NDB* 11/1 (April 1922): 9-11.

"Liu Ma Yana" 劉馬亞拿 (Obituary of Liu Ma Yana). *Nianjian* 5 (1918): 230.

Lodwick, Kathleen, comp. *The Chinese Recorder Index: A Guide to Christian Mission in Asia, 1867-1941.* 2 vols. Wilmington, Deleware: Scholarly Resources, 1986.

Long Deyuan 龍德淵. "Zhongguo jiating de gaijin" 中國家庭的改進 (Reforming the Chinese family). *Nüqingnian* 7/2 (1928): 26-34.

Lu Shiqiang 呂實強. "Wanqing Zhongguo zhishi fenzi dui Jidujiao yili de pichi (1860-1898)" 晚清中國知識分子對基督教義理的闢斥, 1860-1898 (Chinese intellectuals' criticism of Christian doctrines in late Qing, 1860-1898). *Lishi xuebao* 歷史學報 (Journal of history) 2 (1974): 139-159.

——. *Zhongguo guanshen fanjiao de yuanyin* 中國官紳反教的原因 (The origin and causes of the anti-Christian movement by the Chinese officials and gentry). Taibei: Institute of Modern History, Academia Sinica, 1966.

Lu Xun 魯迅. "Nuola zouhou zenyang" 娜拉走後怎樣 (What happens to Nora after she leaves?" In *Fen* 墳 (Graves), collected in vol. 1 of *Lu Xun quanji* 魯迅全集 (Collected works of Lu Xun). Beijing: People's Press, 1973.

"Lun tianfu erzi zhi jie" 論天父二字之解 (On the meaning of the two characters tianfu ["heavenly father"]). *WGGB* 10 (11 August 1877): 4b.

Lutz, Jessie Gregory. *China and the Christian Colleges, 1850-1950.* Ithaca, N.Y.: Cornell University Press, 1971.

MacGillivary, D. "Women's Work." *Year Book* 2 (1911): 425-442.

Macgowan, John. *How England Saved China*. London: T. Fisher Unwin, 1913.

MacNeil, Eleanor, "Women Students in 1926, As Seen by a Y.W.C.A. Secretary." *CR* 57 (1926): 875-883.

Mai Zhanen (George H. McNeur) 麥湛恩. *Liang Fa zhuan* 梁發傳 (Life of Liang Fa). Hong Kong: The Council on Christian Literature, 1959.

"Maliya tu shuo" 馬利亞圖說 (A portrait of Mary), *NDB* 1/1 (April 1912): 21-23.

Mann, Susan. "Widows in the Kinship, Class, and Community Structure of Qing Dynasty China." *Journal of Asian Studies* 46/1 (February 1987): 37-55.

Martin, W. A. P. "Is Buddhism a Preparation for Christianity?" *CR* 20 (1889): 193-203.

Medhurst, W. H. *China: Its State and Prospects, with Special Reference to the Spread of the Gospel Containing Allusions to the Antiquity, Extent, Population, Civilization, Literature, and Religion of the Chinese*. Boston: Crocker and Brewster, 1838.

——. "An Inquiry into the Proper Mode of Rendering the Word God in Translating the Sacred Scriptures into the Chinese Language." *Chinese Repository* 17 (1848): 105-133, 161-187, 209-242, 265-310, 321-354.

——. *Mazupo shengri zhi lun* 媽祖婆生日之論 (On the birthday of Mazu). Singapore: Jianxia shuyuan, 183?

——. "Reply to the Essay of Dr. Boone on the Proper Rendering of the Words *Elohim* and *Theos* into the Chinese Language." *Chinese Repository* 17 (1848): 489-520, 545-574, 601-646.

——. *Sanzi jing* 三字經 (Trimetrical classic). N.p., 1843.

Melvin, M. "The Curricula of Five Representative Mission Schools for Girls in China." *WWFE* 21/1 (May 1900): 5-16.

Milne, William. "Some Remarks on the Chinese Term to Express the Deity." *Chinese Repository* 7 (1838): 314-321.

——. *Xiangxun shisan ze* 鄉訓十三則 (Thirteen sermons). Xiamen: Huaqi yusuo, 1855.

——. *Zhang Yuan liangyou xianglun* 張遠兩友相論 (Dialogue between the two friends Zhang and Yuan). Fuzhou: Huaqi yusuo, 1849.

Miner, Luella. "Jidujiao nüzi jiaoyu" 基督敎女子敎育 (Christian women's education). *Nianjian* 1 (1914): 79-85.

——. "The Place of Woman in the Protestant Missionary Movement in China." *Year Book* 9 (1918): 321-341.

Montgomery, Helen B. *Western Women in Eastern Lands: An Outline Study of Fifty Years of Women's Work in Foreign Missions*. New York: Macmillan Co., 1911.

Morrison, Eliza A., comp. *Memoirs of the Life and Labour of Robert Morrison, D.D.* 2 vols. London: Longman, Orme, Brown, Green, and Longmans, 1839.

Myers, Angie M. "Medical Training in Amoy." *WWFE* 21/2 (November 1900): 151-153.

Naquin, Susan. *Millenarian Rebellion in China: The Eight Trigrams Uprising of 1813*. New Haven: Yale University Press, 1976.

National Committee of the Y.W.C.A. of China, *Diyici guanguo dahui jilu* 第一次全國大會紀錄 (Report of the first national convention). Shanghai: National Committee of the Y.W.C.A. in China, 1924.

Needham, Joseph, and Wang Ling. Vol. 2 of *Science and Civilization in China*. Cambridge: Cambridge University Press, 1956.

Nelson, R. "The Relation of Christianity to Polygamy." *CR* 1 (1869): 169-173.

Nevius, Helen S. *Yesujiao wenda* 耶穌教問答 (Christian catechism). Fuzhou, 1880.

Nevius, John L. *China and the Chinese: A General Description of the Country and Its Inhabitants; Its Civilization and Form of Government; Its Religious and Social Institutions; Its Intercourse with Other Nations; and Its Present Conditions and Prospects*. New York: Harper and Brothers, Publishers, 1869.

Newton, Ella J. "Women's Meetings in Foochow." *Life and Light* 22 (1892): 162-164.

Newton, G. "What Our Girls' Schools are Doing for Christian Womanhood?" *WWFE* 20/2 (November 1899): 138-141.

"Ni Suen" 倪素恩 (Obituary of Ni Suen). *Nianjian* 5 (1918): 228.

"Ningbo Yinxian gaoshi" 甯波鄞縣告示 (Proclamation prohibiting females from entering Buddhist temples). *JHXB* 6 (14 March 1874): 190.

Noyes, Harriet Newell. *History of the South China Mission of the American Presbyterian Church, 1845-1920*. Shanghai: Presbyterian Mission Press, 1927.

——. *A Light in the Land of Sinim: Forty-five Years in the True Light Seminary, 1872-1917*. New York: Fleming H. Revell Co., 1919.

"Nü yishi Jin Yunmei jilue" 女醫士金韻梅紀略 (Biography of the woman doctor Jin Yunmei). In vol. 2 of *Jindai Zhongguo nüquan yundong shiliao, 1842-1911* 近代中國女權運動史料 , 1842-1911, edited by Li Youning and Zhang Yufa, 1386-1388.

Nüduobao 女鐸報 (The woman's messenger). Shanghai, 1912 et seq.

"Nüzi canzheng hui de zhiyuan hui" 女子參政會的職員會 (Committee of the Woman's Suffrage Association). *NDB* 11/10 (January 1923): 57-58.

Ogborn, Kate L. "A Self-Propagating Church, the Goal of All Mission Work" *CR* 45 (1914): 276-280.

Overmeyer, Daniel L. "Alternatives: Popular Religious Sects in Chinese Society." *Modern China* 7/2 (April 1981): 153-190.

——. *Folk Buddhist Religion: Dissenting Sects in Late Traditional China.* Cambridge, Mass.: Harvard University Press, 1976.

Pan Xunru 潘恂如 . "Shenghao lun" 聖號論 (On holy titles). *WGGB* 10 (22 September 1877): 71b-72.

Peng Jinzhang 彭錦章 . "Jidujiao shi mieshi nüxing mo?" 基督教是蔑視 女性麼 (Does Christianity despise women?). *Zhenli zhoukan* 42 (13 January 1924): 1-2.

"Pijiu zhi yanjiu" 啤酒之研究 (Study on beer). *NDB* 4/10 (January 1916): 14-17.

Pitcher, P. W. *A History of the Amoy Mission.* New York: Board of Publications of the Reformed Church in America, 1893.

Pixie jishi 辟邪紀實 (A record of facts to ward off heterodoxy). 4 juan. N.p., 1871.

Pyle, Martha E. "The Present Situation of the Anti-Foot-Binding Movement." *Year Book* 12 (1924): 419-421.

Qiu Yinlan 仇蔭蘭 . "Jiating jiaoyu shou zai xianmu" 家庭教育首在賢母 (A virtuous mother is most important in family education). *NDB* 2/4 (July 1913): 45-46.

Ququ zi 區區子 . "Shenghao lun" 聖號論 (On holy titles). *WGGB* 10 (15 June 1878): 590b-591.

Rawlinson, Frank. "Christian Co-operation for a National-Wide Task." *CR* 51 (1920): 419-425.

——. *Naturalization of Christianity in China.* Shanghai: Presbyterian Mission Press, 1927.

Rawski, Evelyn S. *Education and Popular Literacy in Ch'ing China.* Ann Arbor: University of Michigan Press, 1979.

Records of the General Conference of the Protestant Missionaries of China, Held at Shanghai, May 10-24, 1877. Shanghai, 1878.

Records of the General Conference of the Protestant Missionaries of China, Held at Shanghai, May 7-20, 1890. Shanghai, 1890.

Report of the Tenth Session of the Foochow Woman's Conference of the Methodist Episcopal Church. N.p., 1894.

Report of the Twenty-fifth Session of the Foochow Woman's Conference of the Methodist Episcopal Church. N.p., 1909.

"Report on Medical Schools in China Connected with Christian Missions." *The China Medical Journal* 36/6 (November 1922): 509-525.

Richard, Mary Martin (Mrs. Timothy Richard). "The Christian and the Chinese Idea of Womanhood and How Our Mission Schools May Help to Develop the Former Idea." *CR* 31 (1900): 10-16, 55-62.

——. "Weiladi Falangshi nüshi zhuan" 未辣底法郎士女士傳 (Biography of Miss Frances Willard). *NDB* 4/5 (August 1915): 45-48; 4/6 (September 1915): 48-51; 4/7 (October 1915): 49-53.

Richard, Timothy, *Forty-five Years in China: Reminiscences by Timothy Richard, D.D., Litt. D.* New York: Frederick A. Stokes Co., 1916.

——. *Jiushi jiaoyi* 救世敎益 (Teachings to save the world). Shanghai: Guangxue hui, 1899.

——. "Xinü youyi Zhongguo shuo" 西女有益中國說 (Western women are beneficial to China), translated by Cai Erkang. *WGGB* n.s. 8/129 (October 1899): 1-2.

Ricoeur, Paul, *Interpretation Theory: Discourse and the Surplus of Meaning.* Fort Worth, Texas: Texas Christian University Press, 1976.

Roberts, John. "Shenghao lun lieyan" 聖號論列言 (Preface to the discussion on holy titles). *WGGB* 9 (21 July 1877): 675-675b.

——. "Shengshu tiwen" 聖書題文 (An essay based on a biblical passage). *WGGB* 10 (10 November 1877): 177-178.

Rong Tiesheng. "The Women's Movement in China before and after the 1911 Revolution." *Chinese Studies in History* 16/3-4 (Spring-Summer 1983): 159-200.

Ruether, Rosemary Radford. *Sexism and God-Talk: Toward a Feminist Theology.* Boston: Beacon Press, 1983.

Ruether, Rosemary Radford, and Eleanor McLaughlin, eds. *Women of Spirit: Female Leadership in the Jewish and Christian Traditions.* New York: Simon and Schuster, 1979.

Ruether, Rosemary Radford, and Rosemary Skinner Keller, eds. *Women and Religion in America.* Vol. 1, *The Nineteenth Century.* San Francisco: Harper and Row, Publishers, 1981.

Safford, A. C. "Gleanings." *Woman's Work in China* 4/2 (May 1881): 148.

Sangren, P. Steven. "Female Gender in Chinese Religious Symbols: Kuan Yin, Ma Tsu, and the 'Eternal Mother'," *Signs* 9/1 (1983): 4-25.

Schüssler Fiorenza, Elisabeth. *In Memory of Her: A Feminist Theological Reconstruction of Christian Origins.* New York: Crossroad, 1983.

Schwartz, Benjamin I. *The World of Thought in Ancient China.* Cambridge, Mass.: Belknap Press, 1985.

Scott, Nancy F. *The Bonds of Womanhood: "Women's Sphere" in New England, 1780-1835.* New Haven: Yale University Press, 1977.

Shanghai Y.W.C.A. "Nüzi duiyu shehui zhi yiwu" 女子對於社會之義務 (Women's duty toward society). *NDB* 3/3 (June 1914): 2-5.

Shaw, Ella C. "The Work of Bible Women in China." *Year Book* 6 (1915): 343-347.

Sheffield, (Mrs.) D. E. "Missionary Societies among Native Christians," *Woman's Work in China* 6/1 (November 1882): 3-9.

Shen Caizhen 沈彩珍. "Gaizao shehui de funü lingxiu" 改造社會的婦女領袖 (Women leaders who transform society). *Nüqingnian bao* (April 1923): 1-4.

Shi Meiyu (Mary Stone) 石美玉. "What Chinese Women Have Done and Are Doing for China." *Year Book* 5 (1914): 239-245.

——. "Zhongguo xianjin funü jiaoyu shiye zhi jinbu" 中國現今婦女教育事業之進步 (The progress of Chinese women's educational enterprise). *Nianjian* 1 (1914): 89-93.

Simpson, Cora E. "The Training of the Chinese Pupil Nurse." *China Christian Advocate* 2/6 (June 1915): 4-5, 7.

"Sketch of Kwanyin, the Chinese Goddess of Mercy." *Chinese Repository* 10 (1841): 185-191.

"Sketch of Teën Fe, or Matsoo Po, the Goddess of Chinese Seamen." *Chinese Repository* 10 (1841): 84-87.

Smith, Arthur H. "How Christian Work Looked When I Came to China." *CR* 55 (1924): 9-15, 88-95, 167-173.

——. *Qingnian xingguo zhunfan* 青年興國準範 (Guidance on how young people can strengthen the country; a shortened translation of *The Uplift of China*). Shanghai: Christian Literature Society for China, 1913.

——. "Sketches of a Parish Church." *CR* 12 (1881): 245-266, 316-344.

——. *The Uplift of China.* New York: Young People's Missionary Movement, 1907.

Smith, Carl T. *Chinese Christians: Elites, Middlemen, and the Church in China.* Hong Kong: Oxford University Press, 1985.

——. "The Protestant Church and the Improvement of Women's Status in 19th Century China." *Ching Feng* 20 (1977): 109-115.

Smith, Hilda L. "Women's History and Social History: An Untimely Alliance." *Organization of American Historians Newsletter* 12/4 (November 1984): 4-6.

Smyth, (Mrs.) R. "C.M.S. Women's Hospital, Ningpo." *WWFE* 21/2 (November 1900): 101-102

Snow, Helen F. *Women in Modern China.* The Hague: Mouton and Co., 1967.

Songzhu shengshi 頌主聖詩 (Chinese hymnal). Beijing: Meihua shuju, 1875.

Soothill, W. E. *A Typical Mission in China.* New York: Fleming H. Revell Co., 1906.

Spence, Jonathan. "Opium Smoking in Ch'ing China." In *Conflict and Control in Late Imperial China*, edited by Frederic Wakeman, Jr., and Carolyn Grant. Berkeley and Los Angeles: University of California Press, 1975.

Stacey, Judith. *Patriarchy and Social Revolution in China.* Berkeley and Los Angeles: University of California Press, 1983.

Stauffer, M. T., ed. *The Christian Occupation of China: General Servey of the Numerical Strength and Geographical Distribution of the Christian Forces in China, 1918-1921.* Shanghai: China Continuation Committee, 1922.

Stock, Eugene. *The Story of the Fuk-kien Mission of the Church Missionary Society.* London: Seeley, Jackson, and Halliday, 1890.

Sun Wenxue 孫文雪. "Jidujiao duiyu funü yundong de gongxian" 基督敎對於婦女運動的貢獻 (The contribution of Christianity to the women's movement). *Nüqingnian* 7/3 (April 1928): 22-24.

Tan Huiran (Mrs. Ou Bin) 譚惠然(歐彬夫人). "Duiyu nüquan yundong zhi wojian" 對於女權運動之我見 (My views on the feminist movement). *NDB* 11/11 (February 1923): 1-3.

Tay, C. N. "Kuan-yin: The Cult of Half Asia." *History of Religions* 16 (1976): 147-174.

Taylor, Howard. *Hudson Taylor and the China Inland Mission: The Growth of a Work of God.* London: Morgan and Scott, 1920

Thomas, Hilah F., and Rosemary Skinner Keller, eds. *Women in New Worlds.* Vol. 1, *Historical Perspectives on the Wesleyan Tradition.* Nashville: Abingdon Press, 1981.

Thompson, R. Wardlaw. *Griffith John: The Story of Fifty Years in China.* New York: A. C. Armstrong and Son, 1906.

Thurston, Matilda C. (Mrs. Lawrence Thurston), and Ruth M. Chester. *Ginling College.* New York: United Board for Christian Colleges in China, 1955.

"Tianfu shangdi bian" 天父上帝辯 (On God the father). *WGGB* 7 (3 July 1875): 599b-600.

Tong, T. E. "The Chinese Missionary Society." *CR* 68 (1937): 690-694

Tsai Kuei 蔡葵 and Lily K. Haass. "A Study of the Young Women's Christian Association of China, 1890-1930." *Chinese Studies in History* 10/3 (Spring 1977): 73-88; 11/1 (Fall 1977): 18-63; 11/4 (Summer 1978): 48-71.

Tu Wei-ming 杜維明. *Confucian Thought: Selfhood as Creative Transformation.* New York: State University of New York Press, 1984.

Tucker, Sara Waitstill. "The Canton Hospital and Medicine in Nineteenth Century China, 1835-1900." Ph. D. diss., Indiana University, 1983.

Turner, J. A. *Kwang Tung, or Five Years in South China.* London: S. W. Partridge, 1894?

Tuttle, A. H. *Mary Porter Gamewell and Her Story of the Siege of Peking.* New York: Eaton and Mains, 1907.

Varg, Paul A. *Missionaries, Chinese, and Diplomats: The American Protestant Missionary Movement in China, 1890-1952.* Princeton: Princeton University Press, 1958.

"A Visit with Deng Yuzhi (Cora Deng)." *China Update* (August 1983): 11-12.

Wagner, Rudolf. *Reenacting the Heavenly Vision: The Role of Religion in the Taiping Rebellion.* Berkeley: Institute of East Asian Studies, University of California, 1982.

Wang Bingkun 王炳堃. "Huihao yi" 徽號議 (On honorary titles). *WGGB* 10 (26 January 1878): 325-328.

Wang Ermin 王爾敏. "Jindai Hunan nüquan sichao xianqu" 近代湖南女權思潮先驅 (Pioneers in Hunan feminist thought in the modern period). In *Zhongguo funü shi lunwen ji* 中國婦女史論文集 (Collected essays on the history of Chinese women), edited by Li Youning and Zhang Yufa. Taibei: Commercial Press, 1981.

Wang Fanglian 王芳連. "Wo geren de zongjiao jingyan" 我個人的宗教經驗 (My own religious experience). *Shengming* 3/7-8 (April 1923): 1-2.

Wang Huiwu 王會悟. "Nüquan yundong yu nü Jidutu" 女權運動與女基督徒

(The feminist movement and female Christians). *Nüqingnian bao* (October 1922): 8-9.

Wang Liming (Mrs. Herman C. E. Liu) 王立明(劉湛恩夫人). "The Chinese Woman's Movement and Magazines." *CR* 69 (1934): 85-88.

——. "Funü jiezhi hui" 婦女節制會 (Woman's Christian Temperance union). *Nianjian* 8 (1925): 243-245.

——. "Funü wenti" 婦女問題 (Women's problems). *Jiezhi yuekan* 5/10 (December 1926): 1-9.

——. "Jiating wei shehui fuwu" 家庭爲社會服務 (The family serving society). *Jiezhi yuekan* 5/3 (March 1926): 1-6.

——. "The Woman's Christian Temperance Union." *Year Book* 11 (1923): 257-259.

——. "Zhonghua funü jiezhi xiehui" 中華婦女節制協會 (The Chinese Woman's Christian Temperance Union). *Nianjian* 12 (1933): 171-173.

——. *Zhongguo funü yundong* 中國婦女運動 (Chinese women's movement). Shanghai: Commercial Press, 1934.

Wanguo gongbao 萬國公報 (The globe magazine). Shanghai, 1874-1883; n.s., 1889-1907.

"The W.C.T.U. in China." *CR* 55 (1923): 567-568.

Welter, Barbara. "The Feminization of American Religion, 1800-1860." In her *Dimity Convictions: The American Woman in the Nineteenth Century.* Athens, Ohio: Ohio University Press, 1876.

West, Philip. *Yenching University and Sino-Western Relations, 1916-1952.* Cambridge, Mass.: Harvard University Press, 1976.

"What Ginling Girls Do for Their Community?" *WWFE* 40/3 (September 1919): 94-98.

White, Laura M. "Maliya de muyi" 馬利亞的母儀 (The motherhood of Mary). *NDB* 11/7 (December 1922): 1-4.

——. "Maliya zhi yu Guanyin" 馬利亞之與觀音 (Mary and Guanyin). *NDB* 1/9 (December 1912): 1-4.

——. "Temperance Literature." *WWFE* 42/1 (March 1921): 16-17.

——. "Xiawa beiyou tu" 夏娃被誘圖 (A portrait of the temptation of Eve). *NDB* 1/3 (June 1912): 24-25.

White, M. C. "Evangelistic Work among Women." *Year Book* 11 (1923): 146-154.

Williams, S. Wells. "The Controversy among the Protestant Missionaries on the Proper Translation of the Words *God* and *Spirit* into Chinese."

Bibliotheca Sacra 35/140 (1878): 732-778.

Witke, Roxane Heater. "Transformation of Attitudes towards Women during the May Fourth Era of Modern China." Ph.D. diss., University of California, Berkeley, 1970.

Wolf, Margery. *Revolution Postponed: Women in Contemporary China.* Stanford: Standford University Press, 1986.

Wolf, Margery, and Roxane Heater Witke, eds. *Women in Chinese Society.* Stanford: Stanford University Press, 1975.

"Woman's Conference of the M. E. Church in the Fuhkien Province." *CR* 20 (1889): 88-89.

Woman's Work in China. Interdenominational organ of Protestant missionary women in China. Shanghai, 1877-1889.

Woman's Work in the Far East. Successor to *Woman's Work in China.* Shanghai, 1890-1921.

Women Leaders of Present Day China: Chinese Christians Worth Knowing. Boston: Women's Board of Missions, n.d.

"The 'Women's Army'—A Sequel." *WWFE* 34/1 (March 1913): 33-35.

"Women's Work at the National Conference." *CR* 53 (1922): 267-273.

Wong, K. Chimin, and Wu Lien-teh. *History of Chinese Medicine: Being a Chronicle of Medical Happenings in China from Ancient Times to the Present Period.* Tientsin: Tientsin Press, 1932.

Wood, Myfanwy. "Women at the National Christian Conference." *CR* 53 (1922): 195-196.

Woodhull, Katherine C. "A.B.C.F.M. Hospital for Women and Children, Foochow City." *WWFE* 21/1 (November 1900): 92-95.

Woodin, Simeon Foster. *Jiuzhu xingzhuan* 救主行傳 (The life of the savior). Fuzhou: Meihua shuju, 1876.

Woods, H. M. "Woman's God-Appointed Sphere as Set Forth in Scripture." *CR* 27 (1896): 467-475.

Wright, Arthur F. "The Chinese Language and Foreign Ideas." In *Studies in Chinese Thought*, edited by Arthur F. Wright. Chicago: University of Chicago Press, 1953.

Wu Liming 吳利明. *Jidujiao yu Zhongguo shehui bianqian* 基督教與中國社會變遷 (Christianity and social change in China). Hong Kong: Chinese Christian Literature Council, 1981.

Wu Ming-ying. "Women and Education." *Ginling College Magazine* 1/1 (June 1924): 22-23.

Wycloff, E. G. "Reform in Foot Binding." *Life and Light* 34 (1904): 575-576.

Xie Wanging 謝婉瑩. "Yanjing daxue" 燕京大學 (Yenching University). *Shengming* 2/2 (September 1921): 1-8.

Xu Baoqian 徐寶謙. "Liangxing daode biaozhun zhi bianqian ji Jidu jiaoyi" 兩性道德標準之變遷及基督敎義 (Changes in the moral standard between the sexes and Christian doctrine). *Zhenli yu shengming* 2/16 (1927): 500-503.

Xu Guifen 徐桂芬. "Nüzi aiguo lun" 女子愛國論 (On women's patriotism). *NDB* 1/6 (September 1912): 29-30.

Xu Maoli 許茂利. "Jinri nü xuetang yi zengshe shiye ke lun" 今日女學堂宜增設實業科論 (Recommending that girls' schools offer practical subjects). *NDB* 1/11 (February 1913): 44-45.

Xu Zhihe 許致和. "Fakan ci" 發刊辭 (Remarks on the beginning of publication). *NDB* 1/1 (April 1912): 2-3.

Yang, C. K. *Religion in Chinese Society: A Study of Contemporary Social Functions of Religion and Some of Their Historical Factors*. Berkeley and Los Angeles: University of California Press, 1970.

Yao Fubao 姚福寶. "Wenming jiehun" 文明結婚 (Civilized marriage). *NDB* 4/9 (December 1915): 67-68.

"Ye Cai shi" 葉蔡氏 (Obituary of Ye Cai shi). *Nianjian* 9 (1927): 278-279.

"Yesu zhi mu Maliya" 耶穌之母馬利亞 (Jesus' mother, Mary). *Zhenguangbao* 5/12 (February 1907): 17b-19.

Ying Mei Chun. "The Place of Woman in Social Service." *Year Book* 5 (1914): 289-293.

Yizhi zi 一知子. "Guanbao zhiyan" 觀報直言 (Comments on reading the newspaper). *WGGB* 12 (19 June 1889): 395b-396.

Yuan Peifen 袁培芬. "Wo weihe wei Jidutu" 我爲何爲基督徒 (Why am I a Christian?). *Nianjian* 6 (1921): 239-240.

Yuan Yuying 袁玉英. "Chanzu lun" 纏足論 (On footbinding). *NDB* 8/11 (February 1920): 21-26.

——. "Funü yu zhanshi zhi guanxi" 婦女與戰事之關係 (The relationship between women and war). *NDB* 2/3 (June 1913): 5-8.

——. "Zhongguo nüjie baozhi zhi xianzhuang" 中國女界報紙之現狀 (The present condition of Chinese women's newspapers). *Nianjian* 5 (1918): 167-169.

Yunying 雲英. "Guomin geming sheng zhong zhi Jin nüda" 國民革命聲中之金女大 (Ginling College in the midst of national revolution). *Ginling College Magazine* 4/1 (December 1927): 36-39.

Y.W.C.A. of China. *Chinese Triangles*. Shanghai: National Committee of the Y.W.C.A. of China, 1924.

——. *Introduction to the Young Women's Christian Association of China, 1933-1947*. Shanghai: The National Committee of Y.W.C.A. of China, n.d.

——. *A 1915 Message from the Young Women's Christian Associations of China*. Shanghai: Presbyterian Mission Press, 1916.

——. *The Widening Circle: The Y.W.C.A. of China, 1919*. Shanghai: National Committee of the Y.W.C.A. of China, 1919.

——. *Y.W.C.A.—China, 1917*. N.p., n.d.

Zeng Baosun (P. S. Tseng) 曾寶蓀. "China's Women and Their Position in the Church." *Church Missionary Review* 68 (1917): 372-376.

——. "The Chinese Woman Past and Present." In *Symposium on Chinese Culture*, edited by Sophia H. Chen. Shanghai: China Institute of Pacific Relations, 1931.

——. "Christianity and Women as Seen at the Jerusalem Meeting." *CR* 59 (1928): 443.

——. "Wo de Jidujiao xinyang" 我的基督教信仰 (My Christian faith). In *Jidujiao yu xin Zhongguo* 基督教與新中國 (Christianity and a new China), edited by Wu Yaozong 吳耀宗. Shanghai: Qingnian xiehui shuju, 1940.

——. *Zeng Baosun huiyilu* 曾寶蓀回憶錄 (The memoir of Zeng Baosun). Hong Kong: Chinese Christian Literature Council, 1970.

Zhan Yanlai 詹雁來. "Zhongguo funü yu zhengqu dao nannü pingdeng de genben wenti" 中國婦女欲爭取到男女平等的根本問題 (Basic issues of Chinese women's struggle for sexual equality). *NDB* 14/7 (October 1925): 12-13.

Zhang Qinshi (C. S. Chang) 張欽士. *Guonei jin shinian lai zhi zongjiao sichao* 國內近十年來之宗教思潮 (Religious thought in China during the last decade). Beijing: Yenching School of Chinese Studies, 1927.

Zhang Qunying 張群英. "Wo de zongjiao xinyang de kunnan" 我的宗教信仰的困難 (The difficulty of my religious faith). *Shengming* 3/7-8 (April 1923): 1-2.

"Zhang Zhujun nüshi lishi" 張竹君女士歷史 (History of Miss Zhang Zhujun). In vol. 2 of *Jindai Zhongguo nüquan yundong shiliao,, 1842-1911* 近代中國女權運動史科, 1842-1911, edited by Li Youning and Zhang Yufa, 1379-1382.

Zhang Zimou 張子謀. "Jiaohui gaizao de wojian" 教會改造的我見 (My

opinion on church reform). *Shengming* 2/9-10 (June 1922): 1-12.

Zhao Minshu 趙敏淑. "Nüxing yu zhiye" 女性與職業 (Women and jobs). *Nüqingnian* 8/7 (July 1929): 11-13.

Zheng Yuren 鄭雨人. "Yintai jinhui da Jueyi zi" 燕臺浸會答決疑子 (Reply to Jueyi zi concerning a misunderstanding of mission work). *JHXB* 1 (6 February 1869): 96-97.

"Zhiyan zhi mohai" 紙煙之魔害 (The harmful effects of cigarettes). *NDB* 4/4 (July 1915): 11-14.

Zhonghua Jidu jiaohui nianjian 中華基督敎會年鑑 (The Chinese Christian church year book). Shanghai, 1914-1936.

Zhu Shouheng 朱壽恒. "Gaizao shehui de funü lingxiu" 改造社會的婦女領袖 (Women leaders who transform society). *Nüqingnian bao* (February 1923): 1-9.

Zhu Yansheng 朱延生. "Liangceng lijiao xia Zhongguo nü xintu de hunyin wenti" 「兩層禮敎」下中國女信徒的婚姻問題 (Chinese Christian women's marriage issues in a society with double moral standard). *Shengming* 5/3 (December 1924): 74-77.

Zikmund, Barbara Brown. "Attacking the Male Power Structure in American Protestantism." Paper presented at the Fourth Annual Berkshire Women's History Conference, Mount Holyyoke College, South Hadley, Massachusetts, 1978.

Glossary

Ban Zhao	班昭
Bao Guangxi	鮑光熙
Book of Odes	詩經
Cai Chang	蔡暢
Cai Erkang	蔡爾康
Cai Kui	蔡葵
Cai Sujuan	蔡蘇娟
Cao Fangyun	曹芳雲
Cao Jingrong (Cao Ziyu)	曹景榮（曹子漁）
Chen Yingmei	陳英梅
Chen Yuling	陳玉玲
Cheng Guanyi	誠冠怡
Cheng Jingyi	誠靜怡
Cheng Yi	程頤
Cheng Wanzhen	程婉珍
Dao	道
Deng Yuzhi	鄧裕志
di	地
di	帝
Ding Mingyu	丁明玉
Ding Shujing	丁淑靜
ditan	地壇
duo	鐸
Empress Wei	韋后
Empress Wu	武則天
Fan Yurong	范玉榮

Fang Suxin	房素馨
fengshui	風水
Feng Yuxiang	馮玉祥
Fuyin cuoyao	福音撮要
Ginling College	金陵女子大學
Gongaihui	共愛會
gonglao	功勞
Guanyin	觀音
Guanyin sutra	觀音經
Guo Fangyun	郭芳雲
Hong Xiuquan	洪秀全
Hu Binxia	胡彬夏
Hu Jinying	胡金英
Hu Shi	胡適
Hua Guang	華光
Hua Mulan	花木蘭
Huang Pinsan	黃品三
Huang Ying (Lu Yin)	黃英（廬隱）
Huangdi	黃帝
Hwa Nan College	華南女子文理學院
Jiang Hezhen	江和貞
Jiaohui xinbao	教會新報
Jie chanzu hui	戒纏足會
Jiezhi jikan	節制季刊
Jiezhi yuekan	節制月刊
Jin Yunmei	金韻梅
Jinhua furen	金花夫人
Kang Cheng	康成
Kang Youwei	康有爲
koutou	叩頭
Kuang Rixiu	鄺日修
Laozi	老子

li	理
Li Dequan	李德全
Li Guanfang	李冠芳
Li Zhezhen	李哲眞
Liang Fa	梁發
Liang Fa (Mrs.), née Li	梁發妻黎氏
Liang Qichao	梁啓超
Luo Youjie	羅有節
Ma Yana	馬亞拿
Mazu	媽祖
Mei Yunying	梅雲英
Ni Suen	倪素恩
North China Union College for Women	華北協和女子大學
Nüduobao	女鐸報
Nüqingnian	女青年
Nüqingnian bao	女青年報
Nü xiaojing	女孝經
Pan Xunru	潘恂如
Pangzhuang	龐莊
Pixie jishi	辟邪紀實
qi	氣
Qingnian nübao	青年女報
Qiu Jin	秋瑾
Qiu Liying	邱麗英
Qiu Yinlan	仇蔭蘭
Quandi wu dazhou nüsu tongkao	全地五大洲女俗通考
Quanshi liangyan	勸世良言
ren	人
Sanzi jing	三字經
shangdi	上帝
shangtian	上天
shangtian shenzhu	上天神主

Shi Meiyu	石美玉
shen	神
Shen Caizhen	沈彩珍
Shen Shoukang	沈壽康
shenghao	聖號
Shengming	生命
Shengming she	生命社
shentian	神天
shentian shangdi	神天上帝
shenzhu	神主
shizu	始祖
Song Qingling	宋慶玲
Sun Wenxue	孫文雪
Sun Yat Sen	孫逸仙
taiji	太極
Taiping jie fuyin tang	太平街福音堂
tian	天
tiandi zhi dazhu	天地之大主
tianfu	天父
tiantan	天壇
tianting	天庭
tianzhu	天主
Tianzuhui	天足會
Ti Ying	緹縈
Wang Fanglian	王芳連
Wang Huiwu	王會悟
Wang Liming	王立明
Wang Tao	王韜
Wanguo gongbao	萬國公報
wenming jiehun	文明結婚
wu	物
wu	巫

Wu Leichuan	吳雷川
Wusheng laomu	無生老母
Wu Yifang	吳貽芳
Xiang Jingyu	向警予
Xie Wanying (Ping Hsin)	謝婉瑩（冰心）
xinde	信德
Xu Baoqian	徐寶賺
Xu Guifen	徐桂芬
yamen	衙門
Yang Guifei	楊貴妃
yangjiao	洋敎
yin yang	陰陽
Yu Cidu	余慈度
Yuan Peifen	袁培芬
Yuan Yuying	袁玉英
Zeng Baosun	曾寶蓀
Zeng Guofan	曾國藩
Zhang (Mrs.)(Mrs. Ahok)	張謝氏
Zhang Qunying	張群英
Zhang Zhidong	張之洞
Zhang Zhujun	張竹君
Zhao Zichen	趙紫宸
Zheng Guanying	鄭觀應
Zheng Yuren	鄭雨人
Zhenguangbao	眞光報
Zhonghua Jidu jiaohui nianjian	中華基督敎會年鑑
zhu	主
Zhu Xi	朱熹
Zixi cudong	自西徂東
zui	罪